"Seldom does an author share his soul. Not just his life and experience, but the people and events that inspire him; the art, the music and the encounters that feed his imagination; the passion that drives him. That is what Chris Pramuk does in *Hope Sings, So Beautiful*. His passion is nothing less than overcoming every form of discrimination, but especially racism, to gaze on Christ 'in ten thousand places.' It is spiritual theology at its most satisfying. His publishers have also produced a book in the same spirit, intended to move the senses as well as the mind. If you want uplift and are not afraid to be turned upside down and inside out, this is the book for you."

—Drew Christiansen, SJ
Former editor of *America*
Visiting scholar, Boston College

"Kiss 'doubt and small living' goodbye and prepare to take a tremulous step across the color line. *Hope Sings* gracefully shepherds the reader beyond isolated, self-centered prisons into inspiring worlds of scholarship, story, and song. Pramuk does not present a simplistic diagnosis of race problems, but an 'alternate horizon'—painful, partial, mysterious, but nonetheless resonant with music. To those who help us see, we owe the deepest reverence; this author is one."

—Kathy Coffey
Author of *The Best of Being Catholic*

"Pramuk creatively interweaves music, scholarship, art, the natural world, theology, personal experience, spiritual writings, and much more to examine discipleship in a racist and fractured world. But above all he unveils the everyday mystery of divine love that beckons us to new life and a new way forward."

—Timothy Matovina
University of Notre Dame
Author of *Latino Catholicism:
Transformation in America's Largest Church*

"*Hope Sings, So Beautiful* dares to interrupt readers, inviting them to reflect more deeply still on systemic racism's dehumanization of us all. Pramuk writes with eloquence, integrity, and urgency."

—Kimberly Vrudny
University of St. Tl

# Hope Sings, So Beautiful

*Graced Encounters across the Color Line*

Christopher Pramuk

A Michael Glazier Book

**LITURGICAL PRESS**

Collegeville, Minnesota

www.litpress.org

A Michael Glazier Book published by Liturgical Press

Cover design by Ann Blattner.

Cover art: *Ruby Green Singing*, 1928. James Chapin, American, 1887–1975. Oil on canvas, 38 X 30 inches (96.5 X 76.2 cm). Norton Museum of Art, West Palm Beach, Florida. Bequest of R. H. Norton, 53.29. ©Estate of James Chapin, James Cox Gallery at Woodstock, NY.

1    2    3    4    5    6    7    8    9

**Library of Congress Cataloging-in-Publication Data**

Pramuk, Christopher.
    Hope sings, so beautiful : graced encounters across the color line / Christopher Pramuk.
        pages    cm
    "A Michael Glazier book."
    Includes bibliographical references.
    ISBN 978-0-8146-8210-4 — ISBN 978-0-8146-8235-7 (e-book)
    1. Spiritual life—Catholic Church.    2. Church and minorities.
3. Christianity and the arts.    I. Title.

BX2350.3.P725    2013
241'.675—dc23                                                    2012046001

See, I am doing something new!
  Now it springs forth, do you not perceive it?

  ~ Isaiah 43:19


Jesus said to him in reply, "What do you want me to
do for you?" The blind man replied to him, "Master,
I want to see."

  ~ Mark 10:51


Hope rings, so defiant.
Hope stings, so deferred.
Hope sings, so beautiful.

  ~ Author's notebook, April 2012

# CONTENTS

# ACKNOWLEDGMENTS

*Welcome to My Ghetto Land*, 1986. Jean Lacy. Paint, gesso, and gold leaf on wood panel. Overall: 6 x 3 in. (15.24 x 7.62 cm). Dallas Museum of Art, Metropolitan Life Foundation Purchase Grant. Used by permission.

Girls Praying during Church Service, Port-au-Prince, Haiti. Photo © by Mev Puleo. Used by permission of Mark Chmiel, www.bookofmev .com.

Henry, author's son, at Sturgeon Bay, Michigan. Photo by author.

Tanisha Belvin, 5, holds the hand of fellow Hurricane Katrina victim, Nita LaGarde, 89, as they are evacuated from the Convention Center in New Orleans, Louisiana, Saturday, September 3, 2005. AP photo/ Eric Gay.

Billie Holiday at New York's Apollo Theatre, 1937. Ken Whitten Collection. Reproduced with permission from Robert O'Meally, *Lady Day: The Many Faces of Billie Holiday* (New York: Arcade Publishing, 1991), 50.

View from Christ in the Desert Monastery, Abiquiu, New Mexico. Photo by author.

Peace Wall Mural with Kids. Photo copyright John (Jack) Ramsdale, jackramsdale.com. Mural painted by Jane Golden and Peter Pagast for the Philadelphia Mural Arts Program, © 1998.

Etty Hillesum. Collection Jewish Historical Museum, Amsterdam. Used by permission.

The Passion of Matthew Shepard, Fr. William Hart McNichols. www .frbill.org. Used by permission.

Sr. Thea Bowman, Holy Child Jesus Parish, All Saints Day, 1984. Sr. Thea coaxes a group of sleepy children to sing. Photo © John Feister.

Lauri, author's wife, with children, rural Guatemala, 2012. Photo provided by author.

\*\*\*

Excerpt from "Men (and Women) Finding God's Feminine Presence" by John Kane, *Leaven*, e-vol. 3:3 (Jan. 2011). Used by permission.

At time of publication, permission for use of the following lyrics from Hal Leonard Corporation were pending: "Strange Fruit," written by Abel Meeropol and performed by Billie Holiday; "Russians" by Sting; "Big Brother" and "Village Ghetto Land" by Stevie Wonder.

# FOREWORD

"A body of broken bones." This is how Thomas Merton described us humans—our fractured disunion, our immersion in egoism, our imprisonment in hatreds, our instinctive recoil from sacrifice and pain and sorrow.[1] This is a book about how our vicious essentialism breaks the bones of the body of our humanity; more importantly, this is a book about hope and, above all, grace.

We are a body of broken bones—in need of resetting, in need of love. As a person of faith, a husband, a father, a theologian, a writer, a lover of the natural world and its Creator, Christopher Pramuk digs deep into his own intentionally expanding lifeworld in order to write in elegant, penetrating prose how we might go about resetting those bones with deep, passionate love for one another through authentic encounter, that is, through engagement that evokes a new relationship one with another or perhaps with the natural world and that brims over with the mystery of God.

Pramuk pioneers what he calls a *method of catholicity*. Taking the mystery of the incarnation with utmost seriousness, he enacts a conversation that presumes goodwill, is sympathetic in principle to multiple voices, is committed to discipline and generous listening, nurtures and enriches the imagination, thrives on the question, requires attentiveness of eye and ear and mind and heart, and relies on hope. The horizon of Pramuk's concern is wide—cultural, social, historical; but his focus is spirituality and pastoral practice. We are a body of broken bones—in need of resetting-love. He asks: "To whom do we belong and are we responsible? Who is the 'God' in whom we place our trust, and what does this God ask of us in building a world of greater justice, compassion, and solidarity? How does the memory of Jesus' life, death, and resurrection shape and expand our imagination, the very ways we see, judge, and act in society and in relationship to the natural world?"

"The church fathers," Marie-José Mondzain reminds us, "believed that truth only obtained its authority by means of emotional power, its direct access to the heart."[2] We are a body of broken bones in need of resetting-love. With great simplicity, deep emotional power, and humble authority, Christopher Pramuk offers us a mosaic of images and sketches for our reflection, prayer, and action—a kind of prescription for resetting-love for our body of broken bones, a prescription that pierces the heart with the truths he tells.

M. Shawn Copeland
Boston College

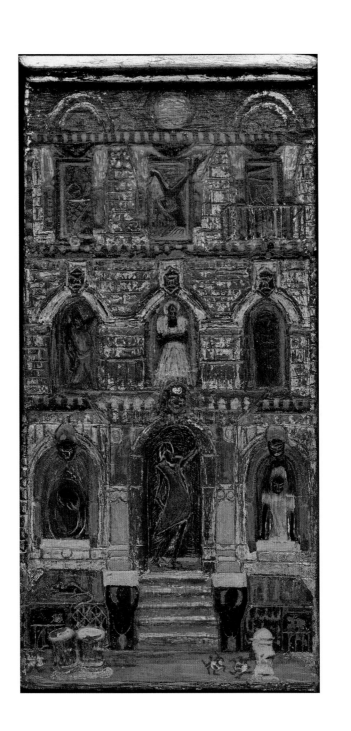

# INTRODUCTION

*"I see people looking like trees and walking."*
~ Mark 8:24

For much of my career as a teacher in Jesuit Catholic institutions, I have had my feet in two very different worlds: the world of privileged, and largely white, Jesuit education, and the world of black Catholic worship. It would be hard to overstate the cultural gap between these two worlds. One of the most moving, if rare, cross-cultural experiences I can remember was an Advent prayer service conceived and organized collaboratively between my students at Regis Jesuit High School in Aurora, Colorado, a largely white, wealthy, suburban community, and the youth choir of St. Ignatius Loyola Catholic Church in Denver, a mostly black, lower-income, inner-city parish, where I played piano. For the all-male white students of Regis Jesuit, travelling some thirty minutes into the inner-city environs of St. Ignatius Loyola was akin to visiting a third-world country; for the all-female black youth choir of St. Ignatius, their white counterparts more or less did come from another country.

Over the course of two intensive weeks of rehearsals, I watched in wonder as the imaginative worlds of both groups, along with their stereotypes and prejudices, were broken wide open. Through the medium of shared creed, storytelling, and song, discomforts faded

*Welcome to My Ghetto Land, 1986. Jean Lacy. Paint, gesso, and gold leaf on wood panel. Overall: 6 x 3 in. (15.24 x 7.62 cm). Dallas Museum of Art, Metropolitan Life Foundation Purchase Grant. Used by permission.*

and tenuous friendships began to form. The presumption of goodwill made room enough for give and take, for trial and error, for spontaneity and laughter: in a word, for grace. The gathering of both communities on the evening of the service, with parents and grandparents, brothers and sisters, and all manner of folks in all style of dress, was a beautiful sight to behold. Not a few left the church that evening with smiles of joy and tears, and rumors of possibilities never before imagined.

Nearly forty years ago, Motown recording artist Stevie Wonder released a double-album masterpiece called *Songs in the Key of Life*, seventeen songs that gave brilliant voice to a world largely hidden from mainstream, middle-class, white America. I vividly remember, as a young white kid, listening to the record for the first time. Though I was too young and far too insulated to grasp the social and racial complexity of the songs, I was mesmerized by the music. Forty years later I am still mesmerized, and the full genius of Wonder's artistry still eludes me. Today, when I introduce his music and his remarkable story to my college students, I never cease to wonder how the encounter with such an artist opens their social horizons, much as mine were broken open as a child. *"Would you like to go with me / Down my dead end street / Would you like to come with me / To Village Ghetto Land?"* How strange, sad, and beautiful that a blind man would be teaching us how to see.

For some forty years and much longer, black artists, preachers, theologians, and public intellectuals have challenged their white colleagues and fellow Christians not only to see and to hear but also to *feel* the presence of God rising from the struggles and joys of life in the black community. They have asked white Christians to take seriously the hopes and dreams of a faith written and sung, so to speak, "in the key of black." Unfortunately, it is a call that remains largely unheeded today.

With this book, I join my voice with other scholars and artists seeking to sow seeds of racial justice, healing, and hope in a society and church where, as Martin Luther King Jr. often lamented, "eleven o'clock Sunday morning" is still the most racially segregated hour in America. Of course, with a topic as rich, complex, and hazardous as race, no single book can serve every purpose, satisfy every reader, or come anywhere near to being comprehensive. My aims here are modest, frankly experimental, and at times quite personal. Above all, what binds the following meditations and case studies into a coherent vision is the theological virtue of hope. And hope, like people, is multivalent. It manifests in different shades and colors. It sings in many voices.

*Hope rings,* so defiant. *Hope stings,* so deferred. *Hope sings,* so beautiful. I take my title from the epigraph that opens this book, lines which came to me late one evening as I struggled to express the beautiful but complex "music" I hear rising from the histories of peoples of color in America. The image of "Ruby Green Singing" on the cover of the book expresses this music, this paradoxical mystery of beauty and hope-in-struggle, much better than I can say. Hope comes toward us, as it were, from the future, from God's own future, just as surely as it rises from the lessons and wisdom of the past. Ruby Green stands rooted firmly in the present, gazing in faith and hope toward the future of God's imaginings, while her song rises on the tide of memories laid down, and terrible prices paid, by her ancestors in the past. "Ruby Green Singing" embodies for me the promises of hope, as does Stevie Wonder, a blind man who shows us the way to see.

## Racial Consciousness and the Problem of Starting Points

Repeatedly in the gospels, Jesus is seen healing the blind. Yet for me the most compelling of all these miracles is the one that did not "take" the first time, the blind man of Bethsaida.

> Putting spittle on his eyes [Jesus] laid his hands on him and asked, "Do you see anything?" Looking up he replied, "I see people looking like trees and walking." (Mark 8:23-24)

Of course, Jesus finishes the healing and sends the man on his way. But it is the man's shadowy, *in-between state* of partial sight and partial blindness that most intrigues me, and seems an almost perfect metaphor for our human condition. Slow the story down and stretch it out over the course of a lifetime, generations, and then centuries, and the blind man of Bethsaida, before Jesus finishes the job, becomes a fitting parable for race relations in America. We are all still on the way, each of us stumbling forward in partial blindness, seeing people "looking like trees and walking." But the face of Christ is there, hidden in light and shadow, calling us forward into our freedom.

White, black, brown, red, or yellow, our healing and growth into the freedom of love is rarely so miraculous or complete as that of the blind man of Bethsaida. We are social beings, persons-in-community. Like a rope woven together by many different strands, we grow into our freedom and capacity for love *together* in families, communities, and complex societies through the interplay of countless relationships, encounters, and transformations—and, to be sure, many tragic failures, sins, and mistakes—along the way. Communities grow stronger and weaker by degrees over the course of generations, just as individuals transform in love and social empathy over the course of a lifetime. Our starting point matters, but rarely, thank goodness, is it the end of the story.

Conversations about race are difficult enough without imposing the impossible condition that every person's starting point should be the same. Like the rope made of many different strands, our collective strength and wisdom depends on the recognition that each of us enters the conversation (or refuses it) from a unique social location and developmental stage in the drama that is a human life. It takes empathy and patience, especially among strangers, to hear the converging strands of *what is* and *what has been* in the story of our respective lives and then to imagine together a future vision of *what is possible* in the shared task of building what Dr. King called the Beloved Community. Complicating but vastly enriching the task is the realization that very few of us come to the table tethered to a single social location. Like a river swollen by many streams, I am the confluence of many inheritances. Who I am cannot simply be reduced to any one of them.

This book offers a mosaic of images and sketches-in-progress for thinking and praying through difficult questions about race in a way that seeks to honor the complexity of the subject and the persons we are who seek to engage it. At times it is quite personal, as theology or spirituality in general, and race discourse in particular, cannot help but be. Because its horizon is both transcendent and deeply personal—Is there anything more intimate or elusive than one's relationship with God?—theological reflection in any setting invites vulnerability, humility, and risk. The risks I take here are my own, of course, as well as any successes or failures; yet, in truth, they also belong to the beautiful but broken body of God's people of which I am a part.

I set the stage in chapter 1 by reflecting on three very different but valid entry points into the conversation about race. The first is the "world" of academic discourse on race. The second is the global "world" of the poor, behind which lurks the onerous weight of European and US history in relation to nonwhite peoples and poorer nations across the globe—here my focus is on Haiti. The third is "the song circle," by which I mean the "world" embodied in the African American spirituals tradition and, more broadly, any community of faith and memory, solidarity and wisdom, to which we may belong. Like the tributaries of a river, each of these three worlds represents major influences in my own life and distinct social locations from which I seek, as a white Catholic theologian, to do theology. As such, they also reflect the blind spots and biases I may bring to the table as someone who is still very much on pilgrimage.

Chapters 2 through 9 each takes as its focus one or more themes, stories, or case studies from the worlds of literature, music, art, or theology, which then serve as an entry point for exploring, as the subtitle puts it, "graced encounters across the color line." By "graced" I mean having the character of a gift from God. Such gifts are often paradoxical: they disturb and console at the same time. Grace *interrupts* our habitual ways of seeing, judging, and acting from day to day, even where it illumines a truth that already is but was hidden from our sight. A "graced encounter" is an illumination that leaves us without words to describe it, save perhaps "thank you." Grace issues in wonder and amazement, for, as the famous hymn by former slave trader John Newton goes, "I once was lost but now am found, was blind but now I see."

By an "encounter" I mean more than an experience or isolated event that happened and then was done with. An encounter involves not just "me" or any individual but a whole situation, climate, or atmosphere in which a person is drawn beyond themselves, sometimes unexpectedly or unwittingly, into a new relationship with others or perhaps with the natural world—and thus, at least implicitly, with the mystery of God. The most significant encounters in our lives stand both in and outside of time, pregnant with presence and dense shades of meaning in memory and imagination long after the fact. The face of Jesus will forever haunt the man of Bethsaida, shaping his whole way of interpreting the world, reorienting his whole climate of thought.

Several years ago my wife Lauri and I adopted two children from Haiti. When we were married almost twenty years ago, neither of us could have predicted this path or the shape our family would take. Early in our marriage we spent a month working in rural Honduras at an orphanage and nutrition center for malnourished children. I can see today how that formative experience, a graced encounter of the most difficult and beautiful kind, transformed our whole climate of thought as a young couple, awakening desires in us that would later bear fruit in our family. There is a hidden line, unpredictable, meandering, and wholly mysterious to me, linking our falling in love with the people of Honduras and the adoption of our two children from Haiti. As it happens, partly because of such grace-filled encounters, the "color line" now passes right through the center of our family.

Historically the color line divides not just white Euro-American peoples from Africans and African Americans but whites from every other so-called (and so negated) nonwhite community in the New (Old) World: Caribbean and Latin American peoples, Native Americans, Mexicans and Mexican Americans, Asian Americans, and so on. Certainly various prejudices and "colorisms" pass between and within these communities as well. I grew up in a white suburban neighborhood in central Kentucky and had little contact with *any* of the above communities until my midtwenties, when I moved to a larger city and was quickly plunged into more diverse environments. Since then, my religious imagination has been shaped by the movement across various color lines, including immersion in Mexican American and black Catholic parishes in Denver, South Bend, and Cincinnati, as well as the study of black and Latino literature, art, and theology. More recently, the horizon of Native American history and spirituality has opened up to me, thanks in part to a friend and artist whose world of the American Southwest is the focus of one of these chapters.

In sum, as the title of this book intimates, a Christian vision of hope and racial solidarity rises implicitly from a theology of grace, or, more concretely and explicitly, from experiences of friendship and grace across the color line. While itself based in Christology, or the revelation of God's love in Jesus, the language of grace orients the Christian imagination before a theocentric horizon often neglected in exclusively Christ-centered or church-centered spiritualities. Bound up with risk, surrender, and trust, the *experience* of grace throws light on the neighbor as the person in whom we meet and serve God, such that we begin not only to acknowledge but to positively expect to discover God's presence "out there" in the city, over there in that neighborhood or church, or, to be sure, in distant, unfamiliar countries—in short, all those places which conventional wisdom about the "real world" urges us to avoid.

Of course the Christian call to love reaches well beyond differences of culture, class, religion, race, and ethnicity. In chapters 7 and 8, I enlarge the field of imagination to consider how our assumed images of God, religious ritual practices, and cultural language-worlds shape the ways we perceive and manage difference not only with respect to race but also in the orders of gender, sex, and sexual orientation. The insight that I develop here in more explicit theological terms is implicit throughout the book: namely, that we are still learning how to give full voice to the mystery of the incarnation. In our stumbling efforts to realize the mystery of Love-becoming-flesh we must attend carefully to the Scriptures and appeal to reason but we also must drink deeply from the wellspring of human experience in all its mosaic, sacramental diversity. To do so is not an act of daring or theological development for its own sake; it is an act of trust in a God revealed in Christ to be Love, a covenantal God who breathes life into all things.

## A Method of Catholicity

Theology at its best is a "catholic" conversation, attentive in principle to a universal horizon of voices, insofar as Christian and Catholic faith rises from the mystery of incarnation. God reveals God's very self in and through all creation and consummately in the mosaic, infinitely diverse human community. As the Second Vatican Council expressed this principle so beautifully and fearlessly, Christianity in full bloom comprises a vision and way of life in which "Nothing that is genuinely human fails to find an echo in [our] hearts."[1] Throughout these pages the reader will encounter the perspectives of artists, poets, and theologians from many different ethnic and racial communities, including not a few Jewish, European, and Latin American voices. In the interest of economy of style, most of my scholarly resources are referenced not in the main text but in the endnotes. The reader need only "follow the notes" to meet some of the most prophetic and creative minds writing in the field of theology and spirituality, critical race theory, and social ethics today.

Though I do rely on experts in race theory, sociology, and the like, the questions I pose here are not primarily sociological or ethnographic but are theological, with a focus on spirituality and pastoral practice. To whom do we belong and are we responsible? Who is the "God" in whom we place our trust, and what does this God ask of us in building a world of greater justice, compassion, and solidarity? How does the memory of Jesus' life, death, and resurrection shape and expand our imagination, the very ways we see, judge, and act in society and in relationship to the natural world? Perhaps above all, *for what do we dare to hope*, and how might our hope translate into pastoral strategies for racial reconciliation and solidarity across the color line?[2]

Where I use the term "we"—especially hazardous in race discourse!—I have in mind the global ecumenical Christian community, inclusive of all races, which "we Christians" call, in a rather staggering but wondrous leap of faith, the One Body of Christ. If I presume to speak for people beyond my ken, even those who reject belief or institutional religion, I do so from the conviction that what unites the human family, both within and beyond the Christian fold, far exceeds that which divides us. I do so also because there are far too few opportunities and safe spaces to practice the art of listening across the color line, to share our stories, hopes, and dreams for the church and society in which we live. Everything gets politicized, too quickly polarized, and effectively reduced to zero. To "wade in the water" of race discourse is to expect and even welcome a certain troubling of the waters. The risk, I believe, is well worth my hope: namely, that this book might stimulate fruitful conversations and fresh thinking on a difficult topic, whether in private study or prayer, in classrooms, churches, and reading groups, or among friends and family around the dinner table.

A website has been developed with the generous support of Liturgical Press to serve the catholic and ongoing conversational aims of this book. The site, www.HopeSingsSoBeautiful.org, includes links to many of the works of music, art, literature, and film discussed in these pages, reflection questions for each chapter, and a blog feature that allows for the sharing of stories, related articles and links, and other resources. With input from a diverse range of contributors from my own Cincinnati-area community and friends and colleagues far and wide, we hope the website offers an additional venue for creative and practical support, especially for folks laboring in the trenches, as it were, seeking to build bridges between the many communities—pastoral, political, academic, ecumenical, interreligious—who hold a critical stake in the dialogue about race in US society today, in the churches, and indeed around the world.

### *Racism and the Imagination*

It is sometimes said that the problem of racial justice becomes much more personal and urgent when you have your own "skin in the game." Most white people remain blind to racism, as the logic goes, because whites in the United States and across the globe have the luxury and privilege of not seeing. They have no skin in the game. While I grant validity to the point in the realm of political self-interest, I reject the cynicism that would make the principle into a law. Self-interest, as I intimate throughout this book, does not describe our whole truth, our deepest truth as human beings, nor our deepest desires and motivations. Racism is not a black, brown, red, or white problem; racism is a *human* problem, crippling something far deeper in us than blood or family ties. The truth is we all have our own skin in the game. The tragedy is how little we care, and how often we fail, to realize it.

To say it more boldly, God, in whose freedom and likeness all human beings are made, has skin in the game. Racism, I will argue in this book, is the symptom of a profound poverty, a terrible captivity, of theological imagination. From a religious-ethical perspective we are called to a way of being in the world, a radically inclusive way, because of who God is and who God calls us to be. God invites, God demands, God needs our participation in the work of social justice and racial reconciliation. At the same time, ethical commands of "should" and "ought" are not enough to heal the disease of racism. A disease of the imagination calls for responses that nourish, free, and enlarge the imagination; thus the artistic spirit that I aim to nourish and give free play in this book.[3]

I have already alluded to the fact that long before I had any direct encounters with peoples of different racial and ethnic backgrounds, music was my doorway to worlds otherwise hidden from me. From Stevie Wonder to the ragtime romps and plaintive ballads of Scott Joplin, whose artistry gifted me as a child with my first real revelations at the piano, it is from a lifetime of such experiences of being drawn, as it were, into *the mystery of unity-in-difference*—experiences that I deem trustworthy—that I write here, sometimes in a frankly personal key, and invite the reader to reflect on their own memories and experiences of grace across the color line.[4]

Finally I want to acknowledge two figures in the Catholic tradition who have deeply shaped my own religious imagination and thus my approach in these pages, if not always explicitly. The first is Thomas Merton, the American Trappist monk whose writings on the contemplative life and prophetic essays on race remain remarkably relevant today; the second is Ignatius of Loyola, whose lively incarnational spirituality tutors our imagination in the way of "finding God in all things." The mystical tradition as witnessed in these two spiritual masters is fully engaged with the world; it is a paschal and prophetic option. It calls us to reflect deeply on our life stories, critically and prayerfully in light of the gospel, for signs of God's grace as well as the call to repentance and conversion. With respect to race and all manner of differences, what I take from both Merton and St. Ignatius is the commitment to listen to the other receptively, contemplatively, as one in whom the very presence of God comes before us, challenging from difference and loving with freedom.[5]

I dedicate this book to my students, past and present, and to my four children, Isaiah, Grace, Sophia, and Henry. Their hidden future comes toward me in the present, beckoning me to be and become my better self. I am especially thankful to M. Shawn Copeland and Edward Kaplan for joining their voices with mine in this conversation; both have long been important teachers and role models to me in their lives of courageous and humane scholarship. I thank my wife

Lauri, who after twenty-plus years remains the most amazing grace of my life. I am deeply grateful to Liturgical Press for their commitment to new works in theology and spirituality, from the ground up, in service to the people of God everywhere. Above all, I thank the artists, poets, theologians, and ordinary people of faith who have inspired my thinking in these pages.

# 1

# ENTRY POINTS

Whiteness is not my point of entry
But whiteness is my point of entry
Is my whiteness your point of entry?

Let my whiteness be your point of entry
I don't mind (but I do mind)
Whiteness is not my point of entry
But surely, whiteness is my point of entry

> ~ Author's notebook, University of Notre Dame,
> March 2004

None of us enters the conversation about race as a fully developed, completely integrated, whole person. Each of us needs to be challenged by each other, but we also need room to imagine and grow into a future different from where we are now and where we have been over the course of our lives. Of course, truthful, meaningful conversation in any human context, especially among strangers, is a kind of delicate dance, structured and spontaneous, tenuous and free,

*Girls Praying during Church Service, Port-au-Prince, Haiti. Photo © by Mev Puleo. Used by permission of Mark Chmiel, www.bookofmev.com.*

1

a difficult *breaking of silence* and interruption of the status quo. Conversations about race are all the more disruptive, calling for a great deal more intimacy and risk than many of us are accustomed to sharing with strangers. To what degree are we prepared to make room in our consciousness for the stories of strangers, much less to linger together in the sheer expanse of our differences? Where we will find the kind of open, compassionate spaces needed for such conversation?

Perhaps in a monastery or a Quaker meeting house, where silence is the order of the day and one speaks only with great care and deference for the spirit of the other. Maybe in church basements and meeting halls or around dinner tables where the first and last item of "business" is simple hospitality and shared sustenance, and conversations unfold naturally when bellies and spirits are full. Maybe even in classrooms where teachers set aside their full agendas and open up circles in space and time where students can simply be and be themselves for a while, sharing their stories, hopes, and dreams for the future.

A tall order, indeed, but these are just the kinds of fertile playing fields we need to imagine and cultivate, where roots can be fertilized and new shoots of interracial encounter and friendship are given room to grow. Without question, no matter the setting, clearing a space for the conversation about race is a delicate gamble rooted in freedom and hope, and the determination to overcome fear and inertia and to act *so as to make something different happen with words.*[1]

## Race and Academic Discourse

Some years ago I attended a conference at the University of Notre Dame on the state of race relations in US society and, particularly, in the Catholic Church. The keynote speakers were superb, the breakout sessions intense and emotionally demanding. It was unlike any other academic conference I have attended before or since, engaging participants not only intellectually but addressing our hearts and moral imaginations in passionate, poetic, and often disruptive ways. It was one of the dozen or so times in my life I have been palpably conscious of my whiteness, sometimes uncomfortably so, in a sea of mostly brown and black faces.

For the bulk of the sessions I was content simply to listen, learn, and be challenged by the diverse perspectives offered by primarily black Catholic scholars but also by white, Native American, Asian, and Hispanic American scholars and conference participants.[2] From beginning to end I felt a great energy pulsing and rising up in our shared desire to talk and learn from one another across the color line. Not a few times I found myself slipping between thought and prayer, one moment giving thanks for the breathtaking scholarship of a speaker or the courageous witness of a participant, the next moment praying for patience and understanding when someone—perhaps the same person—said something that caused my intellect to recoil, my pulse to quicken in protest. More than once it struck me that language itself, when it comes to race, can build up barriers as quickly as it seeks to break them down, even from the best of intentions.

During one of many presentations on the theme of "white privilege,"[3] I scribbled the lines that open this chapter in the margins of my notebook. Is it a poem, a plea, a white man's creed or screed about the hazards of race discourse? I'm not sure, but as I revisit the lines again today they still evoke something of the tension and ambiguity I feel about race discourse as it is often practiced in books and in much of academia today.

Not unlike the social construct of race itself, the term white privilege, for example, seems to risk substituting an idea and a cause, even a valid and urgent one, for *persons*. A great deal depends, of course, on how the term is introduced and used in a particular context and the perceived intentions of the speaker. Yet even in the best of conditions where a degree of mutuality and trust has been established, it is not too surprising that many whites—if those at the conference or more recently in my college classroom are any indicator—will hear the language of white privilege more or less as follows, especially when it serves as the sole entry point or defining framework for conversations about race: "You are white. Therefore you benefit from white privilege. Therefore *you* are the problem." Never mind your name, your family history, your story. "Your whiteness tells me everything I need to know." Presented carelessly, the construct risks overshadowing and effectively obliterating the persons in the room— and not, I think, just the whites.

Thus by a peculiar irony the usual white/nonwhite hierarchy is reversed and the white listener, reduced to silence, is spotlighted as the oppressor. In religious or theological settings the biblical prophets are often invoked to sanction the reversal, alongside the powerful theme of the "preferential option for the poor,"[4] as developed by liberation theology and Catholic social teaching. But the problem of *reception* remains. What begins as descriptive language employed to shed a necessary and urgent light on societal injustice—"white privilege"; "white racist supremacy"; "white hegemony"—risks obscuring, if not erasing, the specificity and dignity of the persons such language aims to educate and transform. The irony, especially in religious settings, is the effective maintenance of race-based exclusionary practices and race-based censorship by means of language.

The problem, by now familiar, seems intractable. Where once upon a time (and often still) the literal blackness of the "Negro" constituted his or her inescapable point of entry into the public square—and thus his or her point of exclusion—today in academic and progressive religious circles whiteness is often foregrounded as an unjustly privileged entry point and therefore, functionally, if not ontologically, as a point of exclusion. "Your task today, thank you, is not to speak but to listen." The circle remains closed, but now it is whites—especially white heterosexual males—who sit penitently on the outside, paying the painful but necessary price for four hundred years of black exclusion, silence, and suffering at the hands of whites "like me." Thus the price of entry effectively precludes the possibility of real dialogue or conversation—if by dialogue we mean something like mutual vulnerability, self-disclosure, and risk, person to person, across the color line.

*Is my whiteness your point of entry?* There is, I dare say, an act of humility and surrender that recognizes the affirmative answer to this question in the eyes of the beholder and quietly concedes, "Let it be." *Let my whiteness be your point of entry. I don't mind.* I recognize my stores of unearned privilege. I accept my "guilt by common association"[5] with white supremacy as it manifests in the academy, church, and in these not-so United States of America. I see, I understand, and I am sorry. But then, if truth be told, *I do mind*, because my whiteness and your blackness (that is, your nonwhite-ness) loom like an unforgiving wall between us. The circle remains closed, and the best I can (or am allowed to) offer from this side of the color line is my silent lamentation for the fact.

On the other hand, this experience of being shut out or silenced—rendered *visibly* invisible—is not an occasional or isolated experience for so-called minorities or peoples of color in American society or in the academy. It is inescapable, *lo cotidiano*, woven into the fabric of everyday existence and survival.[6] That whites are rendered uncomfortable by race discourse and find themselves squirming silently in their seats is not altogether a bad thing! Indeed, in such situations the terms of race discourse move quickly from abstractions into the realm of experience or realization. To be shut out of "mainstream" discourse is to *feel* something of what nonwhites are haunted and imprisoned by every day, even by means of the language we habitually employ to describe what is normal, mainstream, or good, and what is not. "Welcome, my friend, to the back of the bus."

Still the question of the reception of the race critique both in and beyond the academy remains an important one. If race discourse as practiced among scholars is not going to remain merely self-referential preaching to the choir—even if the choir is slow to get it—one eventually has to ask how it will be communicated to ordinary white Christians in the pews. The question may be put this way: What response does race discourse seek from white Christians: guilt or relationship, hand wringing or solidarity? If the answer is truly the latter, then not only *what* is communicated but *how* matters as well. Whether or not the message is received will depend not a little on genuine understanding of, if not empathy or affection for, one's particular audience.

Perhaps the clearest conclusion to draw from all of this is that the greater burden of responsibility for raising racial consciousness among whites and white Christians lies squarely on the shoulders of whites, not blacks or Latinos, Asians or Indians: white pastors and priests, politicians, teachers, lawyers, social scientists, and theologians. For fifty years and much longer, nonwhite communities have rightly been asking: Where are the prophetic voices among our white brothers and sisters?

We will return to the academic context before the end of this chapter. I turn now to a very different point of entry, above all a memory, very far from the hallowed halls of academia, when my wife and I found ourselves in the beautiful but tortured country of Haiti.

## *Race and the World of the Poor*

There is nothing especially unique or profound about the following story. In fact, its significance may dwell more in its banality—the everyday, unquestioned normalcy of the truth it describes—than in any intellectual, spiritual, or emotional meaning I attach to it. I think any reader from any background who has visited Haiti or other severely impoverished places outside of the United States, and not just as a tourist, may recognize something of themselves in the following account.

The American Embassy in Port-au-Prince is the requisite "point of entry" for tens of thousands of Haitians each year seeking exit visas to the United States, hoping to find work, visit family, or attend school. As such it is also a sobering checkpoint and heartbreaking symbol of exclusion, a narrow gate where hope flickers for a few moments and then dies, without comment, at the window of a dead-eyed government bureaucrat.

Before sunrise every morning long lines begin to form outside the embassy gate, hundreds of Haitians dressed in their Sunday best hoping to gain an interview with an official. Fathers with sons, mothers with daughters, young men and women, all standing patiently in queues that extend from the heavily secured entrance out to the plaza and into the busy streetscape beyond. They journey by buses, bicycles, hitchhiking, and foot from every part of the country. Each pays around $400—nearly a year's wages in Haiti—simply for the privilege *to apply* for an immigrant visa to the United States; applicants for a nonimmigrant visa pay $150. Most scrape together what they can over the course of several years and borrow the rest from whomever they can to make the payment. No refunds are granted in the case of refusal. Of the tens of thousands who apply each year, less than two percent will be granted a visa. Yet day after day they come to wait in line.

My wife and I travelled to Haiti several years ago as prospective adoptive parents. We went with both excitement and trepidation to meet the two orphan adoptees with whom we had been matched, to help as we could at their orphanage, and to file the first of many rounds of paperwork at the US Embassy in Port-au-Prince. Our appointment, arranged by telephone months in advance, was at eight o'clock on a Wednesday morning. We had learned by now to expect the unexpected. Bouncing and careening our way to the embassy in our host's thirty-year-old pickup truck, we were a nervous wreck but promised each other we would hope for the best and celebrate small victories. Caught up in a sea of my own concerns—Did we have the necessary paperwork in order? Are they really expecting us? Will they require some kind of "extra" payment?—I was unprepared for the sight that greeted us as we pulled up to the curb one hundred yards from the front gate.

The long lines of people in front of the embassy were one thing; their extraordinary beauty and dignity as they waited was quite another. As our host guided us unhindered across the plaza toward the entrance reserved for US citizens, I felt a sudden rush of shame. *Ah, the VIP entrance*, I thought, fixing my eyes ahead and then down at my feet to avoid the gaze of onlookers. But Lord, how I wished I could stop just for a moment to talk with a few of those waiting, to ask their names and hear their stories. To do so, of course, would have required an enormous amount of *chutzpah*. Given the circumstances, it also would have appeared ridiculous. I held my breath, swallowed my sadness, and gripped my wife's hand tighter as we were ushered quickly into the doorway. The armed guards, serious and efficient young Haitian men, clearly saw and understood our station, the privilege written on our skin. They quickly parted a way through the crowd for us to enter.

For a flash I thought of the camel, the needle's eye, and how difficult, Jesus said, it would be for the rich man to enter the kingdom of heaven. But here in Haiti it was precisely the opposite. Was this the kingdom of hell, over which my wife and I were set as Lord and Lady?

Yet, truth be told, it did not look or feel like hell. What I saw were *people*, ordinary, beautiful people of every kind, waiting with dignity, courage, and something like hope. I dare not guess what they saw in me and my wife as we walked across the plaza and into the entrance. I can only hope that a few recognized something familiar and perhaps even worthy of trust: our humanity, our vulnerability, even our self-preoccupied hopes for our own family and a future a little closer to the scandalously inclusive reign of God. But that would require a different kind of seeing than what was "obvious" to everyone (including me) on the surface of things: the rich, white American, strolling up the plaza with his beautiful wife, entitled to see and do with the world as he pleases.

Beneath the surfaces of the scene lurk many terrible ironies, not least the fact that so many (black) Haitians would look with longing toward (white) America for hope. There is certainly irony in the fact that a "rich white" American couple would look to the shores of "poor black" Haiti in their desire to adopt. Beneath the surfaces of our story pulses the tragic weight of history.[7]

When Christopher Columbus and his flagship *Santa Maria* ran aground on Christmas day in 1492 on the island that would come to be known as Hispaniola, an estimated quarter million indigenous Arawak peoples resided there. The Arawak were initially tolerant of Columbus, helping him to build the first Spanish settlement of La Navidad. Within twenty years, however, the Arawak were almost completely decimated by disease and brutal treatment under their European colonizers, their numbers reduced to a staggering fourteen thousand. Indeed within ten years of Columbus' arrival, the Spanish began importing African slaves to replace the dying Arawak. In so doing, they established Hispaniola not only as a rich agricultural colony but also as a pivotal way station for the slave trade.

By the mid-seventeenth century the western third of the island (today's Haiti) had come under French control and was the most lucrative colony in the West Indies, known to Europeans as "the pearl of the Antilles." Vast plantations of sugarcane raised by slaves of African descent formed the backbone of a rich port economy of goods flowing between the Americas and Europe, including the commodity of African slaves crucial to the rising agricultural economy of the American South. Thus within one hundred fifty years an ancient indigenous culture was "disappeared" to make way for the white, European, Christian, and peculiarly "American way of life," built on the backs of slaves, themselves torn violently from ancient home-lands, religious practices, and the proud African cultures of their birth. It was a pattern that repeated itself with devastating success all across the New World.

The more piercing irony is yet to come. In 1802 a slave revolt led by former slave Toussaint Louverture provoked Napoleon to send twenty thousand troops to pacify the island that had produced so much wealth for France. Met by fierce slave resistance and decimated by yellow fever, the French troops withdrew, and in 1804 the new nation of independent Haiti was declared. What might have become a flourishing independent black republic, however, was not to be.

The success of the slave revolution sent shock waves throughout the New World, especially in the American South where slave owners feared it would inspire a similar uprising. Pro-slavery factions pointed to the slaughtering of French whites during the Haitian revolution as proof that "violence was an inherent part of the character of blacks," a logical fallacy not unfamiliar to us today, which ignores the violent and authoritarian rule of white people over enslaved and subjugated blacks for centuries. Following the revolution, European powers and the United States (led by Thomas Jefferson and other slave holders) refused to recognize Haiti; France demanded compensation for French slaveholders who had "lost their property"; and Haiti spiraled into a long history of unmanageable debt, environmental degradation, and corrupt leadership.

Herein lurks the onerous weight of what Catholic social teaching calls "social sin," the historically entrenched web of institutionalized injustice against a whole people, and the present context in which tens of thousands of impoverished Haitians risk their hearts and fortunes every day against all rational odds for a chance to escape to the United States. Why risk such an irrational venture? The short answer, of course, is hope, hope defiant and beautiful, and the simple desire for a more humane future for themselves and their children. That hope-against-hope is made all the more poignant by the history of white, colonial, and Christian hubris joining the histories of Europe, the United States, and this Caribbean way station for African slaves once called Hispaniola.

As for me and my wife, why Haiti? The short answer also has to do with desires and hopes that elude rational explanation, including the gradual realization that our lives are somehow bound together with Haiti and, by some mystery, with the lives of these two beautiful children that we now call our own. I will say more about this in later chapters, but suffice it to say that "rich," "white," and "American" do not adequately describe our deepest identities as human beings, still less our felt calling as a couple, notwithstanding the empirical surface of things.

*If anybody asks you who I am, you can tell them I'm a child of God.* So goes the great African American spiritual, which I am thinking of now as I reflect on these things. It is a song I first heard in what may seem like the unlikeliest of places. Let us consider now a third point of entry and a body of music that claimed me some twenty years before Haiti. To my mind it both includes and transcends the racial dynamics of the previous two contexts we have considered.

## *Race and the Song Circle*

In the summer of 1988, at the tender age of twenty-three, I packed up my belongings and left my hometown of Lexington, Kentucky, to study music at a small Buddhist college called the Naropa Institute (now Naropa University) in Boulder, Colorado. One of my first courses was a tour de force called "Building a Vocal Community," taught by guest professor Dr. Ysaye Barnwell, long-time member of the all-female African American acapella singing group Sweet Honey in the Rock.[8] For two weeks Dr. Barnwell took her fifty or so students—most of us white, middle-class, and somewhat fragile twenty-somethings still unsure of our place in the world—on an intense and wondrous ride into the terrible beauty of the African American spirituals tradition.

It is one thing to think and talk *about* race and race relations across the color line in the academy, society, and church. It is quite another to accompany a great storyteller, artist, and musician as she plunges you headlong into the deep river of black suffering, resistance, and grace. It was in this class, and indeed in Dr. Barnwell herself, that I first encountered the living God whose face happens to be black. It was here that I first contemplated the black Jesus, who still lives (and dies) deep down in the dangerous memories and slave songs of the African American community. I will never forget the power of Dr. Barnwell's storytelling, her strength and gracious presence, and the haunting power of her voice, which stirred something ineffable in me. I can still feel the thrill of our final evening concert, in which we led the whole campus community in storytelling, song, and celebration of the living tradition we had begun to learn together.

Thomas Merton, the famous American Catholic monk and spiritual writer, once observed that the psalms hold a certain advantage over the New Testament because we *sing* them. In singing the psalms, says Merton, "we lay ourselves open as targets, which fire from heaven can strike and consume."[9] Such is the case, I quickly discovered, with the spirituals. Black or white, yellow or brown, rich or poor, sinner or saint, one cannot hide from the particular beauty and haunting power of the spirituals. Moreover, by singing them with others and not just studying them alone in quiet libraries, we lay ourselves open *to one another* in ways we might never before have risked. Is there any act of greater vulnerability, and potential intimacy, than singing, full-bodied and shoulder to shoulder, with another person? In laying ourselves open we can truly be and become "a vocal community."

But what claim, if any, can a white man have on the spirituals? None at all, save when someone from the black community graciously invites me, the stranger and oppressor at their gate, into the song circle. In truth, when I sing the spirituals, especially when I am encircled by five or ten or fifty others, I make no claim on them whatsoever, intellectually, spiritually, historically, or otherwise. It is the spirituals that claim me, or better, we. Paradoxically, I discover myself by losing myself in the song circle, by giving myself over to the memory and experience of the black community. And it is this particular community, represented by four hundred years of suffering, fidelity, and grace, which claims me. Not incidentally, herein lay a crucial difference between the academy and the church, the lecture hall and the church choir. Where the academy remains more or less beholden to "objective" analysis from a comfortable distance, a faith community not only allows but demands personal engagement and commitment, the kind in which we "lay ourselves open as targets."[10]

Merton goes on to suggest that the peculiar ability of the psalms to ignite a fire in the listener can only be accounted for "by the fact that we, in the Spirit, recognize the Spirit singing in ourselves."[11] Their impact, in other words, is *theological* and not just psychological. No less is true of the spirituals. To sing the spirituals is to be drawn into the very life and pathos of God, poured out and enfleshed in the human community. In our singing and physically embodying them, the spirituals are not merely signs pointing to historical events from which we remain far removed. They become *sacraments*, instruments of real presence and grace for a people still on pilgrimage in history.

The false "I" of individualism and self-absorption—even my socially constructed identity of whiteness—gives way to make room for a new (and eternal) creation, the "we" of our shared life in one another and in God. If only for the duration of a song, the spirituals reveal "not merely what we ought to be but the unbelievable thing that we already *are*." No less than the psalms, they make us to believe that "we are at the same time in the desert and in the Promised Land."[12]

## *Hope Sings, So Beautiful*

I have described just three of many possible entry points from which to enter into the conversation about race. Each represents formative moments and graced encounters in my own life, and just so, each reflects my own limited horizon and biases. To be clear, as a white Catholic theologian and teacher I accept much of the discourse surrounding white privilege and believe it is necessary and even urgent to engage with this reality in a sustained way, as I do with my students. The term is more than a sociological construct insofar as it exposes (and seeks to dismantle) a painful general truth, if not the whole truth, which is empirically impossible to deny. Like racial bias itself, the fact of white privilege remains one of the greatest obstacles to societal justice, racial reconciliation, and, for people of faith, our shared life in God. It ought to make us very uncomfortable.

Academic discourse at its best refuses to smooth over or anaesthetize the sting of exclusionary practices and stubborn biases based on race. The scholar is charged to serve the truth in humility as best as he or she is able to judge it, and indeed to speak the truth defiantly wherever it is denied, manipulated, or paved over by the roar of more politically expedient concerns. *Hope rings, so defiant*, in lecture halls and scholarly discussions of race insofar as all hope begins with telling the truth. Understandably, sometimes necessarily, that refusal to sanitize difficult truths can sanction (or appear to sanction) a blunt reversal of power arrangements that leaves white folks like me sitting uncomfortably outside of the circle. But honesty also compels me to ask, at what cost? What are the costs when *literal* whiteness (or non-white-ness) remains the defining paradigm, the implicit entry or exclusion point, for the conversation? The circle remains closed, the wall remains standing.

In short, as a person of faith I grow uneasy when categorical descriptors, including racial ones, so define and circumscribe our conception of reality that they prevent our naming (and singing) the deeper mystery that binds us together as human beings, citizens of the world, and children of God. Whether we call that something more the Beloved Community, the Reign of God, the Body of Christ, or the hidden ground of Love, the point is that for people of faith, such a vision—and sometimes the transforming experience—of our shared life in God *is no less real because it is hidden* than are the twin evils of racism and white privilege. The act of faith as I imperfectly understand and try to live it involves a commitment to bind myself to the deepest, most real source of all that is, and to speak words of longing and hope from that place of covenantal relationship. There is a greater mystery at play in the sum of people's lives than what lay under the control or purview of scholarly discourse. The mystery of a love that knows no human boundaries is no less worthy of expression because it remains so widely and painfully unrealized.

But then my experience in urban America and in places like Haiti confronts me with the realization of how my literal whiteness *literally* benefits me and my family, even where those benefits have not been asked for or have filled me with shame. To be human is to feel the sting of hope wherever hope has been too long deferred, and to protest whenever justice—right and equitable relationships between persons, communities, and nations—is too long denied. *Hope stings, so deferred*, because in so many ways we still stand gazing impotently across the color line, unable to remove the "beam in the eye of our global village."[13] When and where shall we find the resources to discover in the stranger, even in the oppressor at our gate, something of our very selves, our mutual vulnerability, our common dreams for life's flourishing on this side of the heavenly banquet?

If only for the duration of a song I have felt these barriers fall and something new coming to birth between myself and one-time strangers as we enter the song circle together—something impossible by all lights of practical reason. *Hope sings, so beautiful*, when we find the courage to remove our masks, shed our pretenses, and allow ourselves to love and be loved in communities of storytelling and song. Hope sings *sideways*, not from above to below but from person to person when we take the time to share our stories, traumas, disappointments, and dreams across the color line.[14] In communities where we are welcomed graciously as persons with all of our beautiful differences, the anxious question of every spiritual pilgrim, "Who am I?" is transformed into the more patient and forgiving, "*Whose am I? To whom* do I belong?" Such is the gift of communities of faith and wisdom, where Christ meets us where we are, and invites us to fall in love with his suffering people. Such was the gift to me of Dr. Ysaye Barnwell and her freedom songs of resistance and hope.

There is a season for protest and lamentation, to be sure. But there is also a season for mutual risk and vulnerability, for shared labor and worship, and for concrete gestures of peace-making and justice-seeking across the color line. In which season shall we stake our lives? I don't have a tidy answer. Both ways of being in the world, both styles of prophetic discourse, clearly find support in biblical, gospel faith. But it seems to me that the vocation of the Christian is to live fully situated inside this tension and not to flee from it. In other words, the *unknowing* itself is faith's critical moment, where we stand together, as it were, at the foot of the cross, even while we anticipate and sometimes realize in one another the promises of resurrection.

I get that there is no cheap grace. I know for my part that I remain woefully out of touch with the greater part of black experience in America and live day to day unconscious of the scope of my privilege. But Christ stands with us in our poverty and, yes, I believe— "help my unbelief" (Mark 9:24)—even in our blindness and privilege. And the mercy of Christ makes up for it in kind in every one of these gaps: in the academy, where he sits "in the midst of the teachers, listening to them and asking them questions" (Luke 2:46); in the city streets and prisons, where he calls us to befriend those who live "among the tombs" (Mark 5:1-20); and in our churches, where his spirit sings, so beautifully, in the pathos of our hope.

May Christ be with us in our poverty, heal us in our blindness, and sing through us in our collective strength. Let hope come to sing in us, so beautiful.

# 2

# AWAKENINGS

When I see your heavens, the work of your fingers,
the moon and stars that you set in place—what are
humans that you are mindful of them, mere mortals
that you care for them?

> ~ Psalm 8

There is something which is far greater than my will
to believe. Namely, God's will that I believe.

> ~ Abraham Joshua Heschel

I cannot escape Thy Scrutiny!
I would not escape Thy Love!

> ~ Howard Thurman

Late one afternoon in the midst of summer vacation near Lake Michigan, my family and some close friends packed a picnic and drove north to arrive at Sturgeon Bay just before sunset. As we settled onto the beach and began to take in the moment, our adopted son

*Henry, author's son, at Sturgeon Bay, Michigan. Photo by author.*

Henry, then two and a half years old, looked up from his food to catch the red-orange sun as it fell toward the water. He ambled down to the surf, and after a few minutes playing at the water's edge, noticed the swirls of flaming light in the surf at his feet. Mesmerized, he turned his body and slowly raised his head, following the light as it danced across the luminous bay and out to the shimmering boundary where the crimson sun and purpling sky met the water.

The rest of us sat on our beach blankets, mouths agape, watching the scene unfold. As the sun touched the water Henry raised both hands to the sky, one of them still clutching his sippy cup, and then— I'm not making this up—he began to chant and sing and sway from side to side. For what seemed like the next ten minutes, the child sang the sun into the water.

*What in God's name was he singing? What compelled this child, who cannot stand still for 30 seconds, to remain fixed in that spot and sing with nonsensical abandon to the surf and sky?*

Anyone watching might have reasonably concluded it was nothing, an explosion of random neurons, a flurry of toddler gibberish. I'm not so sure. Perhaps he was singing the forgotten mother tongue, the language of wonder and radical amazement, before he has a chance to grow up and forget. Maybe he was chanting his plain ecstasy before we, with our adult sophistication and sober "reality checks," have a chance to teach such music out of him!

## In the Womb of Something More

The great African American theologian and mystic Howard Thurman recalled a similar memory from his boyhood in Florida, walking on the beach at night "in the quiet stillness,"

> when the murmur of the ocean is stilled and the tides move stealthily along the shore. I held my breath against the night and watched the stars etch their brightness on the face of the darkened canopy of the heavens. I had the sense that all things, the sand, the sea, the stars, the night, and I were one lung through which all of life breathed. Not only was I aware of a vast rhythm enveloping all, but I was a part of it and it was a part of me.[1]

Do such moments teach us anything, *really*, about reality? In a word, are they trustworthy?

There are certain gifts and realms of meaning that, no matter my relative power or privileged status in society, I cannot give to any person, impose upon them, or ever steal away. One of these gifts is the encounter with the mystery and wonder of Life itself and with the greatest of all mysteries we name God. For Thurman the experience of the sheer *gratuitousness* of life itself—unexpected, unearned, simply given—is the pulsing womb from which all other concerns ebb and flow, inclusive of social and political concerns. Here the individual stands "face to face with something which is so much more, and so much more inclusive, than all of his awareness of himself that for him, *in the moment*, there are no questions. Without asking, somehow he knows." Knows what? The reality that we and all things in the universe are, in fact, "one lung" through which all of life breathes is not new, says Thurman; "The thing that is new is the *realization*. And this is of profound importance."[2]

Indeed this palpable sense of the unity of oneself and of all things in God is so transforming that it leads the biblical psalmist and wisdom writers to surmise that in the human race there is an uncreated element, an eternal dimension.[3] Herein lay the disarming paradox of religious experience. On the one hand, the realization of the One in the Many, the Many in the One, feels like something altogether new: it is "so much more, and so much more inclusive" than our default mode of consciousness, a Cartesian mode of experience which divides the world into Subjects and Objects, Me and You, and most ominously, Us and Them. On the other hand, in coming to an awareness of the whole—and of God, not as another object or separate being out there but as the One in whom we live and move and have our being—the person comes into possession, says Thurman, "of what he has known as being true all along."[4] It is like coming home to where we have never been before.

We reach feebly for language to utter such an insight: "sometimes it is called an encounter; sometimes, a confrontation; and sometimes, a sense of Presence."[5] Psychologists, religious philosophers, and skeptics alike have tried to classify, tame, and sometimes dismiss such experiences: they are "peak moments," probably linked to the "ecology of imagination in childhood."[6] In truth, says Thurman, the experience of God is "beyond or inclusive of" all such descriptive terms and attempts at rational, analytic control. The mind has to expand its palette through poetry, psalms, parables, and chant. The mark of God is written eternally on our forehead, says Thurman, citing the book of Job. God's language of desire, what Rabbi Abraham Joshua Heschel calls the "forgotten mother tongue,"[7] is written eternally in our hearts.

So what? Even granting the unmistakable fact that human societies and cultures always and everywhere have reflected something of the religious element, what can religious or mystical experience have to do with the race problem or any practical social and ethical question in society? For Thurman, the realization of God has everything to do with the race question. He writes:

> In the last analysis the mood of reverence that should characterize all man's dealings with each other finds its basis [in the experience of God]. The demand to treat all human beings as ends in themselves, or the moral imperative that issues in respect for personality, finds its profound inspiration here. To deal with men on any other basis, to treat them as if there were not vibrant and vital in each one the very life of the very God, is the great blasphemy; it is the judgment that is leveled with such relentless severity on modern man.[8]

Would that people today in the public square, not least religious folks, could approach one another with something of this "mood of reverence" that issues from the realization that everyone, without exception, pulses "vibrant and vital" with "the very life of the very God." It is no wonder Thurman calls the realization of God "the most daring and revolutionary concept" known to the human race: specifically, "that God is not only the creative mind and spirit at the core of the universe but that [God] . . . is love." Such a conclusion, Thurman grants, cannot be arrived at "by mere or sheer rational processes. This is the great disclosure: that there is at the heart of life a Heart."[9]

Nowhere are Thurman's writings more powerful or moving than where he writes of Jesus of Nazareth as the lens for this great disclosure of the Heart—Jesus, who had "what seems to me to have been a fundamental and searching—almost devastating—experience of God."[10]

To Jesus, God breathed through all that is. The sparrow overcome by sudden death in its evening flight; the lily blossoming
on the rocky hillside; the grass of the field and the garden path
. . . ; the madman in chains or wandering among the barren
rocks in the wastelands; the little baby in his mother's arms;
the strutting arrogance of the Roman Legion; the brazen que-
ries of the craven tax collector; the children at play or the old
men quibbling in the market place; the august Sanhedrin
fighting for its life amidst the impudences of Empire; the fear-
voiced utterance of the prophets who remembered—to Jesus,
God breathed through all that is.[11]

Repeatedly Thurman draws our attention to how Jesus prayed, how
often Jesus prayed, and how the whole of Jesus' life *was* a continuous
prayer.

The time most precious for him was at close of day. This was
the time for the long breath, when all the fragments left by
the commonplace, when all the little hurts and the big aches
could be absorbed, and the mind could be freed of the immediate demand, when voices that had been quieted by the
long day's work could once more be heard, where there could
be the deep sharing of the innermost secrets and the laying
bare of the heart and mind. Yes, the time most precious for
him was at close of day.[12]

And repeatedly Thurman counsels us to do as Jesus did, to "wait in
the quietness for some centering moment that will redefine, reshape,
and refocus our lives."[13]

Thurman acknowledges that cultivating a life of prayer and "the
art of being still" might seem to be a luxury "while the world around
is so sick and weary and desperate." Yet he compares our situation—
and specifically, the terrible challenges facing African Americans in
the decade of the 1950s—with the prodigal son, who could not reconcile the "warring parts" of his existence until he recognized the
contradictions of his situation and came home to his father's house.

It is as if he saw into himself, beyond all his fragmentation,
conflicts, and divisiveness, and recognized his true self. The
experience of the prodigal son is underscored in the religious

experience of the race—when he came to himself, he came to his father's house and dwelling place. The experience of God reconciles all the warring parts that are ultimately involved in the life of every man as against whatever keeps alive the conflict, and its work is healing and ever redemptive. Therefore there is laid upon the individual the need to keep the way open so that he and his Father may have free and easy access to each other. Such is the ethical imperative of religious experience.[14]

For Thurman, the encounter with God is a coming home to one's true self, where we can love and *allow ourselves to be loved* even with all of our inner fragmentation, conflicts, and divisiveness. This is why prayer is not peripheral but essential to the "discipline of reconciliation" on all sides of the color line. It is not a new (or fourth) entry point into the conversation about race, but for people of faith its very source and wellspring. *O love of God, love of God, where would we be without Thee? Where?*[15]

Again there are certain gifts and realms of meaning such as the encounter with God's love which I cannot give to any person, impose, or take away. But I qualify: Consider how often God can and does give such gifts through us, through our embodied presence, and through the communities of family, work, and faith to which we belong. My son Henry's reverie before the sunset was not mine to give. And yet our bringing him to that place of beauty, our sharing it with him, opened up a circle in time and space for the ordinary miracle that unfolded and which so unexpectedly gifted us. Indeed the gift that the Christian tradition calls grace comes in so many unpredictable, spontaneous, and hidden ways: in our awe before the beauty of nature; in kind gestures passed between a parent and child, between friends, or colleagues at work; in "the long breath" and "deep sharing" between spouses or lovers at the close of the day. But torn from that sense of wonder, torn from the art of silence and stillness, torn from the discipline of exposure and surrender to the One who breathes through all that is, what hope can we have for reconciling our fragmented selves, much less for making peace with other persons and communities in the public square?

To say it more darkly, growing in the awareness of God helps us to guard against what Thurman calls the "constant threat of error" that would turn my limited experience and perspective, or that of my social identity group, into a dangerous idol or prison.[16] The tensions and contradictions of life as I see and feel them from within the womb of my social group are not, and must not be, the final word or arbiter of truth. Against the constant temptation to take refuge in the closed circle of self, blood, race, party, religion, or nation, knowledge of God cultivates humility and a profoundly open, "many-sided" awareness. Thurman writes:

> There is a spirit in man and in the world working always against the thing that destroys and lays waste. Always he must know that the contradictions of life are not final or ultimate; he must distinguish between failure and a many-sided awareness so that he will not mistake conformity for harmony, uniformity for synthesis. He will know that for all men to be alike is the death of life in man, and yet perceive harmony that transcends all diversities and in which diversity finds its richness and significance.[17]

To paraphrase the great Protestant theologian Reinhold Niebuhr, left to our own manner of measuring things we human beings and communities are "too ambiguous" to understand ourselves unless our judgments are rooted in a faith that we are "comprehended from beyond the ambiguities" of our own understanding.[18] As Thurman puts it, no community can "feed for long on itself; it can only flourish where always the boundaries are giving way to the coming of others from beyond them—unknown and undiscovered brothers."[19] Sometimes it is the ineffable God who grasps us "from beyond" ourselves; sometimes it is nature; sometimes it is the ineffable human *other*: a beloved, a child, a neighbor, our enemy. In every case the question is, are we willing to let the circle of familiarity be broken open, and the boundaries give way to the coming of the Lord?

To feel ourselves come home into God's wide-open love is to realize that there are many rooms in this house, far more than can be seen or imagined inside rigidly self-enclosed walls of religious, political, racial, gender, or class identity. This is not to render those identities superfluous, self-serving, or false; it is to see them, however, as partial and contingent to the one great fellowship and gift in which we all—inclusive of the natural world—live, move, and have our being. Like the parables of Jesus, revelation has a dialectical character. The light of God's scandalously inclusive love and creativity throws into sharp relief every shadowland and dark prison cell where persons, groups, and nations are turned in upon themselves, or, like the older son in Jesus' parable, turned outward in resentment and animosity against others, grasping aggressively for "our share" and more of society's or the earth's gifts. Indeed, from a biblical perspective our alienation from self, God, and others is bound up from the very beginning with our alienation from the earth, flowers, mountains, fields, animals, trees and waters. Why? Because, like a single lung, God breathes in and through all things. We lose touch with this fundamental insight to our great peril.[20]

At the end of the day, Thurman seems to ask: *Whose are we?* In whom do we place our ultimate trust? The source of life is God, who saturates all things in a sea of reverence. Can we see it? And can we afford "while the world around is so sick and weary and desperate" to bind our lives to such a contemplative foundation? Can we afford not to? "Do not shrink from moving confidently out into the choppy seas. Wade in the water, because God is troubling the water."[21]

### *The Terror of the Closed Circle*

With Thurman I have suggested that for people of faith the realization of God is not simply one of many possible entry points into the conversation about race so much as it is the very source and wellspring. It is the reason for our hope (see 1 Pet 3:15) when we consider the many and steep obstacles that lay ahead. The encounter with the God of Jesus, who breathes in all things, transforms the way believers see, judge, and respond to everything—or ought to—right? If Thurman is correct about the "ethical imperative of religious experience," then how to explain the utter failure of so many self-identified religious people to live in the house of love? How to explain, for example, the refusal of white Catholics, historically, to share the same sanctuary and the one eucharistic body and blood of Jesus with black Catholics?[22] How to explain the regular spectacle of lynching in the American south, where whole communities of "good Christian folks" could imagine, as a kind of ritual entertainment, turning magnolias into lynching trees? Can anything but exorbitant

self-concern and human-centered disdain for God and God's gratuitous love explain the horrors of man's inhumanity to man or the
ongoing desecration of nature?

During an interview some years ago, black Catholic theologian and
Dominican Sister M. Shawn Copeland recalled the first time she became aware of these kinds of painful questions. She was twelve years
old, learning about the Holocaust during summer school. "It struck
me quite forcibly," she said, "that people who have a great disregard
for human life, if they can stigmatize you and identify you and if they
are in charge, they can make laws which can eradicate you."[23] It would
not be a stretch to measure the whole of Copeland's remarkable theological career in view of this early, troublesome awakening. If theology
asks not only "Who is God?" but also, and intimately related, "Who
is the human person?" Copeland answers with an image borrowed
from Thomas Merton: We are "a body of broken bones."[24]

I turn to Copeland's thought here as a counterpoint to Thurman's.
Though they do so from distinct confessions and different emphases
from within the Christian tradition, both seek to illumine reality
beyond the closed circle, and both find hope for the disinherited
persons of society in the person of Christ. Above all, Copeland seeks
to unmask the *thought systems* that allow for the stigmatizing, identifying, and eradicating of whole groups of persons—persons deemed
different, inferior, dangerous to society. For her the premier concern
of Christian theology today must be the defense of the vulnerable
not only from invisibility in society but from evils that render them
*all-too-visible* in the body public, evils such as racism, classism, sexism,
and homophobia. By diagnosing these crippling ailments—by telling
the truth—theology serves the body's healing and anticipates its
future restoration in "the mystical body of Christ."[25]

One of the hallmarks of Copeland's theology is the telling of stories, narratives that serve to keep our thinking about God tethered
to concrete reality. In an address to her colleagues in the Catholic
Theological Society of America, Copeland relates the story of Fatima
Yusif, a twenty-eight-year-old Somali immigrant in Italy, as it appeared in the *Times* of London:

> The plight of a Somali woman who gave birth unassisted
> beside a road in Southern Italy as a crowd stood by and jeered

prompted telephone calls yesterday of solidarity and job offers. . . . "I will remember those faces as long as I live," Ms.
Yusif, who was born in Mogadishu, told *Corriere della Sera* as
she recovered in the hospital. "They were passing by, they
would stop and linger as if they were at the cinema careful
not to miss any of the show. There was a boy who sniggering,
said, 'Look what the negress is doing.' "[26]

While "any number of current newspaper or historical accounts"
might have been selected for analysis, the story of Ms. Yusif, suggests
Copeland, serves as a particularly dramatic *anthropological signifier*:
"it captures graphically what it means to be an exploited, despised,
poor woman of color."[27]

As black, female human being, Fatima Yusif is *thrown* into a
white world. This white world both makes her race and her
body visible in order to despise and renders her humanity
invisible in order to peer, to gaze. . . . On the grounds of
naive racist empiricism, she is, can only be, 'the negress.'. . .
What they see is generated by a pornographic gaze: there is
no human person, no mother, only an exotic object to be
watched.[28]

The experience of Ms. Yusif points to the everyday quality of racism,
its palpable presence, what Latina theologians call *lo cotidiano*. In the
toxic atmosphere of white racism, to be a poor black or brown woman
is to feel one's embodiment as a problem; it is to be exposed "porno-
graphically" at every moment. Indeed, in an earlier essay Copeland
explains why biological denotation is so problematic in a racist milieu:
"the difference is inescapable, irrevocable, and visible in the very
flesh."[29] "Women of color," she writes, "are *overdetermined* in their
flesh."[30]

For someone like me who has never experienced anything re-
motely akin to the trauma of Ms. Yusif it may be difficult to compre-
hend what Copeland can mean by "overdetermined in the flesh."
The striking description points to the myriad ways racial formation
permeates not only naked acts of racism but also the fabric of everyday experience, even what seems (for whites) to be the most innocu-
ous of circumstances. "The most mundane as well as the most

significant tasks and engagements are racially charged—grocery shopping, banking, registering for school, inquiring about church membership, using public transportation, hailing a taxicab, even celebrating the Eucharist or seeking a spiritual director. We *see* race," argues Copeland. "We see and we interpret."[31]

The "we" here is significant. Racial formation initiates Americans into a well-rehearsed game of survival, a social tap dance in which *everyone* has a circumscribed role. "[We] women and men of color submit ourselves to representations and roles developed for us by whites; we learn and practice compliance and deference, or when the occasion prompts, studied, crafted anger."[32] Returning to the story, Copeland probes the racial bias in the mob of Italian onlookers. The refusal of anyone in the crowd to help Fatima Yusif demonstrates how racism chokes the "natural and spontaneous impulse to help another human being, simply because she (or he) is another human being suffering."[33] At the same time, there are layers of complexity beneath the scene that call for more than simply a self-righteous condemnation of the crowd as racists—the Vatican newspaper, for example, rebuked the bystanders as "not worthy of the word man."[34] While such a rebuke approximates a gesture of sympathy for the victim, it does not account for the hidden dimensions of the story: the bias and cultural decline that had likely poisoned the crowd's view of the other (i.e., African immigrants) long before the injury done to Ms. Yusif.

> It is not unlikely that members of the crowd fear insecurity and loss. In the global economy, even in "first-world" rural towns, it is sometimes difficult to make ends meet. These women and men fear the difference that poor people of color and immigrants represent. . . . The frustration and anger that they cannot express directly to venture capitalists and the affluent is spewed out on a poor immigrant black woman. In every country, corporate downsizing and disemployment leave a remainder—dirty jobs and scapegoats. . . . Fatima Yusif is immigration made flesh.[35]

It is not hard to hear in Copeland's analysis strong parallels with the present political climate of the United States and the animosity frequently directed against those who represent "immigration made flesh." If, however, we wish *to understand* the persons in the crowd, it is not enough to simply condemn the whole lot with a label, say, "inhuman racist pigs." What is rightly condemned as inhuman is not the persons as such in the crowd but their behavior, their objectifying gaze, their racist speech and tragic failure to help a person in need, all fueled by cultural stereotypes long fermenting in Italian society. While recognizing the humanity of the individuals in the mob is extremely difficult, doing so is crucial, even in the midst of the hateful act, lest we "innocent bystanders" reproduce their error: namely, the error of dehumanizing individuals or a whole group simply by taking a look at the surface of things, and so reacting toward them in kind.

Copeland models an alternative, contemplative way of knowing, which seeks to look on *the whole situation*, including the individuals in the crowd, with eyes of understanding, even empathy—dare I say love? What could have led human beings to act and speak in such a way? What are the social conditions that might be fueling such acts of racism and xenophobia? The high cost of framing things this way, of course, is that it requires me to question myself and the whole social fabric in which I participate and from which I very well may benefit. In short, I can no longer pretend to be simply an innocent bystander.

While this is indeed a costly way of seeing, is it not the case that most of us, in our hearts if not in our heads, already feel ourselves implicated in the grave sins of the world? When we watch the news and contemplate for two seconds the terrible things done by human beings in our own city, our nation, or across our world, we feel not just shock and anger but also shame. Painful as it is, that feeling is a sign of love, and the most basic, beautiful human solidarity. It is the deeply humane intuition, in the words of Abraham Joshua Heschel, that while "some are guilty, all are responsible." It takes great effort and prayerfulness to live from that empathetic place in the heart, the very Heart of God. It is the opening circle, the "from beyond" that we allow to seize us.

### "Everybody Here Is Traumatized"

The scourge of racial and ethnic bias is clearly not unique to the United States. Everywhere we look the human family is turned against itself. In Israel the Orthodox Jews of Kiryat Arba look down from their houses toward the Arab town of Hebron and say, "Their souls are different," and "One million Arabs are not worth a Jewish fingernail."[36] In the former Yugoslavia, Serbian and Croat nationalists engaged in ethnic cleansing even while claiming a Christian aura. In Rwanda, machete-wielding mobs turned into systematic, black-on-black genocide while the white world watched stupidly in horror. The stubbornly entrenched character of racial and ethnic bias is all-too-evident in our world today. Mere moralist rhetoric—"Racists are bad"; "Violence is bad"—can neither diagnose nor heal a threat that is supported by the whole texture and decline of a civilization. Is there hope for social change? Is there hope for persons like Fatima Yusif?

The cost to the victims of racial or ethnic hatred is not only physical violation, though it frequently and tragically is that. Racism wounds the spirit of the victim, damaging not only a person's self-image but also his or her capacity for spontaneous openness and warmth toward others. Who can forget the passage in "Letter from Birmingham City Jail," where Martin Luther King, Jr., recounts the shadow passing over his daughter Yolanda's spirit when he had to tell her why she could not go to the local amusement park? It was the first time she became aware of the meaning of her blackness in a segregated world, and her father was powerless to protect her.[37] Moreover, the reliving of a particular trauma in memory can reduce persons or groups to a self-poisoning condition of *ressentiment*. Rooted in conflict, hurt, or shame, *ressentiment* is a reactive emotional state that "is usually directed against powerful persons or groups in a society . . . [and] which may take the forms of envy, malice, hatred, revenge."[38] Fatima Yusif's defiant cry "to remember those faces as long as I live, both discloses her shame and risks the spoiling of her spirit through *ressentiment*."[39]

"Everybody here is traumatized." I will not soon forget these words of Daniel Rossing, a negotiator called upon by both Israelis and Palestinians to mediate local conflicts, speaking to me and a group of interfaith pilgrims in Jerusalem in the summer of 1998. "Here in Jerusalem," Rossing continued, "people remember not just in decades or centuries but in millennia." Events that happened a thousand years ago still hang in the air like a beautiful scent or corrosive vapor. During our six weeks in Israel, as we met with groups from opposing sides of the various divides, it became painfully clear to me that the memory of a people can be either a liberating force that transcends boundaries or a steel trap that maintains them. Very often it is both.

In short, when everybody is traumatized, nobody sees or thinks clearly. It seems that only the truly remarkable person is able to see the kinship between his or her own pain and that of the enemy. Living is no longer the pursuit of the true and the common good; living is survival. The world breaks down into good and evil people, and the only question that remains is, "Whose side are you on?"[40] At best the unfamiliar other is an object of deep cynicism; at worst, the other is inhuman, a threat to be blotted out, "not worth a Jewish fingernail." While animosity between racial and ethnic groups in the United States may not be as openly explosive as it is between the Arabs of Hebron and the Jews of Kiryat Arba, there can be no denying that "all of us who dwell in this house built on race are wounded spiritually." The problem of the color line is indeed "a beam in the eye of our global village."[41]

## *The Time Most Precious*

"The confidence of the Christian," writes Thomas Merton, "is always a confidence in spite of darkness and risk, in the presence of peril, with every evidence of possible disaster."[42] If Thurman's context for the race question is a prayerful confidence in the all-enveloping grace of God, Copeland's horizon is the world of risk and peril facing stigmatized persons in society every day. What joins Thurman and Copeland is the realization that these two worlds are not two but one and the same: God's world, where the rain falls "on the just and the unjust" (Matt 5:45).

Just as Jesus manifests by his astonishing words and deeds that the circle of grace is closed to no one—neither to the "strutting Roman Legion" or the "little baby in his mother's arms"—so does Jesus identify himself especially with the disinherited, those thought by social consensus to be structured out of divine favor and the economy of grace. "Through incarnate love and self-sacrifice," says Copeland, "Christ makes Fatima Yusif's despised body his own. In solidarity, he shares her suffering and anguish."[43] For both Thurman and Cope land we are called to "a way of being in the world," a radically inclusive way, "because of who God is."[44]

In the meantime, the great disclosure who is Jesus teaches us how to live inclusively by teaching us how to live prayerfully from the Heart of God, which means not only to see and speak the truth but also to see through the eyes of understanding, empathy, and love. To see with love, of course, is a paschal option. It hurts. It takes time. It refuses blanket condemnations. It takes the time to linger not only in shadow-lands and prison cells but also in courtyards where children play, in boats where fishermen work their nets, at weddings, on rocky hillsides, along garden paths, and in the foaming shoreline of the Sea of Galilee (or Lake Michigan). The cross, after all, would come soon enough!

There are gifts we cannot give to, impose upon, or steal away from anybody. What we can do is *live*, like Jesus, and be present to each other and to the earth, and thus open circles in space and time for the gifts of God to break through. White and black, brown and red, Catholic and Protestant, Christian and Jew, Hindu and Muslim—we can wait together in the quietness "for some centering moment that will redefine, reshape, and refocus our lives."

Let me conclude with another story of sunset, a precious time of day anywhere on earth. Abraham Joshua Heschel's biographer, Edward Kaplan, recalls a poignant incident in 1927 when the young Jewish student, having just arrived in Berlin to study at the university, was walking through the city's "magnificent streets" when he noticed that the sun had gone down and he suddenly realized that he had forgotten to pray. "I had forgotten God—I had forgotten Sinai—I had forgotten that sunset is my business—that my task is to 'restore the world to the kingship of the Lord.'"[45]

Twenty-five years later, having narrowly escaped the catastrophe engulfing the Jews of Europe, including the murder of his mother and three sisters, Heschel lamented still more our seeming imprisonment in the narrow confines of our own minds and the terrible costs to our humanity of being turned in upon the self. "We are rarely aware of the tangent of the beyond at the whirling wheel of experience. . . . What is extraordinary appears to us as habit, the dawn a daily routine of nature. But time and again we awake. In the midst of walking in the never-ending procession of days and nights, we are suddenly filled with a solemn terror, with a feeling of our wisdom being inferior to dust. We cannot endure the heartbreaking splendor of sunsets."[46]

The twilight at sunset is a boundary condition, a liminal space, a fluid borderland where we delight for a while in the haunting indeterminacies of the light in-between. The life of the God-haunted, it seems to me, is much like the twilight, a strange dwelling place of in-betweens where humanity and divinity, life and death, joy and sorrow, ecstasy and despair, *commingle*, and every moment is pregnant with expectation. The great difficulty for the religious person is to live with trust, even confidence, in the beautiful but perilous twilight spaces of our pilgrimage in history. The future is not a homogenous and empty time for the believer. "Do not be afraid," the Scriptures counsel repeatedly. God is with us, and God comes passionately toward us from the future.[47]

# 3

# INTERRUPTIONS

There is a time . . . for life in the social womb, for
warmth in the collective myth. But there is also a time
to be born, to be liberated from the enclosing womb
of myth and prejudice.

~ Thomas Merton

The shortest definition of religion: *interruption.*

~ Johann Baptist Metz

In his book *Amazing Grace: The Lives of Children and the Conscience
of a Nation,* Jewish educator and activist Jonathan Kozol invites the
reader into the microcosm of Mott Haven, "whose 48,000 people are
the poorest section in the South Bronx. Two thirds are Hispanic, one
third Black. Thirty-five percent are children."[1] The book's power
resides largely in the voices of those the author allows to speak for
themselves: children, grandmothers, pastors, and schoolteachers—

*Tanisha Belvin, 5, holds the hand of fellow Hurricane Katrina victim, Nita LaGarde, 89,
as they are evacuated from the Convention Center in New Orleans, Louisiana, Saturday,
September 3, 2005. AP photo/Eric Gay.*

dozens of people with whom Kozol has forged relationships over many years of visiting Mott Haven. Kozol is no detached observer. Like his previous books on public schools and systemic poverty and segregation in the United States, *Amazing Grace* mediates a kind of revelation of the real through the eyes of children.

Two of the children in this book haunt me. The first is Bernardo Rodriguez, Jr., who died when he leaned against a broken elevator door of his apartment building and fell down the shaft. Bernardo was eight years old. His body was discovered when residents in the elevator noticed dripping blood. The *Daily News* reported "garbage piled five feet high in an airshaft" of the building and noted that the telephone company had been to the building repeatedly because rats had "eaten through the walls" and "chewed through the phone lines." In the postscript of a letter to Kozol, a friend of the family mentions that Bernardo's grandmother is "inconsolable."[2]

The second child is Anthony, age thirteen. In a discussion with Kozol about heaven, Anthony says this: "No violence will there be in heaven, no guns or drugs or IRS. If you still feel lonely in your heart, or bitterness, you'll know that you're not there. As for television, forget it! No one will look at you from the outside. People will see you from the inside. All the people from the street will be there. You'll recognize all the children who have died when they were little. God will be there. He'll be happy that we have arrived."[3] No liberal romanticizing of the poor or academic mystification of "the other" is required to discern, in Anthony's straightforward vision of heaven, one of the most persuasive articulations of Christian hope yet uttered.

Kozol makes no apologies for his appeal to the conscience of a nation. The stirring of white conscience by no means depends on the premise that suffering is unique to blacks, Hispanics, or other non-whites in the United States. In one sense, Kozol opens our eyes to human suffering as such, and Bernardo's ethnicity is irrelevant. In a greater sense, Kozol confronts us with a suffering that is disproportionately and senselessly fixed in black and Hispanic communities. What Kozol asks is not only that we pay attention but also that the nation might recover its capacity to mourn. To *pay attention* and to *mourn*: these two practices, it seems to me, are nonnegotiable in any authentic Christian spirituality. With regard to issues of race, they certainly outrank the contentious rhetoric that reflexively defends itself by assigning blame. Indeed, mourning is a first sign of Christian protest, a first act of solidarity across sinfully constructed social boundaries.[4]

Reconciliation has to do with crossing boundaries, or better, with placing oneself *in* the boundaries that divide alienated persons and groups. Just as Jesus asks us to pray for God's reign to come on earth as in heaven, this chapter gestures toward a hope for reconciliation that transcends not only socially inscribed racial boundaries but even that haunting liminal space between the living and the dead. "The entire life of a disciple of Jesus is essentially a life of reconciliation."[5] Yet reconciliation on earth still seems a distant dream because Christ—"Lovely in limbs, and lovely in eyes not his"—is still senselessly crucified "in ten thousand places."[6] Or, as Thomas Merton wrote under the shadow of World War II, "Christ is where men starve and are beaten."[7]

If Christians wish to do more than talk about love of neighbor, we must discover Christ in such places. More than orthodoxy it is courage that is demanded of the church today, courage to build relationships across racial, ethnic, and economic boundaries. What reconciliation and solidarity will look like concretely on the ground is difficult to say in general terms, divorced from specific contexts, but it begins simply enough by reaching out, as Kozol has done, to people like Bernardo's grandmother: in a word, the inconsolable.

### The Revelation of the Real

Many whites remain blind to the everyday realities faced by African Americans and other communities of color in the United States. This blindness manifests, of course, along a very wide spectrum, from apathy, naiveté, and ignorance, to simmering fear, resentment, and hatred. The first moment of revelation for many whites may have to involve what Jesuit theologian Jon Sobrino calls a new and difficult "honesty about the real."[8] Honesty about the real means assessing the world in its totality, and not simply from an assumed standpoint within one's own racial or class identity. It means seeing the world not from the top but from below, where people actually live, and not just through a television screen or other mass media outlets. Sr. Jamie Phelps of Xavier University in New Orleans frames the Christian commitment to honesty about the real from the perspective of the poor: "Most marginalized and oppressed peoples," she writes, "passionately desire to be in union with one another and all of humankind and creation. Yet true community is only possible if it is founded in the radical truth of our personal and collective history of joy and sorrow."[9]

As simple (or quaint) as it may sound, this kind of honesty takes on its radical meaning when "we stop to consider the status of truth in our world." As Sobrino notes, "We human beings, alien from reality as we are, are incurable in our tendency to distort and manipulate reality."[10] Every tribe remembers its own story, its own heroes, and especially its own suffering first. While no ethnic or racial group is innocent of racial bias, those who benefit from the status quo have a much greater interest in manipulating the reigning discourse and perception of reality, and, we may add, have the power to do so. But revelation, understood as *divine disclosure and interruption*, opens our eyes onto a more universal field of vision to a degree of connectedness that reaches well beyond boundaries of blood, soil, race, class, or religion. If only for a moment, I glimpse my kinship with all things in God.[11]

There is something profound to be learned here in the life of Malcolm X. Even after a life-altering conversion to Islam, it was not until his pilgrimage to Mecca that Malcolm would experience a remarkable opening, an eschatological epiphany of the real: "There were tens of thousands of pilgrims, from all over the world. They were of all colors, from blue-eyed blonds to Black-skinned Africans. But we were all participating in the same ritual, displaying a spirit of unity and brotherhood that my experiences in America had led me to believe never could exist between the white and the nonwhite world."[12] What Malcolm saw and experienced during the Islamic *hajj* came as a shock, an unexpected epiphany, at once both universal and disarmingly personal: "Never have I been so highly honored. Never have I been made to feel more humble and unworthy. Who would believe the blessings that have been heaped upon an *American Negro*?"[13]

The pilgrimage graced Malcolm with both a theocentric revelation of the real—it "proved to me the power of the One God"[14]—and a revolutionary anthropological reversal, casting new light on the human race: "I have never before seen *sincere* and *true* brotherhood practiced by all colors together, irrespective of their color."[15] It was the sudden shattering of what had been a lock-tight, and arguably racist, view of reality: "What I have seen, and experienced, has forced me to *re-arrange* much of my thought-patterns previously held, and to *toss aside* some of my previous conclusions."[16]

Is it possible that for many whites, a commitment to the real will require a comparable interruption and rearrangement of thought patterns? Malcolm continues: "perhaps if white Americans could accept the Oneness of God, then perhaps, too, they could accept in *reality* the Oneness of Man—and cease to measure, and hinder, and harm others in terms of their 'differences' in color."[17] Malcolm's stress on reality (i.e., ontology) should not be overlooked. Reality in its deepest structure is just this: *all* are human beings, children of God, irrespective of differences in color. To behold the senseless suffering of another human being—the broken body of an eight-year old boy in an elevator shaft—without compassion, without mourning, without a word of protest, is to betray not only the God of all life, it is also to deny one's own humanity, the *imago Dei* in us.

It is worth comparing Malcolm's story briefly with that of Fr. Virgilio Elizondo, a Mexican-American priest from San Antonio, Texas, widely known as the father of US Latino theology. Remembering his first pilgrimage as a young boy to the cathedral in Tepayac, Mexico, which marks the place where Our Lady of Guadalupe appeared to Juan Diego in 1531, Elizondo describes the thousands of pilgrims moving "in rhythmic procession" toward the image of Guadalupe "as one collective body." "I was part of the communion of earth and heaven," recalls Elizondo, "of present family, ancestors, and generations to come."[18] As the young boy felt the Virgin's gaze meet his own, he felt embraced and protected as never before, not only by the Woman of the Apocalypse, the Patroness of the Americas, but also by the hosts surrounding him, living and dead.

During liturgies in war-torn El Salvador, after every name spoken in the litany of the missing and dead, the assembly shouts out, "*Presente!*" And so it was for the young Virgilio. The hosts of living and dead gathered under the protective gaze of Guadalupe were for him palpably real, a comforting and all-embracing presence. For myself and others, say, of white, European descent, the presence of the Mayan and Mexican dead—like the millions of souls torn from Africa during the slave trade—might feel more like a threatening storm cloud, an accusing portent. To the degree the dead are kept alive in memory—a highly selective practice—their remembrance, their *real presence*, calls the living into account. They hover over history not only as our guides and companions, but also as our judges.[19]

It is also curious that for both Malcolm X and the young Elizondo, the revelation of the One God in and through the Many, and of feeling themselves for the first time *to belong to a people*, occurred (perhaps could only occur) outside the United States. It is worth asking ourselves, why?

## Hurricane Katrina and Its Aftermath

The realization of kinship with others beyond the circle of familiarity can break through not only in moments of common celebration or religious ecstasy, as with Malcolm X and Elizondo, but also when we are confronted with intensely shared suffering. The outpouring of empathy that united so many Americans in the aftermath of Hurricane Katrina in the Gulf Coast, for example, as well as the moral outrage following the government's bungled response, suggests a painful interruption of national complacency and sobering revelation of the real. Suddenly the twin scourges of poverty and racial segregation in major US cities such as New Orleans were nakedly exposed for all to see.

To the degree that this crisis produced in whites a sense of kinship with poor blacks, whether as fellow Americans or simply as fellow human beings, the underside of this genuine empathy may well have been a deep sense of shame.[20] It is no stretch to surmise that this shame involved more for whites than the shattering of the mythos of American democracy or the so-called American dream. For many whites, as for myself, I expect it rested in the secret recognition of our own power and privilege relative to blacks, the taken-for-granted power to live with basic dignity in the United States, to protect ourselves and our families not only from natural disasters but from politically, economically, and racially fashioned ones, too.

Here again, as noted in chapter 1, the concept of "white privilege" suggests that the awakening to real kinship and solidarity across the color line comes for whites with a certain loss of innocence: the uncomfortable realization of my own social capital in a society that still privileges whiteness.[21] Whether or not we are personally conscious of such privilege, whether or not we guard it jealously for ourselves and our children, the fact of white privilege may be the most cogent, if hidden, reason why many whites flee from discussions of social justice and racial reconciliation. In a social order so bent by group bias and stagnation, so unforgiving to those without access to power, the best that may be said is that many whites resist acknowledging racial injustice in society, whether consciously or not, because of their own diffuse but very real fear of falling.[22]

It also has to be said, and celebrated, that volunteers from every racial and religious background poured into the Gulf Coast region and continue to do so today to help people rebuild their lives, one home and business at a time.[23] But that may be the best we can say. For Hurricane Katrina also surfaced the very worst prejudices in people, stereotypes far too often fueled by religious folks. As Michael Eric Dyson chronicles with sad and relentless detail in his book *Come Hell or High Water: Hurricane Katrina and the Color of Disaster*, not a few conservative religious leaders proclaimed that New Orleans faced divine retribution because it was a haven for sin. "We've known for decades and longer that New Orleans has been a place where immorality is flaunted and Christian values are laughed at," said minister David Crowe, the executive director of the Christian group Restore America. "It is the epitome of a place where they mock God."[24] On national television black minister Wellington Boone blamed "the culture of those people stranded in New Orleans" for their fate, claiming that the "looting of property, the trashing of property, etc. speaks to the basic character of the people." As if the point were not yet clear, Boone goes on to say that "these people who have gone through slavery, segregation and the Voting Rights Act are doing this to themselves."[25]

Conservative television and radio talk show hosts hammered home the view that the poor black population of New Orleans brought their suffering upon themselves. Bill O'Reilly issued this helpful warning to the poor. "So every American kid should be required to watch videotape of the poor in New Orleans and see how they suffered, because they couldn't get out of town. And then, every teacher should tell the students, 'If you refuse to learn, if you refuse to work hard, if you become addicted, if you live a gangsta-life, you will be poor and powerless just like many of those in New Orleans."[26] Rush Limbaugh joined the chorus, arguing that a "welfare state mentality" prevented the black poor of New Orleans from escaping the hurricane's path. "The nonblack population was just as devastated, but apparently they were able to get out." Limbaugh appears to be constitutionally incapable of seeing the beam in his own eye. "Race, in this circumstance, is a poisonous weapon, and it's why the liberals are now gravitating to it."[27]

This brings us back to honesty about the real. Simply the desire to behold reality more honestly, and thus to vigorously resist the premature or biased closure of meaning, is the mark of authentic Christian spirituality in full bloom. Like the Good Samaritan who refuses to close his eyes to the suffering neighbor—and who recognizes the enormous privilege of not being abandoned in the ditch—solidarity begins with the "willingness to be swept along by the 'more' of reality."[28] For white Christians, especially the young, this willingness may manifest tentatively as the dull ache for something more than more of the same in our racially and economically stratified society. With prayerful self-examination and honest discernment of one's place in the world, even of one's own privilege, such a holy restlessness can blossom into the expansive spirituality envisioned for the pilgrim people of God by the Catholic Church at Vatican II: "Nothing that is genuinely human fails to find an echo in their hearts."[29]

## The Complexity of Race Discourse Today

To articulate a national vision of racial reconciliation as King did with the image of the Beloved Community would appear to be even more difficult today. Many blacks today express deep ambivalence about reconciliation with whites, especially if reconciliation is understood as integration. (As James Baldwin put it five decades ago, "Do I really *want* to be integrated into a burning house?") For many Americans the civil rights movement appears to be a distant dream, a moralistic history lesson.[30] To the degree that race is mentioned at all from the pulpit of white Christian churches—once a year, for example, on Sundays adjacent to the King holiday—one can expect a fair amount of pious moralizing about King's "dream" for America. While such rhetoric is not itself a bad thing, surely it cannot be mistaken for meaningful Christian relationship building across the color line.

It is crucial to remember that for the visionaries of the civil rights movement, integration never meant homogenization but rather affirmed racial and ethnic difference and pride in a truly just and inclusive society. For King, just as for Howard Thurman (chapter 2), the movement toward integration was a spiritual movement rooted in the biblical vision of the dignity of all life within the "interrelated structure of all reality." King never tired of repeating his faith in a divine, loving presence that binds all people together in "an inescapable network of mutuality," a "single garment of destiny."[31] In his darkest moments of fear and despair, King felt that presence reassuring and beckoning him forward, giving him new courage and strength to love. Indeed for so many who risked their lives during the movement—black and white, Christian and Jew, young and old—the call to unity was no mere slogan, but the way of sacrifice and redemptive suffering. "Speaking about the oneness of humanity was not innocent Sunday-school talk,"[32] as James Cone reminds us. It was a direct challenge to segregationists at every level. To seek the practical realization of such a vision—"Injustice anywhere is a threat to justice everywhere"—is to invite concerted, even violent pushback.

Complicating the pastoral challenges and certainly the political rhetoric today is what many commentators have called a "crisis of culture" in poor communities of color, where forces of decline and despair have long been closing in not just from outside or above but quite rapaciously from within. With roots in public debate reaching back to the controversial Moynihan Report of 1965 and indeed much further, conservatives from white columnist David Brooks of the *New York Times* to black economist Walter Williams of George Mason University highlight the breakdown of the black family as the greatest threat to racial equality and the root cause of problems ranging from welfare dependency to black-on-black crime. Williams consistently blasts the media for its complicity in "the liberal narrative of the continuing problem of white racism," and black comedian Bill Cosby joined the fray with a controversial speech at the NAACP in which he criticized black parents for failing to instill basic moral standards in their children. Liberal voices from evangelical progressives to Catholic theologians and bishops drawing on Catholic social teaching counter that the conservative narrative ignores the constellation of social obstacles reinforcing poverty and amounts to an elitist and classist strategy of denial and of blaming the victim.[33]

Might the whole truth lie on both sides of the argument? While the fact remains that Americans have never come to terms with "the legacy of material, psychic and cultural assault waged against black people since slavery"—a record of violent physical and cultural uprooting, economic, political, and legal disenfranchisement, and culturally inscribed non-personhood—it is also fair to say, as black theologian Adam Clark observes, that the black community has yet to come to terms with self-destructive behaviors and thought patterns that have prompted not a few to wonder, including African Americans, whether blacks are not their own worst enemy.[34]

> The problem of violence, debated as a credible strategy for social change during the late 1960s, has degenerated into a seemingly endless cycle of fratricidal violence in black communities. The accessibility of guns and drugs, misguided sexual experiences, high rates of incarceration, police brutality, family disintegration, dysfunctional public schools, and blighted communities generate a profound sense of hopelessness. Can things *really* change? Is a new world possible?[35]

Situated in Cincinnati's segregated and blighted inner city, Clark's credibility in addressing the complexity of the black situation at street level far outweighs my own. The strength of his analysis, much like Kozol and Dyson, lay in his refusal to turn the race problem into a blame game, a simplistic either/or diagnosis. Complex social evils must be addressed both from above, at the macrolevel of American society where powerful political, economic, and social forces exert pressure downward, and at the same time from below, at the person-to-person level of education and spiritual formation, where impoverished blacks—indeed peoples of every race, ethnicity, and socioeconomic status—struggle from day to day, and often fail, to live with dignity and responsibility in tenuous networks of family, education, work, and worship. In short, the crisis of culture is in no way simply a black or brown problem rising up from self-destructive patterns in the ghetto; to the contrary, it reflects a crisis that is woven into the whole fabric of civilization.[36]

One would at least like to think that a snapshot of reality, as grasped in the wake of Hurricane Katrina, for example, would be sufficient to put to rest the thin illusion that all would be well for peoples of color in America if they would just "get their own house in order," or that we have entered a new age of post-racial harmony following the Obama presidency. Any such naive optimism is shattered when one begins to consider the status of truth in the world, especially in a culture anaesthetized and polarized further by the mass media.

Constructively what black intellectuals like Clark and Dyson share with Kozol (and myself) is concern for the deepest anthropological and theological convictions pulsing beneath practices at every level of society. In a word: Who really counts as *persons* in American society? And who, in practice, can be ignored, written off, left to fight for survival under long-deteriorating social conditions with the scarcest of educational, economic, and political resources? From a religious ethical perspective, is there really any way around Kozol's position that we are called to pay attention, to care, and to make equitable opportunity and the flourishing of life possible for all children, not only because of who we claim to be as Americans but *because of who God is*? The rather straightforward question of "Who counts as persons?" drives us back to the question of integration and the common good: Are we or are we not committed to building a truly just and inclusive society?

### *The Mutual Risk and Grace of Crossing Over*

White Christians may accept that what is at stake in race relations is not political correctness but our integral relationship with God, that is, our salvation. Whites may also be persuaded that the preferential option for the poor is not peripheral but integral to Christian discipleship. To be moved by the suffering of others means little if we are not literally moved to compassion, political engagement, and solidarity. But to begin with the demand for political action is to risk overlooking the prior source and seedbed of all *loving* action, namely, the graced encounter and subsequent growth in friendship with our neighbor. The point of opening myself to such friendship is neither guilt—liberals are already very good at this—nor punishment, but love and concern for justice. How does one begin to engage a divided reality and one's sinful place in it with desire and love? How does one cross over from a condition of blindness to sight? And are we capable of so moving ourselves?

A range of factors, some toxic and others more benign, may explain (not to say justify) the paucity of relationships across racial lines in many communities. In addition to apathy and fear, cultural ignorance and outright racism, we should not underestimate the lack of invitation as a serious factor. The members of a family long divided have to make conciliatory gestures if they are serious about healing. Solidarity, "the empathic incarnation of Christian love,"[37] is not a matter of preconceived agendas, whether offering help (which risks condescension) or asking for help (which risks pawning dignity). The first step may be mustering enough courage for the smallest gestures of hospitality and shared presence, risks which already place us in the path of grace.

It seems to me that prior to any preconceived political or social agendas, prior to any speeches about integration, reparations, or even shared worship (which is crucial), simple physical *presence* is the greatest gift Christians can offer one another in a divided society. Christians on all sides must cross geographic, economic, and racial boundaries in order to simply be present to one another's experiences, to celebrate them and, indeed, sometimes to mourn them. For me this means leaving my various comfort zones—university, home and hearth, solitude, nature—to engage life as it is for peoples of color in my own segregated city. Once again, Kozol, our elder brother in the Jewish faith, presents an unassuming model. Even at half of the dramatic scale we find in his story, any serious effort to build relationships person-to-person across the color line constitutes a miracle of the first order, the dawning of a "first Christian generation."[38]

In the realm of academic discourse perhaps what is most needed today is a revaluation of values, especially a clarification of the relationship between solidarity and integration. What would interracial solidarity look like today on the ground? How to practically and politically confront white privilege as it lubricates the mechanisms of opportunity for whites and short-circuits them for people of color in our schools, businesses, workplaces, and judicial system?[39] Jamie Phelps, for example, correlates King's vision of the Beloved Community with the mission of the Catholic Church; Bryan Massingale writes movingly of instituting more inclusive ecclesial practices inspired by the black community's hard-bought image of The Welcome Table; M. Shawn Copeland urges Catholics to reject the uneasy alliance between Christianity and American Empire and to extend our welcoming practices especially to those "marked" for exclusion, such as gays and lesbians.[40] What these black Catholic authors share is a vision of integration more or less continuous with King's ethos of integration in multiracial communities of society, family, and church.

Yet other voices in black theology and pastoral life, notably non-Catholic ones, question whether inclusion and racial justice are synonymous with integration. Are racially integrated schools, neighborhoods, families, and churches the most desirable goal for blacks? While progressively-minded white Christians and Catholics like myself tend to assume the value of integration *tout court*, a growing number of black clergy situated among the urban poor "have embraced an Afrocentric framework to practice faithful resistance against the forces of spiritual darkness and social oppression that diminish and enslave black life."[41] While Afrocentricity does not necessarily mean radical separatism, self-segregation, or black nationalism, it tends to look with deep suspicion on Christianity as a white European religion of empire, and thus as more of a danger than a help to the self-determination and liberation of black people.[42] Moreover, reaching back at least to the birth of hip-hop in the 1970s, the icons of black music, culture, and art today tend to be formed *not* in the womb of the black church (and thus tethered to narratives of Christian hope) but rather in the bleaker crucible of the streets, with its discordant codes of survival and perceived social "respect" by any means necessary.[43]

Amid all of these tensions, *hope nevertheless rises* and racial solidarity comes to birth in surprising ways in neighborhoods, churches, and communities all over the United States. In the Catholic world, for example, not a few have discerned the hidden movement of the Spirit in the dramatic demographic shifts now taking place in the United States and in the Catholic Church in particular.[44] As the once-normative model of national or ethnically homogenous parishes disappears, many churches have been forced to integrate or assimilate with other parishes, some adjusting quite successfully, others less so. This breaking open of assumed horizons of "being Catholic" may indeed be our *Kairos* moment, and though painful, our path to grace. For my part, if I am more hopeful than apprehensive about the "browning" of the church it is because many of the young white Catholics I teach (certainly not all) express what I gather to be an authentic desire for vibrant, multiracial faith communities and prefer not to wait for the afterlife to experience them. Are there not people of every color and creed who desire the same?

If the answer is yes, we must find fresh ways to address one of the most vexatious challenges facing race discourse in America, which is the problem of its reception among whites. How to proclaim the race critique in a more unified and effective voice than any small group of scholars, preachers, or prophetic voices could do? How especially to plant the seeds of solidarity in our youngest generation, over against the very real lure of virtual anonymity, political apathy, and the warm glow of consumerism? More pointedly, if the churches are not the leaven for hospitality and communion in society—not uniformity but unity in difference—who will be? From ecumenical and interfaith unity, new strength can arise to confront reality, grieve for it, and change it.[45]

## The Contemplative Mirror

The Trappist monk and spiritual writer Thomas Merton wrote many prophetic essays on race during the 1960s that remain astonishingly, and sadly, relevant today. In fact it was an unexpected encounter in a crowded city, far from his monastery in rural Kentucky, that awakened Merton to his essential kinship with brothers and sisters whose names and stories he did not know. It happened in Louisville, Kentucky, "at the corner of Fourth and Walnut, in the center of the shopping district"[46] as Merton was standing on the crowded street corner watching the faces of passersby, when he suddenly saw the human mosaic and his place in it with brand new eyes. "It was like waking from a dream of separateness," Merton wrote in his journal. "As if the sorrows and stupidities of the human condition could overwhelm me, now I realize what we all are. And if only everybody could realize this! But it cannot be explained. There is no way of telling people that they are all walking around shining like the sun." Finally, he confesses, "I have no program for this seeing. It is only given. But the gate of heaven is everywhere."[47]

There is no program for healing the broken body of Bernardo Rodriguez, still less for healing the body of broken bones that is the human family divided violently against itself. In the end, "It is only given." Yet from the very beginning the call of God springs forth from within the dark breach of everything shattered, beckoning us to play our part. That call is rendered with singular intensity by the Jewish tradition's ancient (and very fresh) memory of historical suffering and its doctrine of *tikkun olam*, roughly, "the reparation," the "making good," "the rescuing to make good of what is left of this smashed world."[48] The wellspring of *tikkun olam* is love received and love freely given, a fierce love that seeks justice and the flourishing of life for all God's children. It is possible for us to love, it is possible to be a human being, because God "first loved us" (1 John 4:19).

Clearly the polarized racial, economic, and political landscape of the United States yields no facile prescriptions, no cheap grace. "Even those who want with their whole heart to love one another remain divided and separate,"[49] laments Merton. Yet living with the pain of disunion would be unbearable without companionship, not least a sense of God's presence sharing our burden. Prayer, or contemplation—what Jesuit Walter Burghardt calls "a long, loving look at the real"[50]—prepares us to sit in silence and reverence not only before God's presence in the sacraments or in the beauty of nature but also before every person we meet: black, white, yellow, red, or brown. Prayer makes room in our overcrowded consciousness for others, especially their pain and suffering. But not only their suffering! Prayer also clears space in our hearts for their cultures, languages, art forms, music, and rituals—in a word, their luminous differences. In our prayerfulness, *God* makes room in our hearts so that we—like Simeon beholding the infant messiah—might be prepared to smile in wonder, in the fresh spirit of goodness, freedom, and possibility that hides in every person.

Feminist theologian Sallie McFague writes most eloquently about healing "the body of God." Her lens is that of a contemplative. "The more I know about it, the more open I am to its presence, the closer

I look at it or listen to it or touch it or smell it—the more amazed I am by it."[51] The point is "that whether we pay attention to the others in nature or to our own kind we do so with love, that is . . . with the 'extremely difficult realisation that something other than oneself is real.' "[52] The contemplative way (and disciplined practice) of seeking God in the world presumes the capacity of human beings to radiate the divine for one another. Poet and novelist Alice Walker writes of this capacity to perceive one another through the eye of love: "I notice that it is only when my mother is working in her flowers that she is radiant, almost to the point of being invisible—except as Creator: hand and eye."[53] In the words of thirteen-year-old Anthony from the South Bronx, to see the world on earth as in heaven is to see people truly "from the inside."

But what can we say, finally, of the dead? Is our perception large enough to claim them in our company of saints, or more precisely, to let them claim us? Dare we to hope *in reality* that Bernardo is now bathed in warm light; that his eight-year-old body, crushed on this side, is now pulsing playfully with life on the other?[54] And is such a hope trustworthy? In this I believe Merton is correct. What Christian faith offers in response to earthly injustice and systematized violence is not a "program" but an eschatological vision and hope-infused way of reclaiming our common humanity, including, most radically, fellowship with the dead—perhaps even forgiveness *from* the dead. While such a vision eludes rational control, it is not therefore irrational; it comes both from within and from beyond the visible world of experience to make its claim on us. Can we see? Are we listening?

Whether we ignite such a vision and hope with Jesus' parables of the Reign of God and the liturgical remembrance of his death and resurrection; King's dream of the Beloved Community; Karl Rahner's or Howard Thurman's theologies of a graced world; Jon Sobrino's spirituality of living as resurrected beings; Vatican II's vision of the pilgrim People of God; the black community's hard-bought image of the Welcome Table; or even (and why not?) Bruce Springsteen's haunting, post-9/11 evocation of "The Rising"[55]—in every case we are talking about an intuition and hope that pulses already deep in our bodies and beneath the visible surface of all things. If only for the duration of a song, a pilgrimage, or a shared task, the contemplative way prepares us to grasp that we already are, with Bernardo, "at the same time in the desert and in the Promised Land."[56]

But to *feel* such a thing, and not just believe or assent to it in our heads, we have to linger with Christ for a while down at the cross, in the desert silences, and among the tombs. Perhaps what paralyzes us most is not a lack of courage but a profound poverty and captivity of imagination.

# 4

# CRUCIFIXIONS

There is no document of civilization which is not at
the same time a document of barbarism.

~ Walter Benjamin

Ah but in such an ugly time the true protest is beauty.

~ Phil Ochs

If we place ourselves inside the imaginative landscape of Mark's gospel, perhaps the most disturbing of all the earliest Christian narratives about Jesus, we find that it is on the very edge or furthest margins of society that God's presence is found breaking into the world. Far from the center of respectable society, the edge is where the untouchables recognize Jesus, when nobody else does, not even his family. The edge is the graveyard, where the Gerasene demoniac cries out day and night among the tombs, slashing himself with stones. The edge is the desert, where Jesus is driven by the Spirit and, in his solitude and

*Billie Holiday at New York's Apollo Theatre, 1937. Ken Whitten Collection. Reproduced with permission from Robert O'Meally,* Lady Day: The Many Faces of Billie Holiday *(New York: Arcade Publishing, 1991), 50.*

human frailty, tormented by Satan. The edge is a hill outside Jerusalem where Jesus is scourged, stripped, and raised up by a mob to his horrifying death on a tree. This indeed is the pivotal moment for Mark, when the veil of the temple is torn in two and the centurion, facing Jesus' dead body, names him "Son of God." For Mark, the liminal space joining earth with heaven is far from all normative centers of wisdom, commerce, religious, or political power, far from every well-ordered and otherwise pleasant framework of meaning.

"The truth of the Christian Gospel," writes the great Protestant theologian Reinhold Niebuhr, "is apprehended at the very limit of all systems of meaning. It is only from that position that it has the power to challenge the complacency of those who have completed life too simply, and the despair of those who can find no meaning in life."[1] Niebuhr gestures here to the question of social location: is there a locus *from which* we are best situated to judge reality in light of the Gospel? This chapter seeks to press our theological imaginations to the very limit or edge of their customary and complacent systems of meaning, here represented by four hundred years of black suffering at the hands of whites in the United States. With the help of singer Billie Holiday, we shall try to linger with Jesus for a while down at the cross and among the tombs.

The song "Strange Fruit," recorded by Holiday in 1939, serves here as a figure for what is a radical limit of meaning, a shadowy realm of unmeaning, for most white Christians in the United States. The images confronting the white listener in the song share something of what feminist theology calls the *abject*, "that site of simultaneous fascination and repulsion based on proximity to something that neither maintains the distance of an object nor attains identity with oneself as a subject."[2] The song sets us on edge, at the *eschaton*, a privileged locus, as Niebuhr suggests, for grasping the heart of Christian revelation.

> Southern trees bear strange fruit,
> Blood on the leaves and blood at the root,
> Black bodies swinging in the southern breeze,
> Strange fruit hanging from the poplar trees.
>
> Pastoral scene of the gallant south,
> The bulging eyes and the twisted mouth,

Scent of magnolias, sweet and fresh,
Then the sudden smell of burning flesh.

Here is fruit for the crows to pluck,
For the rain to gather, for the wind to suck,
For the sun to rot, for the trees to drop,
Here is a strange and bitter crop.[3]

The printed word cannot do justice to Holiday's 1939 recording, much less to her devastating embodiment of the song in live performances, which extended over a period of twenty years. To be sure, the song's revelatory power, past or present, hinges considerably on the receptivity of the listener, to say nothing of the social dynamics of a particular performance. Yet when I have shared the recording or video footage of Holiday's performance with my students, I have been amazed and humbled, and indeed sometimes troubled, by the range of responses it evokes. Before proceeding further, I urge the reader to seek out one of the many available audio or video recordings of the song via the Internet, to listen and linger with it, and even better, to reflect on it with others.[4]

Our task here is to consider the revelatory and theological impact of the song as it reverberates from the not-so-distant past into the present situation of race relations in the United States. A second aim, admittedly more tenuous, is to stir in the reader seeds of lamentation, desire, and hope—a hope that would set its heart and move its feet across the color line.

### Art as Dangerous Memory

The first time Billie Holiday sang "Strange Fruit" in public she thought it was a mistake. It was February of 1939, at New York City's Café Society and, as she remembers it, "There wasn't even a patter of applause when I finished. Then a lone person began to clap nervously. Then suddenly everyone was clapping."[5] The song quickly became a signature part of her repertoire. Whenever Billie sang "Strange Fruit," all service in the club stopped, and the room was completely darkened but for a pin of light trained on her face. When the song ended, the light was extinguished. No matter what kind of applause followed, the band would play no encores. These rituals, which seem to me almost liturgical in their precision and regularity, were insisted upon by Jewish club owner Barney Josephson, who says he wanted people "to remember 'Strange Fruit,' get their insides burned with it."[6] Holiday herself would often be in tears after the song, and require considerable time before she could pull herself together for the next set.

And no wonder. Drummer Max Roach describes the song as "revolutionary"; record producer Ahmet Ertegum remembers Holiday's rendering as "a declaration of war . . . the beginning of the civil rights movement."[7] The late jazz writer Leonard Feather called the song "the first significant protest in words and music, the first unmuted cry against racism."[8] Jazz musicians everywhere still speak of the song with a mixture of awe and fear. Samuel Grafton, a columnist for the *New York Post*, described the record as "a fantastically perfect work of art, one which reversed the usual relationship between a black entertainer and her white audience: 'I have been entertaining you,' she seems to say, 'now you just listen to me.' The polite conventions between race and race are gone. It is as if we heard what was spoken in the cabins, after the night riders had clattered by."[9] Mal Waldron, the pianist who accompanied Holiday in her last years, was rather more pointed in his appraisal: "It's like rubbing people's noses in their own shit."[10]

The song worked, in part, because of the stark contrast between Holiday's beauty and elegance on stage and the implicit anger of the lyrics and stark musical accompaniment. With her voice accentuating imagery of trees that "bear" and "fruit" that is "plucked," it was clear that Holiday understood the sexual motives unleashed in many acts of lynching, acts which often involved the accusation of rape and mutilation or removal of the victim's genitals. "I am a race woman,"[11] she often said, with the integrity and force of a woman who had herself known the blows of racism.

There is a little-known but extraordinary narrative behind "Strange Fruit" in the story of Abel Meeropol, a Jewish schoolteacher, poet, and musician from New York City. Deeply troubled by a photograph of a lynching he saw in a magazine, Meeropol sat down some days later and wrote "Strange Fruit."[12] Before Billie Holiday ever heard the song, Abel's wife Anne performed it regularly for several years at teachers' union meetings around New York. Given the iconic status of Holiday's association with the song, people are often amazed to learn that it was written by a white, Jewish American. By all accounts Meeropol was a gentle man, very funny, and ill at ease in public. His son Michael, however, remembers his father as "not only one of the funniest people I know, he was also one of the angriest."[13] In an interview in 1971, Abel Meeropol said, "I wrote 'Strange Fruit' because I hate lynching and I hate injustice and I hate the people who perpetuate it."[14]

"Good art must be hard," Henry James wrote, "as hard as nails, as hard as the heart of the artist."[15] Billie Holiday sang "Strange Fruit" on stage until her death at age forty-four. Her recording of "Strange Fruit" was played at Abel Meeropol's funeral in 1986. Since 1939 the song has been recorded by at least thirty-six different artists, including Tori Amos, Sting, and UB40. It is not enough to describe the song as a "classic,"[16] the mother of all protest songs, which it certainly is. Even "Best Song of the Century," the title bestowed on "Strange Fruit" in 1999 by *Time* magazine, risks trivializing more than celebrating its full force and meaning.[17] The song is best described as "a dangerous memory,"[18] and thus a bearer of unexpected hope. It brings the forgotten dead back to life in the deep wellsprings of our receptivity.

### *From Memory to Real Presence*

For Christians whose imaginations have been shaped by the memory of Jesus' passion, "Strange Fruit" cannot help but resonate in the same troubling "negative space"[19] as the haunting Negro spiritual, "Were You There When They Crucified My Lord?" For in the lynching site, just as in the darkness of Good Friday, we behold in fear and trembling the historical irruption of irrational violence and evil, the senseless horror of "man's inhumanity to man." Like "Were You There," "Strange Fruit" functions as a locus of what theologians call a "negative contrast experience": it is revelatory first of all of *what should not be*.[20] But what makes both songs so disruptive, so potentially transforming, is their power to draw us not merely into a performance but into communion with a living history, a real presence. Not only *were* we there, but by entering into the song we *are* there. As one woman said of "Strange Fruit," "When Billie sings [that song], you feel as if you're at the foot of the tree."[21]

It is precisely from this place "at the foot of the tree," far from the center of white meaning, privilege, and power, that I believe white Christians can and must bring themselves to circle around a question that is deeply personal, mystical, and political all at once. What would it mean for us to live in communion with *this particular* cloud of witnesses, this body of broken bones, this face of the living God, which happens to be black?

The cross of Jesus, "before being *the* cross, is *a* cross and . . . there have been many more before and after it."[22] In the United States, the locus of this "many more" includes the bullet-riddled tenements of Chicago, Los Angeles, and the South Bronx, and the bleak schoolyards, emergency rooms, and prisons of a hundred other inner cities, far from the center of the nation's attention. It includes an apartment building in New York City where an unarmed Guinean immigrant named Amadou Diallo was shot 41 times by four NYPD officers (all later acquitted); an intersection in Los Angeles where an unarmed Rodney King was severely beaten by LAPD officers (all later acquitted); a lonely country road in Jasper County, Texas, where an elderly black man named James Byrd was dragged to his death behind a pickup truck at the end of a logging chain; and a gated suburban community in Sanford, Florida, where teenager Trayvon Martin was followed, confronted, and shot to death by a Neighborhood Watch volunteer who had determined that the boy (being black and wearing a hoodie) looked "suspicious." The scandal of this cross is not death itself, but *senseless* death, the needless suffering and dehumanization of inconvenient, exploited, and "worthless" persons and "the possibility, a thousand times actualized, of putting them to death."[23]

It is never easy to stand in the presence of the dead, especially when their presence implies a judgment, an accusation. The bloodletting of Jesus' cross foreshadows the revelatory power of "Strange Fruit" as a divine word of judgment: You were there, and you killed him. Whether by what we have done or what we have failed to do; whether caught up in the irrationality of the mob or acceding to the cold rationality of the system; whether we wash our hands clean like Pilate or spend our days warming them by the fire, like Peter, far from the ugliness of the cross; no matter what our level of personal complicity, for every Christian the good news of Easter presupposes Good Friday, with its purgatorial dark night of judgment, lamentation, and repentance.

Of course the further I am from the specter of bald systemic racism—the failing schools of our inner cities, racial profiling, the shocking selectivity of the so-called War on Drugs and inhumanity of the federal prison system[24]—the more likely I will rebel against any suggestion of my complicity in such injustice. My defense will be eminently *reasonable*, and echoes the cynicism of Cain: "Am I my brother's keeper?" Or perhaps, on judgment day, I will cling to the sincere fiction of all innocent bystanders: Lord, when did we see you hungry, naked, in prison? (Matt 25:31–46) But the Christian community formed in the memory of Jesus knows it is deeply involved every time lives are crushed under the weight of humanity's collective sin.[25]

There is a time and a season, observes Thomas Merton, "for life in the social womb, for warmth in the collective myth. But there is also a time to be born, [to be] liberated from the enclosing womb of myth and prejudice."[26] If the first moment of conversion is to be awakened to the unjust suffering of our neighbor, the second moment is the costly grace of contrition, repentance, and mourning. The black cloud of witnesses moves the white Christian to say, "Brothers and sisters, this should not be, and I am deeply sorry."

## *Defiant and Beautiful*

As noted in chapter 3, the stirring of white conscience by no means depends on the premise that suffering is unique to blacks or other nonwhites in the United States.[27] While in one sense "Strange Fruit" exposes the dangers of prejudice and mob violence against any person or group in American society, in a greater sense it focuses our attention on a legacy of suffering that remains disproportionately fixed in scope and intensity in the black community and in other communities of color. Crucial to any authentic Christian spirituality is not only that we pay attention to such suffering, the bitter fruit of the entrenched sins of the nation, but also that we recover our deepest human capacity to mourn, a first sign of empathy and solidarity across the color line.[28]

It is important to linger a moment further on the kind of remembering being invoked here, which goes beyond the simple recall of an event that happened in the past and is now done with. The kind of memory at play here is more akin to what the Catholic tradition calls *anamnesis*, living remembrance, "an epiphanic calling forth."[29] Like "Were You There," "Strange Fruit" embodies a kind of apocalyptic unveiling, where the boundaries between past and present, living and dead, become fluid and permeable in our deep listening. In other words, much like the spirituals, the impact of the song is theological and not just psychological. Dare we recognize that it is not just Abel Meeropol and Billie Holiday who gave birth to the song but the Spirit of God—the Spirit of Life itself and life's protest against hatred and violence—who confronts us through their artistry?[30]

At this point even the most sympathetic reader might object that there is nothing redemptive in a song like "Strange Fruit," little of aesthetic value or beauty, and surely nothing akin to the divine presence and transforming hope we behold in the cross of Jesus. Here I would like to interject a comment from one of my undergraduate students, a young white woman who, as she later confided to me, is a survivor of childhood sexual abuse and many desolate years working in the sex industry in northern Ohio. Writing about "Strange Fruit" in a paper, she concluded: "The song itself does not give us anything to be hopeful for, but the act of singing it does." This wise insight— surely intensified by her traumatic memories of sexual objectification and violence—suggests something further about the potentially sacramental power of protest art as exemplified in "Strange Fruit."

There is a crucial difference, as my student intimates, between the act of lynching itself, to which no redemptive or aesthetic value could ever be attached, and the community's response to it in acts of memory and protest. Holiday's truth telling is not just sacramental, voicing God's own protest and lament for the dead; it is also *beautiful*, evoking wonder and galvanizing resistance and hope in the responsive community. Consider Chicago newspaperman Vernon Jarrett's reaction to the song: "I once heard 'Strange Fruit' while I was driving and I tried to park the car, out of respect for her—just to let her voice sink in." There was "this sense of resignation," he continues, "as if 'these people are going to have power for a long time and I can't do a damn thing about it except put it in a song.' . . . This is how most of us felt . . . [but] it enhanced my commitment to changing this stuff, that's what it did."[31]

And yet, as my student also cautioned, with a wisdom once again limned in her own pain: "this kind of 'dangerous memory' is a

double-edged sword, because it can lead to remembering with vengeance, instead of remembering with hope. Only hope brings an end
to the suffering." Here we come to the very heart of things: how to
remember and tell the truth with hope, and not with resentment or
vengeance? And is there something distinctive in the story of Jesus—
especially as remembered by the black church—that illumines this
difficult but crucial question?[32]

## *The Beauty and Paradox of the Cross*

"The God of our ancestors raised Jesus, though you had him killed
by hanging him on a tree" (Acts 5:30). In this terse proclamation resides a whole theology, a memory and experience of God limned in
wonder and hope, not vengeance. Though deeply paradoxical—the
reality it unveils is both wondrous and terrible—it claims to be good
news both for the one raised and for those of whom it is said "You
killed him." Somewhere in this dialectic I have tried to locate the
white believer sitting at the feet of black suffering.

The danger, of course, in speaking of "strange fruit" and "crucified
peoples" is to forget that the victims of history do not want to be
crucified, least of all for our spiritual edification. To say it another
way, blacks and other communities of color cannot and must not
be—no more than Jesus!—reduced to the status of victims, whether
by whites or by blacks themselves. As I noted in chapter 1, even with
the best of intentions the use of categorical, symbolic language such
as victim or oppressor to describe (or "lump") an entire racial group
communicates at best a partial truth and carries unintended costs.
One of the problems with linking blackness ontologically (i.e., in its
very essence) with victimization is that it offers whites no real insight
into the beauty or distinctive gifts of black experience and culture.[33]
Granting that "black experience" is far from monolithic, and speaking
from my own limited experiences from this side of the color line, let
me suggest a few of these gifts.

Nowhere have I experienced as I have in the black community that
mysterious human capacity for celebration and joy in the midst of
suffering, that paradoxical resilience and grace that allows people to
laugh and cry at the same time. Rising from this sensitivity to paradox
and contradiction, black poetry, literature, and art resound with an

honesty and pathos I find irresistible, even where jarring. Much the same can be said for the great names in black comedy.[34] The music of the black church has become for me a profound vehicle of prayer, a disarmingly *intimate* vehicle, I might add. I know of no body of music equal to the spirituals in confessing such tender affection for Jesus and the longing simply to be near him, talk with him, follow him. In terms of the long arc of church history, one arguably has to go back to the first centuries of martyrdom to find a record of prophetic witness and fidelity to the Gospel comparable to that historical era right under our noses: namely, the history of the black church in America rising up from the bloodied soil of slave religion.[35]

And then there is black theology.[36] Any theology committed to the nonsubjects of history is a theology haunted by the memory of the dead, and black theology wants us all to be so. Surely it is this acute *memoria passionis*, this refusal to forget the dead, that makes black theology so troublesome for white Christians like myself, those whose family history, let us say, sums up all that is good about America. If we are honest it is precisely here, under the shadow of the black cross in America, that many of us find the greatest stumbling block. For when we allow ourselves to be touched by the brokenness of the human condition, and further begin to realize our silence and complicity in this brokenness, we are almost guaranteed to falter and lose our nerve.

Yet if the paradox of the Gospel is to be believed, this moment of paralysis at the foot of the cross is the crucial moment—the moment of *kairos*, the *eschaton*—in which the church either finds its true identity or flees from it. For it is here, in this darkly luminous space where moral failure, bitterness, and flight seem to have the last word, that God's mercy comes to meet us—each of us, face to face—in the person of Jesus, the crucified one. Here is the dark ember of our good news, the pearl of great price, the miracle of a love beyond all reason. Consider the words of one of my favorite African American spirituals:

> Down at the cross where my savior died
> Down where for cleansing from sin I cried
> There to my heart was the blood applied
> Glory to his name

I am so wondrously saved from sin
Jesus so sweetly abides within
There at the cross where he took me in
Glory to his name[37]

What could slaves have found worthy of glory in Jesus' death on the cross? I hesitate to answer, having never been so close to violence and senseless death. But what I think can be said is not accessible strictly rationally so much as it is grasped iconically and, so to speak, sonically through the eyes and ears of the heart, in the very act of singing.

From God's side, as it were, what one feels in the song is the miracle of God's unreserved, self-emptying love for all creation (Phil 2:1-11). Through Jesus' suffering God sees and understands, God *remembers* my suffering intimately. The good news is not the "blood" or the act of crucifixion but the wonder that God, the Creator of the cosmos, would freely "suffer in this way" in solidarity and friendship with human beings, an historical reality that is *neither arbitrary nor accidental* for Christians—least of all for slaves and subsequent generations of black Christians who grasped this subversive truth, and grasp it still, well more than their white "masters."

From Jesus' side, what "so sweetly abides" in the cross is *the whole life that led to it*, a life of compassion, self-giving, and mercy, freely embraced even unto death. No less than in living, in dying, too, Jesus meets each of us at the cross and "takes us in" with all our sins, faults, and failings. I emphasize the "freedom" of both Jesus and God in the cross to underscore the obvious contrast with lynching, in every case a horrific violation of freedom, dignity, subjectivity, corporeality. What joins crucifixion with lynching—again, not rationally but iconically, where images touch the heart—is the former grasped as God's unreserved solidarity with every person who faces death but especially those who die in the way Jesus died.

It must be emphasized that Jesus' followers could remember his horrific death with astonishing hope and not bitterness because their whole perception of the event was transformed by the subsequent encounter with the risen Lord, a miraculous, graced encounter that reframed the darkness of Golgotha against the transforming light of the empty tomb. In that light (or dawn half-light) the Spirit of Jesus as *a reconciling Spirit from beyond the earthen grave* appears with its greatest force. Behold: forgiveness and mercy, not vengeance, comprise the very mind and heart of God, and so we also must not forget the deepest heart of human identity and personality. Both in living and dying Jesus reveals the deepest divine-human truth: love received and love given sets the world free from the terrifying closed circle of retribution and scapegoating violence.[38]

The song "Strange Fruit" refuses all such meaning and consolation. "Strange Fruit" tells the bitter truth about lynching without any hint that something else might be the case, that violence and death might not be the last word. And yet Holiday's courageous embodiment of protest at least gestures toward an alternative horizon, something more than more of the same. Through the eyes of faith we could say this: the awful gap between what is and what might still be for history's victims can be bridged, but bridged only *partially*, insofar as faith turns its protest back to God in painful expectation. If not in the firm conviction that God will one day make whole all that is torn asunder, then at least the plea to hasten the day of justice—and a prayer that Christ, in the face of the world's horrors, understands our captivity and makes up for it in our stead with God's mercy.

But faith alone will not serve. The gap between what is and what might be remains un-bridged wherever we do not join resurrection faith with action for justice. God demands, God invites, God needs our participation. From beyond the tight circle of concern for "me and my own kind," Christ himself summons: "What will you do to help take the crucified peoples down from the cross?"[39]

### *Art and the Struggle Itself*

Onstage in Carnegie Hall in 1965, Phil Ochs, the extraordinarily gifted songwriter of the civil rights era, described an effective protest song (with characteristic flourish) as "a song that's so specific that you cannot mistake it for bullshit."[40] Ochs's passion as an artist was history, "to instigate changes in history"; he saw his songs as "subversive in the best sense of the word. They are intended to overthrow as much idiocy as possible."[41] In the context of a world and a nation that has committed itself to so much idiocy, the art of the protest singer is at least the art of "aesthetic rebellion"[42] against the status quo, an artistry of defiance against the eternal return of the same (Nietzsche). In a culture that has perfected the art of selective remembering, the artist tells the stories we would rather forget, memories that irritate the ruling consciousness and challenge our collective myths.

Yet what intrigues me most is how these public and more subversive aspects of art parallel the subversive and paradoxical truth of the Gospel. In both cases something beautiful breaks through, even while reconfiguring our very assumptions about beauty and delivering a painful revelatory sting. In an interview for *Broadside* magazine in 1965, Phil Ochs articulated his artistic vision in words that reflect a wisdom well beyond his twenty-five years: "It's not enough to know the world is absurd and restrict yourself merely to pointing out that fact. . . . It is wrong to expect a reward for your struggles. The reward is the act of struggle itself, not what you win. Even though you can't expect to defeat the absurdity of the world, you must make the attempt. That's morality, that's religion, that's art, that's life."[43]

Not to put too fine a point on it, but it seems to me that there is something of the Gospel paradox in Ochs's expressly secular but hard-bought vision of things. Perhaps truth, goodness, and beauty are found, after all—or find us most ready to receive them—not in what we win but in "the act of struggle itself," the willingness to immerse ourselves body and soul in the history we have been given, and thus to be drawn into that same horizon of grace that rendered Jesus' own struggle unspeakably beautiful, even where it plunges into violence and death on a cross.[44]

Like the Gospel itself, art infused with the contemplative eye of love not only dares to plunge us into the paradoxical and sometimes horrific mystery of the human condition; in doing so, it can help us to *bridge the gap* between the horrors we witness and the more humane and unfathomably beautiful future into which God draws the whole creation, the Beloved Community toward which we struggle in grace. Intuitively, the artist understands what theology sometimes forgets: There is no human path to the Reign of God save through Jerusalem, no way to Easter save through Good Friday.[45] And in that drama each of us incarnates, at different points in our lives, a range of possible roles: I am Peter, fleeing the violence and ugliness of the cross; I am Mary, weeping at the bloodied feet of her son; I am Joseph, anointing the corpse with oils and returning it with infinite care to the earth; I am Jesus, alone in the hell of God's terrifying silence. What is most difficult for the Christian is to live *in* the boundary between Good Friday and Easter and to be able, through memory and experience, to affirm the reality of both.[46]

Let me be clear about this final point, which hinges on faith's grasp of a gratuitous, merciful, healing presence even amid the storms of life. For Christians of every color, solidarity with the stranger and the option for the poor spring not from some idealized notion of the poor, of their innocence, worthiness, or simplicity relative to us; still less does solidarity issue from our own heroic capacity to love, to "keep on keepin' on," which we find, after all, isn't there. Solidarity depends on our having already been seen, touched, and realized by love, lifted up again by mercy. For Christians, it is possible to love the other, the stranger, even those at the furthest margins of society whose very existence terrifies us, because God "first loved us" (1 John 4:19).

"Nothing is more practical," writes Pedro Arrupe, "than finding God, that is, than falling in love in a quite absolute, final way. What you are in love with, what seizes your imagination, will affect every-thing."[47] I have suggested that in a world full of crosses, our task is not to run from them, seeking security only for ourselves, our own kind, and our children. Our task is to pray for the grace to sit beneath the crosses, to let our hearts be broken, our imaginations be stirred, and our feet be moved into action. Whatever might be our particular vocation in society, academy, or church, may God grant each of us the courage to keep our eyes fixed on "the dark tree that springs up in the center of night and of silence, the paradise tree, the *axis mundi*, which is also the Cross."[48]

# 5

# SILENCES

Most of us are used only to the awesome holiness of churches and lofty arches, cathedrals where, with stained glass and brooding silences, priests try to emulate the religious atmosphere that is to be found in the living earth in some of her secret places.

~ Mabel Dodge Luhan, *Winter in Taos*

When I think of death, I only regret that I will not be able to see this beautiful country anymore . . . unless the Indians are right and my spirit will walk here after I'm gone.

~ Georgia O'Keeffe

You can't make a big thing of yourself in New Mexico. It shrinks you down. It shrinks everybody down. People come and go, a lot of famous people, and it's still here.

~ Fr. Bill McNichols

*View from Christ in the Desert Monastery, Abiquiu, New Mexico. Photo by author.*

I was thirty-two years old when I made my first trip into the high desert plains of northern New Mexico, known to many as the landscape that inspired artist Georgia O'Keeffe and to a few as the home of the Taos Pueblo Indians. About an hour's drive from Taos and twenty minutes more up the state highway from O'Keeffe's home in Abiqui, near Ghost Ranch, there is a small Benedictine monastery called Christ in the Desert, set against cliffs of red rock in the Chama River Canyon. Having read about the monastery in the writings of Thomas Merton, I was determined to see the place, so during spring break one year I recruited a fellow teacher to join me. We drove south all night from Denver, parked the car just off the main highway and, at dawn's first light, shouldered our backpacks and set off by foot down the winding, single-lane dirt road that would lead us through the Chama Canyon, and some twelve miles later, to Christ in the Desert.

What I remember most about that long hike with my friend is the palpable, pregnant silence of the place. To leave the city with its constant din of automobiles, machines, and the assault of words, words, and more words (most of them trying to sell something) and to be plunged into the silence of the desert is overwhelming and not a little discombobulating. For me—at the time a high school theology teacher immersed daily in the challenges of communicating the faith—the silence was a liberation. Bathed in the blue-bright exposure of the New Mexico sun, I felt able to breathe again, just to be, without explanation. From head to toe I felt embraced by the stark beauty of things, things heard and seen with sudden clarity under the broad desert sky. The arc of an eagle alighting from a gnarled cluster of pine trees at river's edge seemed almost apocalyptic, hitting me with a force of recognition I had never felt before. The nakedness of the landscape—my own nakedness, suddenly, precariously within it—seemed to strip bare all lesser concerns. I was *alive*, the dry breeze kissed my face, and that was gift enough for the moment.

Many years later, trying to better understand the particular magic of northern New Mexico, I came upon the remarkable writings of Mabel Dodge, a wealthy New York socialite who, in 1918, left her privileged life behind to discover in Taos and its native peoples what she felt was the answer to both her own emptiness and the discontentment of white, "cultured" American society. It was Dodge—later Mabel Dodge Luhan—who lured Georgia O'Keeffe and many other artists to New Mexico, convinced that its austere beauty and Pueblo peoples could teach America something essential and beautiful about itself—that in helping to preserve the sacred lands, waters, and memory of the Indians, we, as Americans, might even save ourselves. That conviction, sincere and wise as it may be, is fraught with at least three difficulties or risks in actual practice.

### The Hazards of Spiritual Tourism

In the first place, it risks perpetuating a kind of naïve romanticism with respect to Native American culture, or more perniciously, a kind of spiritual tourism that, rather than probing the roots of our own spiritual or cultural malaise, would look to Indian culture in a shallow or self-centered way to retrieve something of our own lost innocence. The issue here is that we as outsiders effectively remain at the *center* of such an encounter, seeking to control or selectively plunder Native culture instead of allowing the self-revelation and spiritual wisdom of the Indians *as* Indians to engage and challenge us—and yes, to invite our transformation and conversion, but from a perspective of profound cultural difference and with potentially costly implications.

Second, in ways incomparable to other cultures in the United States, Native American ways continue to elude the most basic epistemological assumptions and categories of non-Natives. As William Hart McNichols (Fr. Bill to most), a well-known and gifted iconographer who lives outside of Taos, said to me recently, "We don't live well with Mystery, we don't like it. But they do here. There's a respect for mystery. I don't know another place like it." The Western mind, in other words, is so accustomed to accumulating *information*, formulating rational *solutions*, and exercising willful *control* over our environment that Indian ways can leave us uncomfortable gazing in from the outside. Rather than sitting *in* and *with* mystery, the Western impulse is "to investigate it, settle it, close it, find an answer." Everything in Indian culture resists that impulse, as Fr. Bill notes. "You can come up close to it and describe parts of it, but the mystery remains." Indeed for Indians themselves, the sacred origins and meanings of many of their religious rituals and narratives lie beyond immediate memory, understanding, or rational explanation. And that is just as it should be. "There's a deep humility there, knowing what you don't know or understand about God. And then in it will come to you in its own way."[1]

Third, it follows that any attempt to engage Indian culture should itself be exercised with humility and reticence to judgment. Erna Fergusson, for example, in her classic guide to Pueblo Indian ceremonials of New Mexico and Arizona, aptly describes the Hopi kiva as "a chamber of mystery."[2] About Pueblo dances she cautions that even "the most painstaking and the most scientific investigators have failed to get the hidden significance of most of the movements of a dance."[3] What hope can the outsider have then, if any, of a true encounter with Native peoples? Everything depends on our contemplative orientation before the other, our epistemic humility and readiness to be changed by the encounter, by the whole-bodied situation in which "I," as objective observer, might recede into the greater dance of the One-in-the-Many. Fergusson writes:

> In looking at any Indian dance, therefore, it is well to imitate the Indian: sit back quietly against an adobe wall, soak into your body and into your soul the stimulating warmth of the sunshine, smoke or chat, watch the *viga* [roof-beam] shadows move along the walls as the hours pass, let the beat of the *tombe* [drum] and the dancing feet get into your blood—and feel what it is about. This method has the enormous advantage of permitting no contradiction; every man's guess is then as good as any other man's.[4]

As Fergusson here intimates, there is an "otherness" that teaches most authentically *when it remains radically other*, when we resist assimilating our multivalent encounter with the other into well-worn intellectual, spiritual, or theological categories. To say it another way, recalling my first pilgrimage into the Chama River Canyon, there is a deep silence, pregnant with possibility and presence, that we respond to best and most naturally with our own attentive silence, spontaneity, and heightened expectation, in our simple acts of being present. Like the silences punctuating the musical figures of a great symphony, we cannot hear the symphony of the other wherever the space between us is laden with the static of our own words, judgments, and opinions. Silence is essential if we wish to grasp anything at all of the person or community before us.[5]

It is in this spirit of an encounter analogous to the tensive interplay between music, speech, and silence that I embrace Mabel Dodge's conviction as my own: insofar as we are prepared to approach with humility, deference, and love, the Indians teach us—they help us to remember—something essential that we have forgotten about ourselves as persons in community with one another, in the mystery of God, and in primordial relationship with the earth.

## Earth as Sacrament: The Battle for Blue Lake

Few stories that I know evoke such lessons more dramatically than the story of the Taos Indians and their seventy-year battle with the US government over the sacred watershed of Blue Lake. Unlike most protracted conflicts in US-Indian relations, this story has a happy outcome. It is potentially happy and fruitful *for us*—a graced encounter of a healing kind—insofar as we take the witness of Native peoples to heart and commit ourselves to respond in kind as they do, radically rethinking how we live and respond in attunement to the suffering earth. For the Taos Indians, Blue Lake has been for seven centuries and remains to this day much more than a body of water. It is their place of worship, communal fellowship, and sanctuary with God. In a word, it is their church.

In 1906 the US government unilaterally appropriated Blue Lake and some 50,000 acres of surrounding watershed in the mountains above Taos Pueblo as part of the Carson National Forest, to be managed and developed as the US Forest Service saw fit. That action dramatized an elemental conflict between Pueblo culture and the so-called "American way of life" that variously raged, flared up, and dragged on for seventy years.[6] In the field of public debate the Taos Indians made their case for the return of Blue Lake largely on grounds of religious liberty, an argument that eventually won the minds and hearts of many non-Native and white Christian Americans to the Indian cause. John C. Reyna, the Governor of Taos Pueblo during the pivotal developments of the 1960s, gave eloquent voice to the Indians' religious relationship with the land:

> The lake is as blue as turquoise. It is surrounded by evergreens. In the summer there are millions of wild flowers.

Springs are all around. We have no buildings there, no stee-
ples. There is nothing the human hand has made. The lake is
our church. The mountain is our tabernacle. The evergreen
trees are our living saints. They are with us perpetually. We
pray to the water, the sun, the clouds, the sky, the deer. Without them we could not exist. They give us food, drink, physical
power, knowledge.[7]

When the government tried to buy the Indians out of their sacred
watershed, Reyna unequivocally rejected the offer, responding, one
might say, in the most basic *theological* terms: "Without energy provided by God, we are helpless. We will never accept money for our
place of worship." One wonders how much it would cost us today—
and quite literally how much it would save us—to see and relate to
the Earth in an analogously holistic, relational, and fundamentally
God-centered way.

Mabel Dodge, in her 1935 book *Winter in Taos*, reaches for metaphor in trying to give words to her experience of Blue Lake and the
Pueblo Indians' religious response to it, albeit as an outsider. Note,
however, that the way Dodge uses language itself to *break the silence*
and give witness to the sacred encounter is itself illuminating, sug-
gesting that she is, in truth, no longer an outsider.

The afternoon passes, the light fades, and evening is coming
when we are upon the cold, treeless ridges in austerity and
awe, utterly removed from everyday life and everything we
are used to in light and sound. As we top the last bleak, shale-
covered edge we see below us Blue Lake. Bottomless, peacock
blue, smooth as glass, it lies there like an uncut, shining jewel.
Symmetrical pine trees, in thick succession, slope down to its
shores in a rapid descent on three sides.

This Blue Lake is the most mysterious thing I have ever
seen in nature, having an unknowable, impenetrable life of
its own, and a definite emanation that rises from it. . . . The
Indians begin to chant, at first in faint, humming tones, that
gradually grow strong and full. They look over to the lake
and sing to it. Their faces show they are deep in communion
with the place they are in. They experience it and adore it as
we do not know how to do.[8]

Such accounts, I suggest, are not merely instructive for our remembering and flourishing; they are revelatory and even *salvific* to the degree they awaken something in us that has died or fallen asleep, long paved over by the roar of what Western culture (still) calls progress, or the logic by which we reassure ourselves that we have mastered all that is wild and not-human. Against that dubious presumption, societal hubris, and often willful blindness, the Taos Indians, pressed to the wall of political conflict and debate over Blue Lake, voiced their ancient and alternative vision of divine-human life in communion with the natural world. The key political voice for the tribe during the 1960s was Indian Paul J. Bernal, who delineated in hearings before Congress the philosophical and, as it were, epistemological differences at the heart of the conflict.

> In all of its programs the Forest Service proclaims the supremacy of man over nature; we find this viewpoint contrary to the realities of the natural world and to the nature of conservation. Our tradition and our religion require our people to adapt their lives and activities to our natural surroundings so that men and nature mutually support the life common to both. The idea that man must subdue nature and bend its processes to his purposes is repugnant to our people.[9]

Lending immediacy to the threat posed by Forest Service plans to timber in the watershed, cut trails, erect cabins, and "manipulate its vegetation to increase conservation policies," Bernal denounced such plans as not only disruptive of the tribe's religious privacy but flatly "destructive of nature" and the divine-human balance. "Our religion is based upon the unity of man with nature in the Rio Pueblo watershed. Any outside interference with natural conditions of the watershed interferes with our religion."[10]

In short, Blue Lake and its watershed, Bernal explained, were both literally and spirituality the tribe's source of life, as central to the Taos Indians' religion "as the cross is in Christianity."[11] Yet the Pueblo people's salvific relationship with Blue Lake was far from passive or purely receptive, as the cross too often functions in Christian belief and practice. Rather to the contrary, Native religion was based on a circle of reciprocal sanctification and blessing between the Indians, Earth, and God. "The people, through their prayers and religious ceremonies, give homage to and fructify the land. The land, in turn, nourishes and sustains the people. Land and people, therefore, are joined in a sacred, symbiotic bond; and any alteration of the land directly threatens this bond. For this reason, the Indians look upon preservation of their wilderness as a sacred obligation."[12]

In an article that proved critical in the national debate, Dean Kelley of the National Council of Churches put it this way: "Anything which mutilates the valley hurts the tribe. If the trees are cut, the tribe bleeds. If the springs or lakes or streams are polluted, the lifestream of the tribe is infected."[13] How much truth, wisdom, and urgency lie in these words! Not only for the Taos Indians, of course, but for the "tribe" that is all of us today. And yet the debate over Blue Lake raged for seven decades, as it rages today over the health of our dangerously imperiled Blue Planet.

## *Polarities*

No less than the polarized rhetoric of environmental debates in our time, the campaign against the Indians by their opponents over the years was often quite ugly, including vociferous attacks on Pueblo religion by the United States government. The denunciations begun in 1921 by the commissioner of Indian Affairs, Charles Burke, were typical of a pattern of governmental intimidation and abuse of power directed against the Indians for almost seven decades. Burke "personally went to Taos, invaded the Tribal Council chamber, and denounced the tribal elders as 'half-animal' for their religious beliefs." Insisting that the council renounce their ancient religion "within a year," he further demanded the cessation of religious instruction of the tribe's children. When the council refused, "Burke had the old men arrested and transported to jail in Santa Fe."[14]

The American public weighed in passionately on both sides of the battle for Blue Lake. "If the Indians get it," objected Roberto Martinez of the regional Livestock Association (which had been granted grazing rights to the watershed by the Forest Service), "everyone else would be out. I thought we were trying to integrate and get along with each other—no matter what race or color. This looks like segregation to me."[15] From the other side, a citizen named Thelma Honey, describing herself as "shocked, disappointed, and disillusioned" by the actions of Senator Clinton Anderson of New Mexico, the tribe's most ardent opponent, voiced her displeasure in the *Albuquerque Tribune*. "I am fully aware that bilking the Indians is an old and lucrative sport. But do you have to add your name to the list of infamous characters who have participated in this recreation for centuries?"[16]

Raymand Nakai, chairman of the powerful Navajo Tribe, spoke poignantly of the Taos Indians' battle with the US government as exemplifying the cultural precipice threatening the entire Indian Nation. "Without this we are but census numbers in a file cabinet in Washington, D.C., waiting to be absorbed into the dominant society." The return of Blue Lake, Nakai concluded, would signify "a new day for all our Indian brethren. Let us hope that it may signify a new day of respect and honor for Indian culture and Indian religion."[17]

Into the breach of these heated and sometimes violent polarities stepped the tribe's elder Cacique, or holy man, Juan de Jesus Romero, who travelled to Washington, DC, to speak before Congress in 1970. Why he did so may be best explained in his own words: "I want to be present with [the] white man. . . . He doesn't know us. . . . He does not visit our village, he does not come and speak to us face to face, man to man."[18] The old man did not simply testify so much "as weave a sort of spell"[19] in his person and words, speaking of the tribe's religious responsibility not in terms of self-enclosed isolation or private worship but as a call to pray for and "love the human being" without discrimination: "I include everyone, the white, the black man, the Indians, and what-have you in this world." The conflict could not be resolved by force of power, he said, but only through "love and care" and mutual understanding. "We want to talk peacefully. We want to talk as brothers. We want to talk as understanding of everything." By all accounts even the tribe's opponents were moved, and praised the Cacique for his "splendid presentation."[20]

When the bill returning Blue Lake and its watershed to the Taos Indians was finally signed into law by President Richard Nixon in December of 1970, Romero praised the signing as a "new day" not only for Taos Pueblo but for all of the nation's citizens, an invitation to embrace our responsibilities for the common good of all with renewed hope. "And this responsibility is more than material things. [It is] to protect the life and to protect what this America is, really beautiful, peace, honesty, truth, understanding, consideration."

What to make of this extraordinary story in which a small community on the brink of cultural extinction prevailed in its determination not to be simply absorbed into mainstream US society, like "census numbers in a file cabinet in Washington, D.C."? What to make of Romero, this ninety-year-old holy man, speaking of love for all people and care for creation before Congress, and sharing warm words of congratulations with President Nixon after the tribe's legislative victory? Is it too much to suggest that the Spirit of God can work in surprising, even miraculous, ways precisely in and through profound cultural polarities and conflicts of difference?[21]

As I contemplate the photograph of a smiling President Nixon at his desk, surrounded by a joyful throng of Indian supporters with the quiet Cacique in the background, an odd thought steals into my mind. It seems to me that Romero's role in this dramatic tale is akin to the paradox of the monk or hermit who prays in quiet solitude for all the peoples of the world. Or perhaps he is like "the poverty of the priest who vanishes into the Mass,"[22] yet who steps forward, breaking the silence to speak the truth in love, calling us back to ourselves when we have lost our way. In this sacramental understanding of prophetic witness, the holy person does not organize, dominate, or even interpret the signs of the times *for us so much as* he or she shows us *how to respond attentively* to every environment—bodies, spirit, animals, trees, earth, cities—in which we find ourselves. This to my mind is the incomparable gift and sacramental legacy of the Indians. It is their witness to life, their protest *for* life, as a prophetic people.

## *Breaking the Silence: Life Out of Balance*

In 1982, filmmaker Godfrey Reggio released the first film of his *Qatsi* trilogy, *Koyaanisqatsi*, followed by *Powaqqatsi* (1988) and *Naqoyqatsi* (2002). Each film takes its title from the Hopi Indian language: "Koyaaniqatsi" meaning *life out of balance*, "Powaqqatsi" meaning *life in transformation*, and "Naqoyqatsi" (released not long after September 11, 2001) meaning *life as war*. A longtime resident of Santa Fe, New Mexico, Reggio spent fourteen years in fasting, silence, and prayer in training to be a Catholic monk before leaving this path and making the first *Qatsi* film. Indeed Reggio's sensitivity to humanity's pro found need for silence amid the din of commerce and fog of war is made disarmingly clear in these three films.

To take just the first film in the trilogy, the Hopi word *koyaanisqa-tsi*—"life in turmoil," "crazy life," "life disintegrating," a "state of life that calls for another way of living"—is chanted slowly at the beginning and end of the film in a deep *basso profundo* over the haunting minimalist score of Philip Glass. The film consists primarily of slow motion and time-lapse footage of cities and massive human construction projects juxtaposed against the panoramic, sweeping silences of natural landscapes and the rhythmic ebb of flowing waters and cloud-drenched skies across the United States. The most arresting sequences involve the camera fixed on human faces—thoughtful, beautiful, diverse—while automobiles and subway trains and jetliners rush by in the background, carrying their human cargo through time like so many insects in a complex web of effects, a chaotic reality far beyond any single person's or society's control. The effect of these sharp juxtapositions is jarring: one wonders just how our lives on the planet became *so* out of balance.

Reggio's visual "tone poem" contains neither dialogue nor a vocalized narration: its tone is set by the juxtaposition of imagery, music, and silence. Why? It is "not for lack of love of the language that these films have no words," Reggio explains. "It's because, from my point of view, our language is in a state of vast humiliation. It no longer describes the world in which we live."[23] Indeed, no feeling person can watch *Koyaanisqatsi* and not be sensually overwhelmed by the "vast humiliation" in which we and our imperiled planet live, and where language itself—including much artistic and religious expression—seems everywhere coopted and colonized by the very technical-economic forces against which so many feel powerless to resist. Reggio notes:

> These films have never been about the effect *of* technology, *of* industry *on* people. It's been that everyone: politics, education, things of the financial structure, the nation state structure, language, the culture, religion, all of that exists within the host of technology. So it's not the effect *of*, it's that everything exists within [technology]. It's not that we *use* technology, we *live* technology. Technology has become as ubiquitous as the air we breathe.[24]

What are the consequences of existing not within nature's womb but within the "host" of technology, at the whim and pace of grandiose economic and political forces that drive human behavior in ways well beyond our control? The interjection of three Hopi prophecies, sung by a choral ensemble and translated just before the end credits of the film, suggests a possible answer:

- If we dig precious things from the land, we will invite disaster.
- Near the day of Purification, there will be cobwebs spun back and forth in the sky.
- A container of ashes might one day be thrown from the sky, which could burn the land and boil the oceans.

How should we interpret these enigmatic Hopi sayings, so strangely resonant with warnings issued today by the scientific community? In its biblical sense the term "prophecy" should not be equated with prediction. The task of prophetic imagination is not to forecast an irreversible future so much as to survey the signs and to *name the present*, speaking the truth of realities unfolding before our eyes but which most of us are unwilling to see.[25] The prophet's intimations of the future, in other words, are conditional, contingent on our response—thus the word *if* that opens the first Hopi prophecy. In short, the prophetic person or community dares to break silence so as *to make something different happen with words*—or in the case of artists like Reggio, through images, silences, music.[26]

Reggio makes clear that the *Qatsi* films are intended to simply create an experience and that it is up to the viewer "to take for himself/herself what it is that [the film] means." Like the Cacique, his charge is not to tell us how to act or what to think but to mediate an encounter with reality, opening our eyes onto a wider horizon than what is permitted by conventional ways of seeing, thinking, and acting. Like the Indians, Reggio speaks from within the people but he is not "of" the people. Standing at the margins the prophet listens and sees, but then dares to speak, showing the people what they will not see. Behold, we are suffering *koyaanisqatsi*, a state of life that calls for another way of living. Whether we have eyes to see and ears to hear is the critical question. If we will not hear the wisdom of the artists, poets, and indigenous peoples of our time, whose authority may not impress us, perhaps we will finally hear our environmental scientists, whose urgent pleas about climate change sound not a little like the Hopi vision of "burning lands" and "boiling oceans."[27]

It must be said, and I daresay Reggio would agree, that technology as such can be framed positively, even spiritually, as the wondrous fruit of evolutionary flourishing: consider the eradication of smallpox, or the uses of social media to empower struggling freedom movements. But we have reached a point where questions about *how* we evolve and *to what purpose* we bend our technologies have profoundly far-reaching implications for social, economic, political, and spiritual life on the planet. How to participate in the sanctification of creation and not its desecration, if not by drawing from our deepest wellsprings of scientific, cultural, *and* religious wisdom? How to choose wisely, with freedom from arrogance or willful blindness about the darker aspects of the American experiment and with a commitment to all of life's flourishing? And can we really trust Exxon Mobile or JP Morgan Chase or the Pentagon to make these choices for future generations?[28]

All of these more or less public and political questions are manifestations of a deep and far-reaching spiritual malaise, a kind of insanity that prevents us global citizens of the supposedly advanced twenty-first century from living, as it were, in our "right mind." It is not that the desert silences of New Mexico or the Pueblo Indians harbor some magic potion to secure our release from what Max Weber called the "iron cage" of Western civilization. Yet surely the Pueblo people's "lack of interest in material wealth, their devotion to communal values, their healthy respect for human limitations, and their adaptation to rather than exploitation of the natural environment" represent sane and even salvific alternatives, as Mabel Dodge Luhan believed, "to a chaotic white civilization that is heading for self-annihilation."[29] How to imagine and embrace, both individually and corporately, a more simplified and integrated life of balance between the human and natural worlds that sustain us, between work and living space, silence and speech, stillness and creativity, play and art?

The greatest silence of all, of course, is death. The desert nakedness of northern New Mexico where the monks of Christ in the Desert dwell is a stark reminder of death, a confrontation with mortality. "It shrinks you down," as Fr. Bill says, "it shrinks everybody down," in ways that human-centered environments such as towering cities and air-conditioned shopping malls do not. Fr. Bill describes that feeling of smallness and vulnerability as a good thing, not least as a precondition for prayer.[30] Yet so long as we remain ensconced in the artificial womb of our own buildings, experiments, and gadgets, and continue to put our faith as a nation in our inhuman and fabulously efficient killing machines, how will we ever taste and see that great mystery of communion in which we live and move and have our being even now and which beckons to us, just maybe, from behind the veil of nature and our own inevitable mortality?

"One has to be alone, under the sky, before everything falls into place and one finds one's own place in the midst of it all."[31] To live in reality is to live reconciled on this side of death with the Earth. It is to approach the lakes as our churches, the mountains as our tabernacles, the evergreen trees as our living saints. To feel the maternity or womb of the earth as the Indians do, submerged in their earthen kivas, is no romantic abstraction or New Age flight from reality. Especially for we dwellers of large cities, bathed in concrete, commerce, and the relentless rhetoric of conflict, when we long for solitude, healing, and replenishment, it is to the Earth that we must return and find ourselves again. Indeed, as we fill the skies in the East (and increasingly here at home) with unmanned attack and surveillance drones, our latest means of communication with the distant and feared other, how much harder will it be to recover our true selves, cut off from nature and others, and resigned to a functionally scientific or utilitarian view of *nature without God*?

For if the skies are nothing more than a theatre of "enhanced security," if nature is only an arid desert wearing a mask of beauty, to be mined, plumbed, penetrated, and "fracked" for its resources, then death and burial for human beings—even for Christ, buried in an earthen tomb!—can be nothing more than void, darkness, suffocation. Artist Georgia O'Keeffe discovered intimations of quite another possibility in the desert landscape of northern New Mexico. "When I think of death," she mused, "I only regret that I will not be able to see this beautiful country anymore . . . unless the Indians are right and my spirit will walk here after I'm gone."[32] It is that hint and rumor of another possibility, seeded in the rocks themselves, that beckons me to be still and hear the silences speaking everywhere in the desert canyons of New Mexico.

### *Remembering by the Eyes and Ears (and Feet)*

"It is the tragedy of Native American history," observed Alfred Kidder, the great archaeologist of the meso-American Southwest, "that so much human effort has come to nought, and that so many hopeful experiments in life and living were cut short by the devastating blight of the white man's arrival."[33] Integral to these "hopeful experiments in life and living" is the belief that all forms of creation depend on one another—rocks, trees, flowers, birds, animals, humans—and that these, in turn, rely for their existence on the clouds, snow, rain, lightning and wind. The harmony of human life within this order emanates out from the Indians' felt sense in all things that our purpose in life is "to adore, thank, and praise the Creator for the continuation of life and harmony within this creation." The Pueblo peoples did this "by fasting in their kivas, sacrificing, offering prayer feathers, and dancing."[34] Above all by dancing!

Fergusson observes wryly that when the Indian farmer finishes his springtime labors of digging, clearing fields, beating out irrigation ditches in the hard desert soil, and finally planting, he "is not content, as the white farmer is," to "sit back and fear the worst or petition Congress to do something about it." Rather, she writes, "He goes quietly and assuredly to work to make things come right. . . . He prays for water, for rain to fall so the ditches may run full. He also prays for renewal of life everywhere, for many beasts, for many children. In short, he dances."[35] If the rain does not come, the Indians "know that something has been done wrong and they will patiently try again." We may shake our heads at such "irrational superstitions," but the Indians say, "White men laugh at our dances, but they are glad, too, when the rain comes."[36]

Far more than any written language or religious text, the dances of the Pueblo Indians secured their way of life from generation to generation; dance was a way of "remembering by the eyes and ears," and, we may add, by *the drum circle and the feet*. Indeed, as Pueblo historian Joe Sando notes, such remembrances "could not be seized or burned like the written word. Even the closest surveillance by the Spaniards could not control this form of communication." By means of their dances and other carefully guarded traditions the Indians "learned to conform outwardly to the religion of the Spaniards while keeping alive their own faith inwardly." Consequently, Sando adds, with pregnant understatement, "few Spaniards realized until too late that conversion by the sword had been a dismal failure in seventeenth-century New Mexico."[37] Fergusson shares similarly pointed observations about the chasm separating Christianity as practiced and preached by their European colonizers and the faith as received, *not* received, or received and *transformed* by the Indians. "Through it all [the Indian] manages to maintain his dignified aloofness. He is not yet a white man's Indian."[38]

Whether or not the same is true today I cannot say. Does the proliferation of Indian casinos on Pueblo lands throughout New Mexico represent a practical lifeline for Indian autonomy and cultural survival or is it an accommodation to the "white man's" worship of *mammon*, with attendant blessings and curses? Is the strangely evocative synthesis of Catholic and Pueblo beliefs and ritual practices to be lamented or celebrated? The whole truth, I expect, lives on both sides of such questions. However the Indians themselves may answer, I do not doubt that God still moves and calls to us in Native ways of listening and responding to the soil and winds and waters, through the eyes and ears and feet. These questions, in the end, turn back upon us: Are *we* listening?

### *In Beauty It Is Finished*

Recently I returned to Taos with my teenage son, hoping he might feel something of what I felt during my sojourn many years ago to Christ in the Desert. As I watched my son skip rocks across the Chama River, my prayers reached beyond my family to embrace the country of my birth. I found myself praying, perhaps in the spirit of Mabel Dodge, for the United States and all its peoples, that we might learn the gift of gratitude and humility from the original inhabitants of this ancient and beautiful land. In the spirit of that prayer, I would like to give Erna Fergusson the last word, as she describes twilight falling over an Indian village, somewhere in 1930s' America. She reminds me that God, too, moves freely, lightly, and beautifully, through worlds of difference.

As night came on, the pines withdrew to become a part of the
mountains, and the fires made spots of light under a skyful of
stars. Suddenly I knew how alien I was in that Indian world.
It is a separate world. The white man sees it, he touches it,
some even have the temerity to break into it, to change it. But
they cannot. For this is a world apart, a brown world of brown
people. They come out of their world sometimes to speak to
us, for they understand our language; but when they withdraw
into their world, we cannot follow. They live close to the earth.
The mass for a pale god who died on a cross did not reach
these people. They do not understand. A religion of an idea,
of an ideal, is foreign to them. Their religion is of earth and the
things of the earth. I thought of all these brown people whom
I had seen dancing their prayers, pounding them with their
feet into the earth, which is their mother. Her ways are close
to them, even when they are hurt. They understand the earth,
they dance their prayers into the earth; and they pray for real
things, for sun and rain and corn. For growth. For life.[39]

When death comes among the Navajo, the family of the deceased
sits for four successive days outside the chamber where the body lay,
facing east "and chanting prayers to help the departing soul on its
way." Their prayers end, as all Navajo prayers end, with the following peroration:

> In beauty, it is finished.
> In beauty, it is finished.
> In beauty, it is finished.
> In beauty, it is finished.[40]

# 6

# STREETS

*Your name is Big Brother / You say that you're watching*
*me on the tele'*
*Seeing me go nowhere . . . .*
*My name is Nobody*
*But I can't wait to see your face inside my door.*

> ~ Stevie Wonder, "Big Brother," *Talking Book*

Much of the real germinating action in the world, the
real leavening, is among the immobilized, the outsiders. . . . Where the good may come from is perhaps
where evil is feared. The streets. The ghettoes.

> ~ Thomas Merton, *Learning to Love*

    In 1976 Motown recording artist Stevie Wonder released a double-
album masterpiece called *Songs in the Key of Life*, giving brilliant and
beautiful voice to the joys and struggles of life in inner city America.
With an original working title of "Let's see life the way it is," the

*Peace Wall Mural with Kids. Photo copyright John (Jack) Ramsdale, jackramsdale.com.*
*Mural painted by Jane Golden and Peter Pagast for the Philadelphia Mural Arts Pro-*
*gram, © 1998.*

album's seventeen songs reveal a world largely hidden from suburban, middle class, white America. I was twelve years old when *Songs in the Key of Life* debuted at number one on the pop music charts. I remember listening to the record with my older brother in our suburban home in Lexington, Kentucky. As I noted in the introduction, though I was too young and certainly too insulated to grasp the social complexity of the songs, Stevie's artistry broke my imaginative horizons wide open. Almost forty years later, I am still mesmerized. No matter how often I listen to the album or plumb its depths with my students, the full genius of *Songs in the Key of Life* still eludes me.

The album's third track, for example, "Village Ghetto Land," juxtaposes disturbing images of "life the way it is" in the inner city over the serene instrumentation of a chamber quartet:

> Would you like to go with me
> Down my dead end street
> Would you like to come with me
> To Village Ghetto Land?. . .
> Children play with rusted cars
> Sores cover their hands
> Politicians laugh and drink
> Drunk to all demands[1]

Two tracks later, as if to say, don't even think you understand me now, or where I come from, Wonder delivers "Sir Duke," an incomparably funky and joyful tribute to the genius of Duke Ellington and other black artists, followed by "I Wish," his playful remembrance of growing up on the streets of Detroit. "Isn't She Lovely" celebrates the birth of Wonder's daughter, Aisha, followed by "Joy Inside My Tears," "Pastime Paradise," and "Black Man"—all hymns to what it *feels like* to be black in America. Like turning a many-faceted diamond, now this way, now that, Stevie refracts the mosaic colors of life as it is for many in inner city America, life held down to street level.

## Life in the Key of Black

Listening to the album today, one might be tempted to celebrate just how much things have changed in a so-called post-racial America, where a black man resides with his beautiful family in the White

House and projects American military power across the world stage. Or one might lament how far too little has changed at street level for peoples of color in the United States. In any case, what interests me here is not the insight into "ghetto life" that Stevie Wonder's music gives us, gives me, as a middle-class white person in America. What interests me is the critique of the *racially unconscious white listener* embedded everywhere in his music. For listeners like myself, Wonder's artistry facilitates a powerful and potentially painful realization: namely, my own nearly complete isolation from black experience, my "confinement in the prison built by racism,"[2] and the degree to which my own white habitus or groupthink—what Thomas Merton called the "conspiracy of the many"[3]—conditions my very manner of seeing and judging reality.

In other words, the opening of "Village Ghetto Land"—*Would you like to go with me / down my dead end street?*—still resonates today as both an accusation and an invitation: an accusation of social blindness but also an invitation to wake up, to come and see life as it is more clearly than I have seen it before from my perspective of social privilege. To say yes to the invitation is to discover that what is at stake is not strictly my grasp of ghetto life so much as the music of life itself, life in the key of humanity, black, white, brown, red, or yellow. It is about the music of human relationships, sorrowful and joyful, broken and redeemed.

In this chapter we consider life as it is in the cities and streets of America by juxtaposing Stevie Wonder's music with select writings of Thomas Merton (1915–68), the Catholic monk and spiritual writer whose prophetic commentaries on race remain remarkably and sadly relevant today. Stevie Wonder and Thomas Merton are both artists, albeit of a very different kind. What joins them is their remarkable capacity to open our imaginations to the life-worlds of people and places well beyond our habitual comfort zones. An elder African American woman in my parish recently reminded me of Merton's significance as a voice for justice during the civil rights movement. She told me that as a young black woman growing up in a racially explosive Cincinnati in the 1960s, Merton's *Conjectures of a Guilty Bystander* was her "bible." "I carried it with me everywhere," she added, with a pained look on her face. "Merton *got it*, when few others did."[4]

There is some irony to that fact. As a cloistered monk living in a remote monastery in rural Kentucky, Merton was about as distant geographically from urban America as one could be. It is true that before he entered the monastery in 1941, Merton had lived the better part of his life in cities throughout Europe and then for five years as a student and teacher at Columbia University in the heart of New York City. Indeed he even considered taking up residency in Harlem, living and working among the poor.[5] But Merton's deep sensitivity to the black situation during the 1960s was rooted not in geographical proximity so much as basic human empathy, that is, his radical openness to the life-worlds of others. "Most of us," as he wrote in 1964, "are congenitally unable to think black, and yet that is precisely what we must do before we can hope to understand the crisis in which we find ourselves."[6]

We begin with Merton's experiences of and reflections on city life down at street level. From there we turn our attention to children and the prominent image of the child in Merton's and Stevie Wonder's work. We conclude by asking, in pragmatic terms, how we might help to nourish and cultivate the seeds of racial justice especially in our youngest generation.

## *Merton and Harlem: 1964*

When Merton was a student at Columbia in the 1930s, he spent a good deal of time listening to jazz with his friends in the crowded clubs of New York City. As detailed in his autobiography, *The Seven Storey Mountain*, Merton in those youthful days was something of a playboy who pushed life to the extremes. With his conversion to Catholicism and embrace of the austere monastic life, one could say Merton took refuge in the opposite extreme. In any case, it is clear that when he entered the Trappist monastery of Our Lady of Gethsemani in 1941, he saw his vocation in the traditional way as *fuga mundi*: flight from the world. By the late 1950s, however, Merton's awareness was turning back to the secular world, to the realities of "life as it is" for ordinary people in America who struggle simply to both make ends meet and live with some kind of dignity. Like the Catholic Church on the eve of Vatican II, he was learning to rediscover God in unexpected places, which is to say, *everywhere*. The contemplative life is not an escape from the world after all, Merton discovered, but a deepening grasp of all things in God, inclusive of the world's social and political problems.

In chapter 3, I referred to a pivotal moment in Merton's life, his well-known epiphany "at the corner of Fourth and Walnut" in Louisville, which he describes in *Conjectures of a Guilty Bystander* as "waking from a dream of separateness."[7] It is not hard to picture Merton standing at the busy street corner, surrounded by a sea of faces of every color.

> Then it was as if I suddenly saw the secret beauty of their hearts, the depths of their hearts where neither sin nor desire nor self-knowledge can reach, the core of their reality, the person that each one is in God's eyes. If only they could all see themselves as they really *are*. If only we could see each other that way all the time. . . But this cannot be *seen*, only believed and "understood" by a peculiar gift. . . . I have no program for this seeing. It is only given. But the gate of heaven is everywhere.[8]

The passage in its entirety is stunning, and rightly celebrated as a moment of conversion in Merton's life. From this moment forward he began to publish on the most contentious issues of the day, including the race crisis now exploding in cities across the country. And still he continued to press the case for the contemplative life in a world of relentless action. Much like Stevie Wonder, albeit in a very different key, Merton was teaching his contemporaries the art of paying attention.

But there is another urban epiphany of sorts that I would like to consider here. Detailed in Merton's private journals, it is much more hidden and, to be sure, rather less idealized than the famous Fourth and Walnut passage. It happened in the summer of 1964, when Merton boarded an airplane for New York City for a meeting at Columbia University with Zen scholar D. T. Suzuki, with whom he had engaged in serious interreligious dialogue for many years. Flying over the city at 35,000 feet, Merton noted in his journal, hearkening back to his life before Gethsemani, "I suddenly realized after all that I was a New Yorker." Arriving at Columbia late in the morning he found his way to his room in Butler Hall, overlooking the streets of Harlem. He writes:

> The noise of traffic and the uninterrupted cries of playing
> children, cries of life and joy coming out of purgatory, loud
> and strong the voice of a great living organism. Shots too—
> and there is no rifle range! Frequent shots—at what? More
> frequent than in the Kentucky woods behind the hermitage
> in hunting season. And drums, bongos, and the chanting of
> songs, and dogs barking and traffic, buses like jet planes.
> Above all the morning light, then the afternoon light, and the
> flashing windows of the big new housing developments.[9]

The passage is vintage Merton. Notice how Merton observes everything and seems to find something beautiful even in the "flashing
windows of the big new housing developments." But there were
gunshots too, at what, he wonders. But then, "drums, bongos, and
the chanting of songs." In sum, *the incomparable music of Harlem*: "Cries
of life and joy coming out of purgatory, loud and strong the voice of
a great living organism."

Just a month later, back at the monastery, the key darkly changes.

> Jim Forest sent me clippings from Monday's New York Times
> about the big riots in Harlem last weekend. It all took place
> in the section immediately below Butler Hall. . . . The police
> shot thousands of rounds into the air but also quite a few
> people were hit, and one man on a roof was killed. In the
> middle of all the racket and chaos and violence a police cap-
> tain was shouting "Go home! Go home!" A Negro yelled back
> "We *are* home, baby!"[10]

Suddenly the description of Harlem as "purgatory"—a place of "purification"—bears much more ominous meaning.

### "The Street is for Celebration"

These memories of Harlem must have been fresh in Merton's mind
when a few years later he wrote "The Street is for Celebration."[11] On
the surface the essay is a much gentler read than his fiercely prophetic
commentaries on race such as "Letters to a White Liberal."[12] Indeed,
race is never mentioned at all. Instead Merton focuses our attention on
cities and streets themselves as reflections of *what human beings do with
space*. How we arrange and navigate the physical spaces of our cities,

he suggests, reveals a great deal about who we are, what we value, and what we do not value in the everyday practices of our lives. The essay hinges on a distinction Merton draws between "alienated spaces," where people simply submit, and "inhabited spaces," where people actually live and can participate in the creation of their lives. The question at hand is this: "Can the street be an inhabited space?" Can the street be a place for living, for creativity, even for celebration? He writes:

> Suppose the street is an impersonal no-man's-land: a mere tube through which a huge quantity of traffic is sucked down toward the glass walls where business happens. Suppose the street is a tunnel, a kind of nowhere, something to go through. Something to get out of. Or a nightmare space where you run without getting away.
>
> Then the street cannot be an inhabited space. . . . [Then] the street is not where [people] live but where they have been dumped.
>
> When a street is not inhabited it is a dump.
>
> A street may be a dump for thousands of people who aren't there.
>
> They have been dumped there, but their presence is so provisional they might as well be absent. They occupy space by being displaced in it. . . .
>
> *An alienated space, an uninhabited space, is a space where you submit.*
>
> You stay where you are put, even though this cannot really be called "living." You stop asking questions about it and you know there is not much point in making any complaint. (Business is not interested in your complaint, only in your rent.) "I live on X Street." Translated: "X Street is the place where I submit, where I give in, where I quit."[13]

Note the crucial point about persons living an alienated life: "their presence is so provisional they might as well be absent." To whom in American society today would such a description apply? To how many children residing in our inner cities? How about the millions of young men of color locked behind bars inside our sprawling prison system?

Here I pause to mention two contemporary authors who have opened my eyes to the trajectory of this line of thought as it applies to systemic racial injustice in the United States today. The first, noted in chapter 3, is Jonathan Kozol, whose books have long cast an ominous spotlight onto the plight of minority children and the state of public education in our cities. The titles of Kozol's books—*Death at An Early Age*; *Savage Inequalities: Children in America's Schools*; *The Shame of the Nation: The Restoration of Apartheid Schooling in America*—tell the story of whole populations of young people, disproportionately black and Latino, whose presence in America "is so provisional they might as well be absent." The second is legal scholar Michelle Alexander, whose critically acclaimed study, *The New Jim Crow: Mass Incarceration in the Age of Colorblindness*, details the devastating effects of mass incarceration and systematic disenfranchisement on communities of color in the United States. Like Kozol, Alexander's painstaking scholarship unmasks patterns of injustice directed against whole populations that most of us would rather not see and many simply choose to deny.[14]

Fifty years ago the face of racial animosity was epitomized in openly racist organizations like the Ku Klux Klan, in men like Bull Connor, the bigoted public safety commissioner of Birmingham, Alabama, and in horrific tragedies like the bombing of the 16th Street Baptist Church in Birmingham. Then it was quite clear what racial hatred and violence meant: it meant to will the nonexistence of black people, to seek their *erasure*. Merton's poem, "And the Children of Birmingham" is a powerful lament for this kind of race hatred; likewise his "Picture of a Black Child with a White Doll," an elegy for Denise McNair, one of the four children killed in the bombing.[15]

Today racial animosity manifests much more subtly than this, though its effects are no less quotidian, oppressive, or potentially violent, as Kozol and Alexander demonstrate in unflinching detail. In the decades since the civil rights movement, racism's implicit strategy has not been the erasure of the feared and marginal other (e.g., young black men) so much as their *eclipse* from meaningful participation in society. To eclipse is to ignore, to refuse to deal with a person as a person, a somebody—a Child of God, as we say—who matters. To eclipse is to blot out the light. As the great Howard Thurman often noted, to destroy a people, I don't have to kill them, I only have to convince them that they are not worth anything—to hold a bushel basket relentlessly over their light.[16] It is this form of violence,

violence by systematic neglect and creeping despair, which concerns Merton here. *X street is the place where I submit, where I give in, where I quit.*

To his credit, Merton acknowledges the temptation to violence among the marginalized, violence as a means of reminding the world "that you are there, that you are tired of being a non-person." Yet violence cannot succeed in making the city inhabitable, he continues, because "it accepts the general myth of the street as a no-man's-land, as battleground, as no place." Violence is "another kind of submission . . . another way of giving up."[17] How, then, can the street become an inhabited space, a place where people are present to themselves, with full identities, as real people, as happy people? Merton begins to gesture toward a positive answer, toward hope.

> To acquire inhabitants the street will have to be changed. . . . The people who are merely provisionally present, half-absent non-persons must now become really present on the street as *themselves*. They must be recognizable as people. . . .
>
> Instead of submitting to the street, they must change it. . . . [They must] transform the street and make it over so that it is livable.
>
> The street can be inhabited if the people on it begin to make their life credible by changing their environment.
>
> *Living is more than submission: it is creation.*
>
> *To live is to create one's own world as a scene of personal happiness.*[18]

Here we come to the heart of things. Living, says Merton, is more than submission: it is creation. And here he contrasts the streets of modern America as places of alienation with the first Mayan cities of North America, which were places of festival and celebration. What is celebration? Celebration "is the creation of a common identity, a common consciousness. . . Celebration is when we let joy make itself out of our love. . . . Celebration is the beginning of confidence, therefore of power."[19] He continues, redirecting our imaginations back to the streets of urban America:

> When we laugh at them, when we celebrate, when we make our lives beautiful, when we give one another joy by

loving, by sharing, then we manifest a power they cannot
touch. We can be the artisans of a joy they never imagined.
　　We can build a fire of happiness in this city that will put
them to shame. . . .
　　*Can the street become an inhabited space?*
　　*Yes, when it becomes a place of celebration.*[20]

Of course to remake the street and one's own life in the face of
creeping despair will not be easy. "We can dance in the street, but
that will not change the fact that our buildings are lousy, the rent is
too high, the garbage is not taken away, and the back yards look like
bomb craters." Nevertheless, Merton continues, "we [can] begin to
discover our power to transform our own world. He who celebrates
is not powerless. He becomes a creator because he is a lover."[21]

Invoking the theme of power as Merton did here was to engage
the aims and rhetoric of the Black Power movement. Implicitly Merton is wrestling with the question of subjugated populations everywhere during the revolutionary 1960s: What are the conditions of the
possibility for the empowerment of the poor, for justice and equal
opportunity, for positive social revolution? Does Christianity, at its
heart *a narrative of power through love and redemptive suffering*, have
any wisdom to offer the black community? What are the implications,
by contrast, when the demand for justice is framed by the logic of
violence and revolution "by any means necessary," as it was by the
Black Power movement? Implicitly Merton is making the case here,
in the tradition of Jesus, Gandhi, and King, for nonviolent resistance
through interracial solidarity and love: love not in the abstract, but
love as it sings and marches and rises up fiercely in an embodied,
joyful, hopeful people.[22]

Two further points are worth noting about this remarkable essay.
First, by the middle of the piece Merton is no longer analyzing the
situation objectively, as it were, from an abstract, third-person distance. Like Stevie Wonder, Merton draws his audience into the
streetscape itself, inviting us, through a kind of imaginative empathy,
to identify ourselves with the occupants of the alienated street. *We
can build a fire of happiness in this city that will put them to shame.* Second,
note how Merton gradually shifts the locus of power from the im-
personal to the personal, from behind the shiny glass walls of sky-
scrapers "where business happens" to the inner landscape of lives

and relationships down at street level, where hope can catch flame and burst forth again in human hearts. Yet such an outcome is tenuous and unpredictable. Merton lays the burden of hope partly, if implicitly, upon the reader. Can I identify *myself*, my own kind—"Kind, which means 'likeness' and which means 'love' and which means 'Child' "[23]—with my suffering brothers and sisters in the city?

## *The Divine-Human Child: Defending God's Image in the Other*

In all of Merton's writings there may be no more poignant or powerful symbol of our shared personhood in God than the symbol of the Child. "We do not hear the soft voice, the gentle voice, the merciful and feminine. . . . We do not see the Child who is prisoner in all the people."[24] The Christ of Merton's mature writings is the Christ Child of the Nativity, who hides especially in those for whom there is "no room" in society, no inhabitable space for dignity, creativity, and happiness: the children of Harlem, for example, with their "cries of life and joy coming out of purgatory." What *kind* of purification, Merton might ask today, are we requiring of the nation's black and Latino children? Whose sins are being paid for as we build more and bigger prisons, fill them with young black and Latino men, and staff them with working class whites who desperately need the jobs?

In one of my favorite passages in all his journals, Merton reflects on some children's drawings that were sent to the monastery from "somewhere in Milwaukee." After noting that the pictures are the "only real works of art I have seen in ten years," he continues, quite poignantly: "But it occurred to me that these wise children were drawing pictures of their own lives. They knew what was in their own depths. They were putting it all down on paper before they had a chance to grow up and forget."[25] What is Merton getting at here? What is it that lives and shines forth especially in children that we "grow up and forget," that we—academics, pundits, common sense adults—fail to behold in ourselves, firstly, but especially in the strange and marginal other?

Perhaps it is that same translucence and secret innocence that Stevie Wonder beheld in his newborn daughter and celebrates in the song "Isn't She Lovely?" wherein he sings, "I can't believe what God has done / through us he's given life to one / but isn't she lovely made from love?" Her name, Aisha, the song tells us, means simply "Life," life made from love. What we grow up to forget is that diamond-like image of God that hides in all people, without exception, the inner potentiality and latent freedom in which God invites each of us *to be* and to participate fully in the discovery, creation, and celebration of our lives. As Merton confessed of the passersby at Fourth and Walnut, "If only they could all see themselves as they really *are*. If only we could see each other that way all the time."[26] Notice the integral link between discovery of our true self and discovery of the other. Yet how often we live under the shadow of eclipse, where neither "you" nor "I" appear as our authentic self, as a person who matters infinitely in the eye of God. *To eclipse is to blot out the light.*

How then to live more fully in the light? How to identify myself more empathetically with the occupants of the alienated street, and so discover myself in discovering them? Merton reminds us that it is not enough for the Christian to spiritualize the struggle, to "build a little chapel for [ourselves] inside the Church to make things more tolerable."[27] One cannot listen to Stevie Wonder records in the suburbs, pray for peace "down there" in the city, and consider oneself sanctified. Nor is it enough to pontificate from the ivory tower, taking refuge in the "illusory dignity of the well-fed spokesman who justifies himself by diagnosis, planning and exhortation."[28] Indeed the Gospel calls us to be transformed from beyond ourselves by love, to risk precisely the kinds of *attachments* to people that will cost us something.[29]

A few years ago I heard black Catholic theologian Sr. Jamie Phelps frame the question quite simply and beautifully this way: "What work are we doing to help re-establish a sense of the image of God in people of color?"[30] Throughout the 1960s Merton confronted his readers, and confronted them theologically, with the same question: "How, then, do we treat this other *Christ*, this person, who happens to be black?"[31] Of course in the process he angered and alienated a great many of his white Catholic readers. Yet he chose to speak, knowing full well he was treading into dangerous waters. Today Merton still challenges us, especially those of us who are white, to look carefully into the mirror of our own neighborhoods, churches, businesses, and schools and to recognize the signs of our self-segregation from peoples of color, our sad confinement in the prison built by racism.

That prison, as I have repeated throughout this book, is in no way a black or brown problem confined to the ghetto but is woven into the whole fabric of civilization.[32]

And so here I raise again the question of reception: How to communicate the race critique, especially to whites, in a manner that it might be heard, and in a more unified voice than any small group of scholars, preachers, artists, or prophetic voices could do? As a teacher I wonder especially how to sow the seeds of social empathy in our youngest generation, in the context of a consumer culture that offers little incentive to do so. How to initiate conversations about racial justice without being dismissed as apathetically as the teenager's deadpan, "Whatever"? Can a theology of solidarity be a theology of life, of celebration, of good news? In whom might such a theology, *a spirituality of discovering the One in the Many*, best have a chance to take root, as seeds falling on good soil?

## *Revisiting the Logic of Solidarity*

In the years before our marriage my wife Lauri and I both lived in an intentional faith community in northwest Denver called Romero House, a project of Jesuit-run Regis University. Named after the martyred Archbishop Oscar Romero of El Salvador, Romero House gives undergraduate residents an opportunity to live, work, and pray among the Mexican immigrant population of the city. After Lauri's year-long tenure in the community, I served as the resident house manager, coordinating communal meals, weekly faith-sharing and liturgy, and working in the neighborhood with five Regis students and a resident seventy-year-old Jesuit priest, Fr. Vince O'Flaherty. Fr. Vince could not bake a casserole if his life depended on it! But he knew how to dream big and live small, and simply be present to each of us in our respective faith journeys as our world was beautifully, sometimes painfully, broken open. Not incidentally, Fr. Vince was also one of the funniest and most naturally joyful and spontaneous persons I have ever known.

During Lauri's year at Romero House, she and her fellow residents conducted house-to-house surveys of neighborhood residents to identify the most urgent health care needs in the community. Months later they opened a free clinic set up in an old house adjacent to the church and staffed by volunteer doctors and nurses to directly address some of those needs. Lauri credits this intense year of living among the immigrant poor with her decision to go to medical school and her one ongoing commitment as a pediatrician to work with underserved populations.

What I remember most about Romero House are the children. On just about any afternoon before dinner you could find us throwing a football in the street with kids from the neighborhood. Their single greatest challenge was surviving the local public school system where the high-school drop-out rate among Hispanic teenagers in a typical year was well over fifty percent. Within a few weeks of living at Romero House, the children of the neighborhood were no longer merely statistics to me, unfortunate "others" to be lamented or argued about abstractly in classrooms or political debates on TV. They were children with beautiful names: Juanita, Jesus, Pablito, Susanna—children of irreplaceable value, and, as I wanted to believe, children with a future in our society. Living *is the creation of a common identity, a common consciousness. It is when we let joy make itself out of our love.*

When I think about Fr. Vince and our sojourn at Romero House, I think of Jesus' encounter with the rich young man (Mark 10:17-21), a story which speaks poignantly to the question of solidarity in our day. In the first place the story opens a window into Jesus' frame of mind in an encounter with a privileged person in his society. As Mark's gospel tells it, Jesus beheld the young man "and felt a love for him." Second, the young man himself took the initiative, approaching Jesus with some urgency (he "ran up" and knelt before him) and with a particular kind of question: "Good teacher, what must I do to inherit eternal life?" It seems the young man was driven to Jesus by an awareness of his own emptiness, a desire for formation in the way of authentic happiness and holiness. *What am I still lacking?* Jesus, of course, challenged him in a way he could not have foreseen: give all you have to the poor and follow me.

Solidarity with the poor offers little in the way of political or economic reward in American society. The logic of solidarity cannot be grounded in an apparent, real, or promised system of rewards and punishments, not even, I think, an eternal one. Nor can solidarity be conjured out of a strictly ethical code of behavior. At the same time, many young Americans today feel deeply unfulfilled by their situation in society. More keenly than their parents' generation they are aware of the world's interconnectedness and of the costs incurred by their own grasping for the "American dream": the costs to the masses of poor persons across the globe; the costs to nonhuman life and the environment; the costs to their human spirit, which manifests as the coarsening of youthful idealism before life in the "real world," and the vague but gnawing hunger for something more. They measure all of these costs against the values and fears of a consumer society deeply embedded in themselves and their parents. They try to make sense of a political (and religious) landscape polarized by cynicism, where participatory democracy gives way to the economics of spin, and whoever shouts the loudest on TV wins.

About the logic or motivation behind solidarity, Gustavo Gutierrez writes: "It is not a matter of 'struggling for others,' which suggests paternalism and reformist objectives, but rather of becoming aware of oneself as not completely fulfilled and as living in an alienated society. And thus one can identify radically and militantly with those—the people and the social class—who bear the brunt of oppression."[33] If my experience at Romero House and in subsequent years as a teacher has taught me anything, it is the happy realization that a great many young people yearn for something more than what the consumer culture and the disembodied world of virtual reality and the global economy offers them. They long for genuine community and local participation in the common good. They want to serve, but like the rich young man, they rarely know how to give words to their desire, much less to identify a course of action. In the pattern of Jesus—and in the pattern of witnesses like Fr. Vince O'Flaherty and others working where needs are greatest—the church ought to be able to turn the imagination of young Christians from self-centeredness to other-centeredness, that is, to the poor, the stranger, and do it in a spirit of love.[34]

There is no question here of watering down the prophetic sting of the race critique or the urgency of telling the truth about white privilege or white racist supremacy. But the church and its teachers must also help young people diagnose their own participation, alienation, and emptiness in a highly stratified racist, consumerist, and militarist society. This interior self-confrontation may be faith's first critical breakthrough in the movement toward solidarity. Like the rich young man, of course, we can expect that some, perhaps many, will turn away in sadness, even contempt.[35] But for those who say yes and risk the turn to solidarity, the beloved multiracial community offers a path of joy and fellowship on this earth that is unfathomable inside the narrow walls of class security, or the pseudo-communities of virtual reality and market success.

To be clear, the turn of the privileged toward the poor can neither be paternalistic ("Let me help you become more like me"), nor sentimental ("Let's go sing '*Kumbaya*' with the smiling poor"). It should neither ignore nor overstate the risks of discomfort and even violence. The invitation to a new way of relating to the world, the invitation to Christian freedom, is a paschal option and requires a difficult break with the past.[36] I know of no better way to facilitate such *positive interruptions* in the lives of young people than by inviting them into structured, communal immersion experiences, the kind of education that meets young people where they are, mobilizes their gifts, and gives them room to grow. Whites in this country—indeed privileged peoples of any color—need not go so far as Latin America or Africa to meet fellow pilgrims and Christians living, praying, celebrating, and surviving, just one or two floors away inside "the master's house."[37]

*Would you like to come with me to Village Ghetto Land?* What will it take to venture beyond our habitual comfort zones and begin to build relationships with those whom conventional wisdom about the real world tells us to avoid? What will I do to help reestablish the sense of the image of God in people of color? What work can we all do to cultivate racial and economic justice in our cities? Asking these kinds of questions and issuing invitations to come and see, person to person, is the risk that places us in the path of meaningful work, genuine happiness, and amazing grace.

Living is not submission to "the way things are." Living is creativity and celebration. It is the forging of a common identity as we walk the path and "let joy make itself out of our love." Though Thomas Merton wrote the words, and Stevie Wonder still embodies them, their truth is written forever for me on the face of a seventy-year old Jesuit priest who died peacefully in his sleep one morning at Romero House. May God free us from every hesitation, and may God's own creativity and joy make itself out of our love.

# 7

# PRESENCES

Sometimes when I stand in some corner of the camp,
my feet planted on earth, my eyes raised towards
heaven, tears run down my face, tears of deep emotion and gratitude.

~ Etty Hillesum, *Letters from Westerbork*, 1942

She smiles, for though they have bound her, she cannot be a prisoner.

~ Thomas Merton, *Hagia Sophia*, 1962

Our growth as persons and communities into the freedom of love
is never as miraculous, predictable, or complete as we should like.
Like a river swollen by innumerable tributaries, or a mosaic dappled
in thousands of disparate colors, all merging and bleeding into one
vibrant and pulsating image, human communities and cultures are
the confluence of many seen and unseen inheritances. New colors
and shades are forever swirling and flashing into the whole, yet many
of these are not new at all, but rise up from ancient and eternal

*Etty Hillesum. Collection Jewish Historical Museum, Amsterdam. Used by permission.*

wellsprings. Only when we step back from the mosaic do we realize with sudden wonder and clarity that many of those pulsating colors had been there all along, dancing in their own circles of shadow and light, yet we had not seen them. How disarming, and yet what a grace it is to behold them! Our view of reality was so much smaller than it might have been.

Is it possible that the very same dynamic applies to our theological imagination, the ways we "see," imagine, speak of, and grow into the mosaic mystery of God? Can we imagine a divine Love so large that it flashes like diamond light from within all the world's peoples and natural landscapes, across every race, ethnicity, and religion, all the earth's continents, oceans, and watercourses?

This chapter is an experiment in the kind of theological imagination that would welcome such a boundless vision of divine Presence, and therefore, of hope. Hope is the fruit of an imagination given room enough to step beyond its place inside the mosaic, as it were, and envision a larger, more humane and joyful future. The imagination that produces hope is fluid, permeable, and catholic, always stepping back from the great mosaic and then plunging in again, convinced that there is something still more to discover, seeking after a greater sense of the whole. The imagination that produces mistrust, cynicism, and despair, by contrast, is like a tightening barbed-wire circle, a succession of closing doors that promises nothing new, only more of the same. Despair cannot see beyond or imagine a way out. It infuses life with a dread weariness.[1]

For the Christian and Catholic sacramental imagination, hope rises from what pulses beneath the surface of things, calling our freedom forward, inviting us to imagine and make room for another possible future, the future of God's own imagining. As a *theological* virtue centered in the incarnation, Christian hope rises not from human vision or effort alone but from the commingling of human and divine freedom, history and eternity, matter and spirit, freedom and grace. In other words, the mosaic is still being imagined and, while promises of great wonders spring forth from the mouth of God, *nothing is fixed ahead of time*. Our freedom as sons and daughters of God hinges on the present moment of imagination and decision, pregnant with possibility and risk. "See, I am doing something new! Now it springs forth, do you not perceive it?" (Isa 43:19)

Authentic Christian hope, it must be said, has little patience with fantasy. Fantasy is a flight from reality, a flight from freedom, creating alternative worlds and a diversity of images largely untethered to human history, memory, and experience. The imagination that produces hope, by contrast, involves a profound engagement with the real and "a refusal to let go until one goes beneath the surface."[2] Where fantasy is the kind of free-wheeling imagination that Hollywood and the masters of the culture industry tend to exalt—and not a few religious and apocalyptic fundamentalists—the sacramental imagination *grasps* reality by starting with the world as we encounter it, the world of the senses, the world in which God became flesh, which is "a broken world with many broken people in need of healing."[3] Authentic hope must begin there, lest it be a false and fantastical hope, pie in the sky hope, merely dreaming.

What follows is an experiment in the kind of religious imagination that bears hope even where despair is fully warranted. We begin with the witness of a young Jewish woman named Etty Hillesum whose story plunges us into the mosaic of racist genocide during the Holocaust. From there we step back and plunge in again, our view of the mosaic shifting to the rural American South and the hidden stories of black women during the early civil rights movement as portrayed in Sue Monk Kidd's novel *The Secret Life of Bees*.[4] Pulsing beneath these two very different worlds is the question of God and God's presence: Where was God during the Holocaust? What kind of cultural and theological imagination could sanction—literally: sanctify—social evils such as genocide, slavery, misogyny, and culturally entrenched racism? An even more important question emerges: *Who* was God during the Holocaust, or amid Jim Crow south? *In whose image*, really, are we made?

The witness of mystics, sages, and ordinary people of faith down through the ages suggests that rising up from within creation there pulses an uncontainable Love, coming toward us in all things. How we imagine, speak about, and pray from that encounter with divine mystery matters urgently. To recover hope in a despairing world we need room enough to imagine again, to step beyond our worlds within the mosaic and let ourselves be seized by God's vision of a more humane and joyful future. I invite the reader to join me in an experiment in heightened imagination, the kind that might even see heaven itself in something so small and unpromising as a mustard seed.

## The Eclipse of God

Etty Hillesum was a young Jewish woman who lived in Amsterdam during the Nazi occupation and was murdered in Auschwitz at age twenty-nine. Her diaries give witness to a spirit in humanity that defies rational explanation, a light and hope that flashes forth even from within the horrors of racial genocide. The following lines, written in May of 1942, just before Etty was arrested and sent to the transit camp of Westerbork, have haunted me since I first read them some twenty years ago.

> *Saturday morning, 7:30.* The bare trunks that climb past my window now shelter under a cover of young green leaves. A springy fleece along their naked, tough, ascetic limbs.
>
> I went to bed early last night, and from my bed I stared out through the large open window. And it was once more as if life with all its mysteries was close to me, as if I could touch it. I had the feeling that I was resting against the naked breast of life, and could feel her gentle and regular heartbeat. I felt safe and protected. And I thought, How strange. It is wartime. There are concentration camps. . . . I know how very nervous people are, I know about the mounting human suffering. I know the persecution and oppression and despotism and the impotent fury and the terrible sadism. I know it all.
>
> And yet—at unguarded moments, when left to myself, I suddenly lie against the naked breast of life, and her arms round me are so gentle and so protective and my own heartbeat is difficult to describe: so slow and so regular and so soft, almost muffled, but so constant, as if it would never stop.
>
> That is also my attitude to life, and I believe that neither war nor any other senseless human atrocity will ever be able to change it.[5]

The passage radiates what Robert Ellsberg calls the "earthy and embodied" sense of the divine that saturates Hillesum's diaries. "For Etty, everything—the physical and the spiritual without distinction—was related to her passionate openness to life, which was ultimately openness to God."[6] Our bodies, the trees, the earth—even the hard soil beneath the camps—pulses with the whisper and protest of life itself, enfolding us "in her gentle and regular heartbeat." It is impossible to overlook the striking feminine imagery with which Etty describes God's presence, "her arms round me" so close and protective that she can scarcely distinguish it from her own heartbeat.

Etty was no naïve romantic. She felt the noose tightening, the impending "cruelty and deprivation the likes of which I cannot imagine in even my wildest fantasies." Yet there pulses throughout her diaries an enduring sense of grace and consolation: "I don't feel [caught] in anybody's clutches; I feel safe in God's arms, to put it rhetorically, and no matter whether I am sitting at this beloved old desk now, or in a bare room in the Jewish district, or perhaps in a labor camp under SS guards in a month's time—I shall always feel safe in God's arms. . . [All] this is as nothing to the immeasurable expanse of my faith in God and my inner receptiveness."[7]

The key image may be the last: her determination to maintain an "inner receptiveness," a spiritual freedom, which no amount of barbed wire or ideological fury could contain. Indeed, Etty's journals reflect an inner freedom and faith that seem to flow much more from sensual receptivity and wordless silence than from any explicit religious creed or ritual action. "Such words as 'god' and 'death' and 'suffering' and 'eternity' are best forgotten," she writes. "We have to become as simple and as wordless as the growing corn or the falling rain. We must just be."[8]

In no small way Etty's sensual openness to God included her closest friendships and intimate sexual relationships. Meditating on a night spent with her elder mentor and lover, Julius Spier, she writes, "Our desire must be like a slow and stately ship, sailing across endless oceans, never in search of safe anchorage. Then suddenly, unexpectedly, it will find a mooring for a moment."[9] With lovers no less than with friends, family, and children, we must learn to "just be," attentive and unconditionally present, whether in passing ecstasies, in evening laughter around the dinner table, or long passages of dryness and mutual loneliness. So is the way of friendship with God, who shares our desire, our solitude, our companionship, our loneliness.

### The Incarnate Open Circle

Two weeks before her internment at Westerbork, Etty speaks directly and intimately to God, confessing her growing realization that the perceived presence or absence of the divine in the world depends considerably upon us, on our "safeguarding" God's hidden dynamism within creation.

> *Sunday morning prayer.* "Dear God, these are anxious times. Tonight for the first time I lay in the dark with burning eyes as scene after scene of human suffering passed before me. I shall promise You one thing, God, just one very small thing: I shall never burden my today with cares about my tomorrow, although that takes some practice. Each day is sufficient unto itself. I shall try to help You, God, to stop my strength ebbing away, though I cannot vouch for it in advance. But one thing is becoming increasingly clear to me: that You cannot help us, that we must help You to help ourselves. And that is all we can manage these days and also all that really matters: that we safeguard that little piece of You, God, in ourselves. And perhaps in others as well. . . . You cannot help us, but we must help You and defend Your dwelling place inside us to the last."[10]

What most defies rational explanation in Etty's story, as in other narratives of courage and resistance during the Holocaust, was her willingness to take suffering upon herself "in solidarity with those who suffer."[11] This was not a masochistic embrace of suffering for its own sake, as Ellsberg notes, but rather a vocation "to redeem the suffering of humanity from within, by safeguarding 'that little piece of You, God, in ourselves.'"[12] *To redeem the suffering of humanity from within*: black or white, Jew or Christian, Hindu or Muslim, Buddhist or atheist, is this not what it means to live in solidarity with friends and strangers alike in the merciful womb of Love? For Christians, does this not describe the very person, life, and teaching of Jesus Christ?[13]

We know very little of Hillesum's childhood or formative teenage years before the war. As Eva Hoffman observes, Etty "comes to us unmediated."[14] Yet it is also true that "an encounter with her is instantly and compellingly direct. From the first [diary] entries she comes across as a wonderfully vivid personality: charming, unaffected, with funds of warmth and an eager appetite for pleasure."[15] Indeed no matter how often I return to her diaries, when I turn the final pages I am overwhelmed with both wonder and sadness. So much vitality, so much erotic warmth and humane goodness, snuffed out by the fury of racist ideology, set into motion with a technocratic efficiency and scope beyond all imagining. Etty's last known writings were scribbled on a postcard thrown from the train that delivered her to Auschwitz. "We left the camp singing,"[16] she wrote.

It is not for me, let alone any Christian, to claim the victory for love, and thus for God, by Etty Hillesum's witness. And yet an almost miraculous spirit endures and comes to life again in our remembering her. Can more be said than this? I think so. And here I want to linger a moment with the striking feminine imagery that Etty uses to express her sense of God's presence, her feeling "that I was resting against the naked breast of life, and could feel her gentle and regular heartbeat."[17]

Of course she is not the first Jew to express the divine encompassing Presence in such vividly feminine terms. From the books of Proverbs and Wisdom to the wisdom sayings of Jesus and much of the earliest christological imagery of the New Testament, the feminine face of God haunts the Bible itself, even where she has largely been marginalized or banished from institutional Judaism and Western Christianity. She saturates Jewish kabbalism's imagery of *zimzum* (Hebrew: "contraction"), a mystical narrative in which God creates and nurtures the world not through sheer omnipotence or "masculine" power, but rather more like a mother, freely and lovingly opening a space in God's very self for the emergence of the material cosmos and consummately for human freedom. Paradoxically, it is the emptiness or womb-like openness of God's expansive love that sustains the ripening fullness of a vibrantly unfolding creation.[18] But what can such imagery have to do with racist genocide or the collective horrors of human history?

In her breathtaking study, *The Female Face of God at Auschwitz*, Jewish theologian Melissa Raphael echoes many other scholars of religion and culture in the observation that our dominant images and conceptions of the divine powerfully shape the ways we see, judge, and relate to one another at every level of society.[19] A bit more provocatively, Raphael joins other feminist theologians in arguing that patriarchal or male-centered images, discourses, and practices have sanctioned a great deal of injustice, misogyny, and violence in society, synagogue, and church, in no small part by obscuring the female face of God:

God's nurturing, indwelling Presence known in the Hebrew Bible as Wisdom, Shekinah, Sophia, or Spirit.[20] Patriarchal forces have veiled the feminine divine "to the point of disappearance," argues Raphael, perhaps nowhere more horrifically than in Auschwitz. Indeed, she suggests, it is not altogether surprising that traditional Jewish theology, with its own patriarchal imagination, could not imagine how the all-powerful God of Moses and the prophets would have been so utterly powerless, so *impotent*, in the face of Auschwitz.[21]

In truth, Raphael argues—and here is her distinctive thesis—God was not wholly eclipsed in Auschwitz but was incarnate in women who turned in compassion and bodily care toward one other, defying the most inhumane and desperate circumstances. With unsparing detail, Raphael unearths the largely ignored and forgotten stories of women in the camps who maintained the practices of Jewish prayer and ritual purification with whatever resources were available to them—not excluding their own bodily fluids where water was nowhere to be found.[22] Within the barbed-wire enclosure of the camps, one woman's body bent in compassionate presence over another woman or a child formed an encircling space where the divine Presence could dwell, where God could be reconciled, as it were, with humanity, over against the patriarchal god of raw power, the false and idolatrous god of nation-states and National Socialism. Even (or especially) in Auschwitz, the most basic gestures of empathy constituted "a redemptive moment of human presence, a *staying there* against erasure"[23]—not only for women in the camps, but through them, for God.

Raphael tells the story of a woman who, torn from her husband and children by SS guards immediately after arriving at the camp, falls weeping on the frozen ground "with the flaming crematoria before her," when she suddenly feels two hands lay a garment around her shoulders. An old Frenchwoman had stepped forward, wrapping her in her own cloak, whispering "It will be over and done soon, it will be over."[24] Raphael recalls another now-iconic story of an old woman who is remembered "for holding in her arms a motherless 1-year-old child as she stood at the edge of the communal pit, about to be shot with the rest of her village by Nazi troops. The old woman sang to the child and tickled him under the chin until he laughed with joy. Then they were shot."[25]

Clearly Raphael's case for the divine presence in Auschwitz does not hinge on numerical or otherwise logical analyses, as if hints and gestures of the good could cancel out the overwhelming weight of evil. Hers is "not a quantitative theology, contingent upon circumstance"; it is "a qualitative, ethical theology,"[26] in which "the truly numinous spectacle was not the horror of the flaming chimneys but the *mysterium* of human love that is stronger than death, the *tremendum* of its judgment upon demonic hate, and the *fascinans* of its calling God back into a world which had cast her out."[27] Indeed the sacramental impulse, as we might here call it, whether Jewish or Catholic, is an impulse that "attaches very large meanings to very small signs."[28]

Let me hazard a personal example much closer to home. Immediately after our adopted son Henry was born, somewhere in the vast slum of Cite Soleil in Port-Au-Prince, Haiti, his mother, believing she had been impregnated by an evil spirit, abandoned him in a latrine. When my wife and I held the infant for the first time at the age of six months, we were told this much about his birth. We also learned that sometime after he was abandoned—whether minutes or hours we don't know—another woman from the area heard the newborn's cries and found him struggling in the latrine, half-submerged in feces. She retrieved him, brought him back to his mother, and insisted that she take him to the orphanage. The rationalist may hear this story and call it a happy accident of circumstance. I call it a miracle of grace, which brought Henry crying and fighting *for life* from one woman's womb into another's sheltering arms, and, less than a year later, into my family's embrace.

Of course for every story like ours there are ten thousand (and six million) more that defy theological meaning. Even ours is haunted by ambiguities. Can grace rise from the horror of an earthquake? I think often of Henry's birth mother and pray that God has freed her from whatever dark spirits, or abusive men, which overshadowed her. Even still, when I contemplate this beautiful child and his beautiful sister who came to us, as it were, "in the fullness of time," from a chain of events and innumerable acts of selflessness well beyond my capacity to understand, I cannot help but fall mute in wonder. Raphael, I believe, gets it exactly right: the restoration or *tikkun* of the world "does not occupy a quantity of space and time; it is the theophanic possibility of a moment."[29] The fearful mystery of grace hinges precisely on the moment—the accumulated constellation of moments—in which we, and people we will never meet, say yes or no to love.

Collectively what such moments reveal, suggests Raphael, is a picture of God's power as manifest in the vulnerability and weakness of incarnate love. "Where the communal fabric of the world was being torn apart, human love was anticipating its renewal."[30] Where racist ideology sought to obliterate God as God-incarnate in the Jews, there were nevertheless women (and men) who "made a sanctuary for the spark of the divine presence that saved it from being extinguished."[31] God asks, God invites, God needs our participation in the indwelling drama of love (Exod 25:8).

We encounter that very same flash of incarnate presence and reconciling power in Etty Hillesum. Etty's witness belies the empirical surface of things, and suggests an alternative view of divine power and presence, albeit a costly one. What seems to be God-forsaken is not and must not remain so: God, life, the earth, await our response, our resistance, our protest, our celebration. Note how the word "Presence" evokes a gift that is both spatial and temporal: *I am here with you now, in this place, in this moment*—not just with you, but *in* you, and *you in me*. God awaits, as it were, our bodily surrender to a communion that is deeper, yet more hidden and tenuous (because free) than any earth-shaking or army-defeating theophany. *Be still and know that I am God* resounds ineffably, like the root note of a minor triad, with *Be still and know that I am a human being*, and more ineffably still, beneath the rapacious machinery and rhetoric of war, *Be still and know that I am the Earth.*

Earth indeed is "the silent memory of the world that gives life and fruit to all," she who "preserves everything in herself," and in whom "nothing perishes,"[32] not even the smallest and most forgotten of creatures. Over and over again Etty describes a sense of divine presence cutting through the fog of anti-Semitic hatred and consoling her from within the silences of nature, as in "the jasmine [outside] and that piece of sky beyond my window."[33] Raphael, too, notes that when no person was capable of a kind word or compassionate touch amid the dehumanizing conditions of the camps, "inanimate natural objects could take on the functions of divine presence for women." She recounts Victor Frankl's story of a girl who told him as she lay dying that a bare chestnut tree "was the only friend she had in her loneliness and that she often talked to it." When Frankl asked the girl if the tree replied, she answered, "It said to me, 'I am here—I am here—I am life, eternal life.'" Raphael concludes: "If God has chosen Israel as God's vehicle of self-revelation then [such stories] must tell us something about the nature and posture of God's presence among us. It may seem little more than a tree stripped of its leaves by an untempered wind."[34]

Thus do Etty Hillesum and the hidden women of Raphael's study teach us that so much that is hard to bear, insofar as we show ourselves ready to bear it, can be "directly transformed into the beautiful."[35]

### *"She Cannot Be a Prisoner"*

We might think of other places today, mostly hidden and marginal places, where the protest of Life itself, of Earth, and a Mother-Love's rebellion against cruelty and arbitrary violence, seek to break through into a human world and social imaginary increasingly engineered for war, violence against women and children, and planetary destruction.

She rises from the threatened rainforests of the Amazon river basin, not least in their mournful lament for the memory of Sr. Dorothy Stang. She speaks to us in the "Mothers of the Disappeared," who dance together in the Plaza de Mayo of Buenos Aires in silent remembrance of their missing sons and daughters, husbands and grandsons, sisters and granddaughters. She weeps and rises defiantly in the story of Somaly Mam, and countless other Cambodian women and children sold into the horrors of sexual slavery, often by their own families. She whispers in the resplendent sophianic icons of the Russian Orthodox tradition, and in the sublime portrait of "Ruby Green Singing," which graces the cover of this book. Painted in 1928 by American artist James Chapin, the image, to my eye, succeeds beyond all human measure in capturing, in Chapin's words, "the beauty of Negro music and the Negro people." She is for me the face of hope.

She speaks in the pages of Georges Bernanos's mournful classic *The Diary of a Country Priest*, in the soulful storytelling of Bill Withers's "Grandma's Hands," live at Carnegie Hall in 1973, and in Sojourner

Truth's still-electrifying "Ain't I a Woman?" She sings in the poetic artistry of Joni Mitchell, Billy Holiday, and Fannie Lou Hamer, and again, from almost every page in Sue Monk Kidd's resplendent first novel, *The Secret Life of Bees*, where the image of the Black Madonna infuses hope into the life of a young white girl who has none. She cries out in the silent aftershocks of destroyed natural landscapes—the "naked, tough, ascetic" earth of Etty's imagination—and in the faces of the global poor and victimized women and children of color.[36]

What binds these diverse figures and narratives into one won-drous yet disturbing mosaic is the affirmation of divine-human pres-ence precisely, urgently, and most intensely, in those persons and places written off by conventional wisdom as inhuman and God-forsaken. Indeed where commonsense understanding about the real world registers no disconnect between our habitual worship of "God" and the systematic violation of women, children, and the planet itself, divine Wisdom cries out from the crossroads in protest, identifying herself especially with the little, the hidden and forgotten ones, and with suffering earth, the Mother of all God's children. Neither blood, nor political alliances, nor religion can contain the reach of God's universal loving presence. "Not that she is strong, or clever," as Thomas Merton wrote in his sublime poem to Holy Wisdom, "but simply that she does not understand imprisonment."[37]

This brings us back to *The Secret Life of Bees*, where August, the matronly black wisdom figure of the story, explains to the young white girl, Lily, why she and her friends, who call themselves the Daughters of Mary, pray to the Black Madonna. The Black Madonna, a.k.a. "Our Lady of Chains," holds forth in the midst of their "house church" in the form of a striking wooden statue, formerly a ship's masthead, of an African woman looking toward the horizon with raised fist in the air. "I wish you could have seen the Daughters of Mary," says August, "the first time they laid eyes on [the Black Madonna]. You know why? Because when they looked at her, it occurred to them for the first time in their lives that what's divine can come in dark skin. You see, ev-erybody needs a God who looks like them, Lily."[38]

What the Black Madonna does for the Daughters of Mary is what no white or male image of God could do, namely, she *redeems their suffering from within* by reflecting back to them in bodily form their own inherent dignity, strength, and beauty. She does not stereotype, she sees, and somehow in seeing her *see you*, you become visible to yourself. Blackness is made beautiful. To borrow from Etty Hillesum, for the women in the story (and a few men too), the Black Madonna is a palpably healing and empowering Presence, especially in the racially explosive and patriarchal culture of the deep South, because she awakens and safeguards that "little piece of You, God, in ourselves."

It is the same grace that August herself incarnates—sacramentalizes, enfleshes, *makes real*—for the young Lily, whose spirit is overshadowed by an abusive father and crippling guilt associated with the death of her mother. In the womb of August's unexpected, gratuitous love, Lily's single prayer is answered: "Mother forgive. Please forgive." In the circle of welcoming community, Lily's spirit is gifted with room enough to heal, to flower forth bodily into womanhood.

"When you're unsure of yourself, when you start pulling back into doubt and small living, she's the one inside saying, 'Get up from there and live like the glorious girl you are.' She's the power inside you, you understand?"[39] From August to Lily such words are no less than a priestly and prophetic grace, a theandric affirmation of the divine presence who hides in Lily and in all things, *a reminder of Lily's dwelling place in God's heart from before the very beginning*. One wonders in what context our children today, especially (but not only) our girls, might be encircled and gifted with such an elemental theological truth about themselves, where God's mercy and strength is sacramentalized in images, discourses, and practices that "look like them."[40]

Indeed *The Secret Life of Bees* is a beautifully realized, almost mythic protest against a whole civilization—and implicitly a patriarchal church—that seems determined to obscure that extraordinary good news about our shared life together in God, reducing men, women, and children alike to "doubt and small living." Without ever using these terms, the story exposes the tripartite evils of racism, sexism, and classism, sins that obscure the divine image in victims and perpetrators alike, and so blaspheme the revolutionary good news of a God who dwells bodily with us. These are diseases of the eye, but no less afflictions of the mind and heart, indeed, of all the bodily and spiritual senses. Above all, they manifest a deep poverty, and captivity, of the imagination.

Surely the unraveling of the world in our time is bound up with our ongoing violence against, and willful theological sundering, of

God. "When the masculine and the feminine aspect of God have been reunited and the female half of humanity has been returned from exile, we will begin to have our *tikkun*. The world will be repaired."[41]

## God Who Is with Us

Jesuit Fr. Alfred Delp, executed for his resistance to Nazism on February 2, 1945, wrote to his friends from prison about the beauty and cost of a life lived freely under the horizon of grace. I invite the reader to take a deep breath, step back again from the mosaic, and allow Delp's words to guide us toward some conclusions in our experiment in imagination, hope, and presence. He writes:

> One thing is clear and tangible to me in a way that it seldom has been: the world is full of God. From every pore, God rushes out to us, as it were. But we're often blind. We remain stuck in the good times and the bad times and don't experience them right up to the point where the spring flows from God. . . .
>
> In everything, God wants to celebrate encounter and asks for the prayerful response of surrender. The trick and the duty is only this: to develop a lasting awareness and a lasting attitude out of these insights and graces—or rather, to allow them to develop. Then life becomes free, in that freedom which we have often looked for.[42]

In every generation, across all times and places, the constant and final barrier to that "freedom which we have often looked for" is *theological*, namely, our inability or willful refusal to surrender to those "insights and graces" that would lead us to an ever greater grasp of the living God. Can we imagine a Love so great—and so small—that it flashes from within all the world's peoples and every natural landscape? Indeed, God "rushes out to us" from every pore. But can we believe it?

German Catholic theologian Johann Baptist Metz once asserted that Christians can pray after Auschwitz only because there were Jews who prayed *in* Auschwitz. The implications are painfully clear: the Christian community has been both the vehicle of grace in history and too often its most tragic obstacle. Wherever Jews struggled in faith before the seeming silence of God to keep the circle of grace open, through resistance, prayer, and loving compassion, they not only helped to redeem humanity from its most vile capabilities, they also opened the way for God to dwell bodily and perceptibly within God's suffering creation. Of course there were many Christians, too, Christians like Alfred Delp, who resisted to their deaths the terrifying closed circle of Hitler's Final Solution. And this fact, too, must be accounted for and celebrated.[43]

But Metz's point stands. Insofar as we have failed to defend the image of God in ourselves and in others, we have condemned ourselves to a self-destructive and sometimes horrific prison of our own making. It is fully in this sense that Christians can pray after Auschwitz only because there were Jews who prayed in Auschwitz. Closer to home we might add that white Christians in America can still pray after the horrors of slavery, Reconstruction, and Jim Crow, only because African slaves and subsequent generations of black Christians have prayed from the depths of their suffering, resisted the evils of racism and segregation, and so preserved, against the ignorance of whites, the deepest truth of the Christian gospel. And there were, of course, white Christians and Jews and all other manner of folks who resisted and persevered in faith as well, many risking their lives to do so. "When I marched in Selma," confessed Rabbi Abraham Joshua Heschel, "my feet were praying."

Metz might put it this way: Without our participation in the work of justice and making a welcome place for all of God's children, which is the way of the cross, there is *no ground from which* to joyfully and credibly proclaim the resurrection. Christian freedom in full flower plants itself bodily, like a mustard seed, in the borderlands between Good Friday and Easter. These borderlands and desert landscapes are found everywhere across the world, and in the church itself, pleading for rain. They teach us that it is not riches or worldly power and authority that unlock the way to freedom but, paradoxically, the startling realization of our own mortality, the vulnerability of spirit joined to flesh, which no person, no government, and no church can escape. We need the wisdom of women and peoples of color to help us in our dying and rising. It is their prophetic witness and perseverance in faith that preserve the world's and the church's sanctity today. And keep our hope alive.

## Postscript: Wisdom-Sophia in Viet Nam

I append this chapter with a story of encounter and grace published a few years ago by a friend and former colleague, John Kane of Regis University in Denver. I hope it will resonate with readers' experiences or even bear some in their doubts, as it does for me, concerning the hidden depths of presence and hope rising from within a beautiful but troubled world.

> I was recently in Da Nang, Viet Nam—a beautiful coastal city that many of us first came to know as the location of one of the largest U.S. military air bases during the terrible "Viet Nam War" (which the Vietnamese more accurately remember as "the American War"). Looking out over the surf during my first evening, I noticed in the distance, in the hills on the northeast rim of the bay, a large and brightly illuminated white statue. It was, I soon learned, a very tall (probably well over 100 feet) and slender statue of Quan-Am, the Buddhist mother of compassion. Later we visited the site, a monastery compound with numerous temples and buildings, all dominated by this magnificent statue overlooking the bay and the city. It happened to be raining quite hard when we were there — rain at once forceful and yet gentle. Quan-Am is typically depicted, as in this statue, holding a water vessel, and sometimes depicted actually pouring the cool water of mercy over a troubled world.
>
> It felt that way to me as I stood, getting drenched, at the foot of this immense statue. I found myself praying, spontaneously, perhaps in part because the statue reminded me of so many statues of Mary, but also because I knew in both brain and heart that it made no difference whether this statue and my prayer were Buddhist or Christian. I was, in that rain and in that place, in the presence of grace — surrounded by love and compassion, called to be my better, more loving and compassionate self. The rain was—it didn't just seem, it really was—God's merciful tears over the former violence of that place and Her cleansing outpouring for the recovery of childlike innocence and kindness.
>
> I think something like this—often less dramatic, but not always—happens to men in the presence of loving women; to be sure, in the presence of feminine beauty mediated by

the women of our lives: our mothers, sisters, wives, daughters, and friends. Yet it can also happen in the typically more sudden experience of beauty and grace reflected by and from a woman we've perhaps never met, or at least not before "seen" in this way—perhaps it's just someone passing on the sidewalk, on a bus, in a classroom, at church, or even on television or in a film. The sad but strong face of actress Juliette Binoche in Krysztof Kieslowski's magical film *Blue* never ceases to grace me in this way.

Yet, sadly, the deliberate and constant emphasis on female sexiness in most of our visual media—even increasingly in the advertising plastered everywhere in Viet Nam—this continual focus on sexiness short circuits the experience of grace. It seeks to immediately provoke my sexual response rather than my deeper need for the companionship and love of women. Indeed it is deliberately intended to blind me to the far more fundamental presence of grace that is mediated by the feminine in women, in nature, and the earth, in the sea and the city and the home, whether in Da Nang or New York, Paris or Platteville.

I know that I risk reverting here to stereotypes of "the eternal feminine" against which feminism rightly warns us and out of which so many women have had to struggle. Yet I believe that what I am saying is fundamentally true, and that a newer, more independent and adult feminine will only succeed in making this grace even more fully present for men.

I will not attempt to say how the feminine also mediates grace for women, but that it does so I have no doubt. Just watch mothers and daughters doing things together, or girlfriends happily sharing a drink or a dance, and you get a very quick reminder of such grace.

Such are the seed-experiences that might ground and flower into our own prayerful awakenings to Wisdom-Sophia.[44]

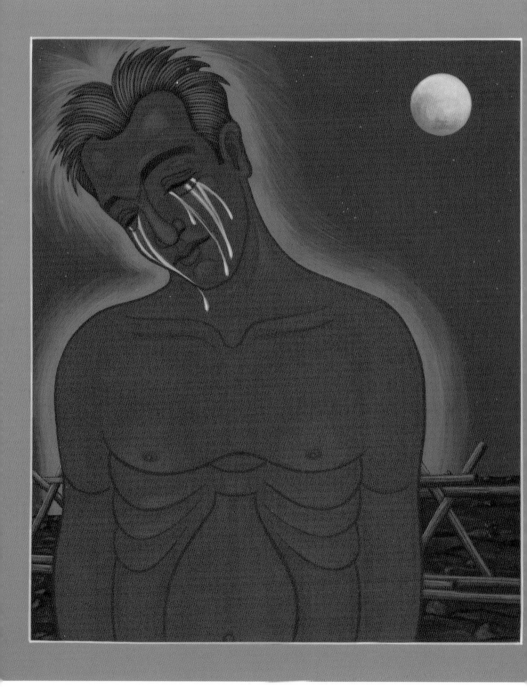

# 8

# DIFFERENCES

*For Christ plays in ten thousand places,*
*Lovely in limbs, and lovely in eyes not his*
*To the Father through the features of men's faces.*

~ Gerard Manley Hopkins, SJ

Theology makes progress by being always alive to
its own fundamental uncertainties.

~ John Henry Newman

Few have captured the heart of the Christian and Catholic sacramental imagination so vividly as the English Jesuit poet Gerard Manley Hopkins. Hopkins's luminous vision of the Christ who "plays in ten thousand places" is not an exercise in literary fantasy. It begins, like all authentic Christian hope, with the world as we encounter it, the world in which God became flesh, "a broken world with many broken people."[1] It is there, through eyes of faith, that we meet Christ, "lovely in limbs, and lovely in eyes not his." Authentic Christian hope—in this respect no different from Jewish hope—begins with the real and refuses "to let go until one goes beneath the surface."[2] But alas, how difficult

*The Passion of Matthew Shepard, Fr. William Hart McNichols. www.frbill.org. Used by permission.*

it is to get beneath the surface of *people*, especially those whom we are inclined to identify ahead of time as suspect, dangerous, dangerously different. How often do we presume, without benefit of encounter, that what lies beneath the surface is not trustworthy?

We might ask ourselves honestly: In whom are we least prepared to meet Christ, the incarnate face of Love? The Jew? The Muslim? The young black man from the inner city? The "welfare mom"? The gay couple down the street? The atheist? The priest behind the altar? This chapter builds on the previous by wrestling with the question of difference, and the ways we handle racial, biological, and cultural differences theologically, in relation to God or the divine realm. The intuition I wish to explore in greater depth has been implicit throughout this book: namely, that theology requires a method and a language, above all an imagination, that does not seek to manage or erase difference out of the gate, but is committed to listening to the other receptively, contemplatively, as "an other with words to speak—words of his or her own that may challenge from difference and may love with freedom."[3] Indeed the question at hand is not only how *we* relate to all manner of differences—racial, cultural, sexual, biological—but also *God's freedom* to love in and through all of God's creation, not least those we hold apart and demonize as different. Theology, for the sake of love, must interrogate the ten thousand ways we cut ourselves off from the unfamiliar or feared other and, thus, from the hidden Christ who plays in all things.

I begin with a montage of contemporary realities that serve to illuminate the challenge of difference in society and church. Like any recitation of images or examples, it is highly selective and leaves aside a great deal of contextual nuance, not least any silver linings or graces that may be hidden or yet emerge in each of these contexts and the different worlds they represent. What follows are only partial snapshots of reality, yet, together they suggest a society and church increasingly, sometimes dangerously, impoverished of theological imagination and hope.

### Language, Reality, and Difference

- An unarmed, seventeen-year-old black man named Trayvon Martin, wearing a hoodie and walking in a gated community in Florida, is identified as "suspicious looking" by an armed twenty-eight-year-old Hispanic neighborhood watch volunteer, then confronted and shot to death as a 911 operator records his screams for help. The shooter pleads self-defense under "Stand Your Ground" laws, and is not charged with a crime for five weeks. Americans are divided along racial lines as to whether racial profiling is self-evident in the case.

- Black parents everywhere describe the ritual of sitting down with their sons to teach them the "Black Male Code," i.e., the rules of how to act and not act in public and in the presence of white people, and above all, how to act when—not if—they are pulled over by the police while driving.[4]

- Analyzing thousands of music videos played on MTV and BET in the last thirty years, media critic Sut Jhally describes the dominant portrayal of young black men as possibly "the most racist set of images ever displayed in public" since D. W. Griffith's white supremacist film of 1913, "Birth of a Nation." The portrayal of women in music video, and black women especially, is almost universally dehumanizing and objectifying, "their value often reduced to a single part of their anatomy." Several infamous hip-hop videos, for example, feature the male star running a credit card through a willing woman's buttocks. Jhally describes the dominant lens or narrative through which men and women have been portrayed in music video since the early 1980s as the "adolescent male heterosexual pornographic imagination," a narrative now so dominant in American popular culture as to be widely considered normal. Jhally's critique presses well beyond the artists themselves or any single musical genre to indict the powerful and mostly white male record company executives behind the camera who envision and dictate the content of music videos for public consumption.[5]

- A 2010 Kaiser Family Foundation survey reports that children between age eight and eighteen in America spend an average of fifty-three hours per week (nearly eight hours per day) engaged with television or some form of electronic media. African American and Hispanic kids spend nearly one-third more time than white kids. Jesuit ethicist Fr. John Kavanaugh describes the consumer society and the advertising imagery driving these media as the dominant form of education and moral formation in our lives, preaching a gospel of unrestrained individualism, consumerism, and militarism, and crippling our deepest capacities for social empathy and loving, committed sexual relationships.[6]

- A study commissioned by the United States Conference of Catholic Bishops reports that between 1950 and 2002, approximately 10,667 children were sexually abused by clergy in the United States. The revelation of widespread sexual abuse in the Roman Catholic Church and ongoing systematic denial and obfuscation by bishops around the world continues to this day.[7]

- Several African American Catholic eighth graders in a Midwestern parochial school habitually refer to one another in casual conversation as "niggers." Their white classmates understand that they are never to use the term, but confess bewilderment as to why the black kids, and presumably their parents, would use it.

- Federal statistics report that one in five college women are victims of sexual assault, most often during the first few months on campus. College women express conflicted feelings about reporting sexual assault in the face of enormous pressures not to do so, especially where incidents involve alcohol (as most do) or high-profile male student athletes. As a University of Notre Dame professor sees it, "Most of my colleagues and almost all of my students tend to be very protective of the institution and our image, and they're not eager to look too closely at anything that might raise questions."[8]

- A best-selling video by rap superstar Snoop Dogg features an "interview" with an admiring female "journalist." Draped by dozens of nearly naked women throughout the film, he sings "You gotta' break these hoes for Snoop." The interviewer herself finally succumbs to Snoop Dog's charms, as he smiles into the camera and says, "Yeah. Another bitch broke. Ain't no f*-in' joke."[9]

- The National Underground Railroad Freedom Center in Cincinnati, Ohio, estimates that some 12–27 million human beings are caught in one form or another of modern day slavery. Between 600,000 and 800,000 people are trafficked internationally, with as many as 17,500 into the United States annually. Nearly three out of four victims are women, and half are children.[10]

- Congress repeatedly fails to pass The Dream Act. Supporters say the legislation provides a rigorous and reasonable route for millions of children and young adults to be integrated fully into American society. Opponents decry any hint of "amnesty" for the children of "illegal aliens."[11]

- During a televised Mass presided by Pope Benedict in Washington, DC, following Prayers of the Faithful and a Presentation of the Gifts marked by diverse languages and spirited Gospel and Spanish singing, a noted commentator on the influential Catholic EWTN network remarks: "We have just been subjected to an overpreening display of multicultural chatter. And now, the Holy Father will begin the sacred part of the Mass." Black Catholic ethicist Fr. Bryan Massingale observes that such a statement is not an isolated incident but reflects an attitude "more typical and widespread than many are willing to acknowledge" in a "white racist church," namely, that "Catholic" equals "white." "In U.S. Catholicism," Massingale writes, "only European aesthetics and cultural products are truly Catholic—regardless of the church's rhetorical commitment to universality."[12]

- The white pastor of an urban black Catholic parish in a Midwest diocese is reprimanded by his bishop for sitting among the parishioners during the Liturgy of the Word instead of remaining situated above them in the presider's chair in the sanctuary, as liturgical norms dictate, and for participating with parishioners in a spirited, wide-ranging, and lengthy sign of peace. Asked to explain, the priest says, "They forget that I, too, like the laity, am the object of the Word."[13]

- The Roman Catholic Pontifical Commission *Ecclesia Dei* clarifies that the newly reinstated Tridentine or Latin form of the Mass does not permit girls to serve at the altar. Pastors in Arizona, Michigan, and Virginia forbid altar girls during *all forms* of the Mass under the logic that "replacing girls with boys as servers leads to more vocations to the priesthood." Facing objections from parishioners, a Phoenix pastor says he did not consult the parish council "because they are not theologically trained." One (female) Catholic blogger applauds the move, describing girl altar servers as a "liturgical aberration" and "one more example of the devastating feminization of worship which has contributed in no small measure to the prevalence of effeminate priests and the sex abuse scandal." A Virginia mother whose pastor instated a boys-only policy says, "That's when I knew, in my heart, that we couldn't stay any longer at this parish." She and her husband and daughters have since "floated around" between area parishes, feeling "heartbroken by our church." The diocese of Lincoln, NE, has forbidden girl servers since 1994.[14]

- Pastoral staff and volunteer teachers in many dioceses across the United States are increasingly required to sign loyalty oaths as a condition of remaining in employment indicating that they personally and "enthusiastically support" the official teachings of the Catholic Church on matters of widespread conscientious dissent such as contraception, gay marriage, and women's ordination. Many choose to sign; some refuse and resign or are terminated.[15]

- A 2012 survey reports that ninety-two percent of American youth aged two through seventeen years old play video games, while some nine percent of players between eight and eighteen are "pathological players," or clinically addicted. By far the most popular games among children are "first-person shooter" games, in which "you approach the world with a deadly weapon, and your job is to kill them before they kill you." A respected medical journal describes video games as possibly "the most effective educational technology ever invented. Players are immersed in an environment where they are rewarded for doing well and punished when they don't. Either way, they get to keep doing it until their performance improves." In the case of the massively popular "Call of Duty: Modern Warfare 3" (one billion dollars in sales in the first sixteen days after its release) and "Grand Theft Auto," mostly what children "keep doing until their performance improves" is kill people. "If you're being rewarded for killing female hookers," worries Dr. Michael Rich of Children's Hospital in Boston, "that's bound to teach you something over time."[16]

- A gay student at Rutgers University commits suicide after his roommate secretly records him engaging in sexual activity with another man and posts the video online. Educators and public health officials describe cyber-bullying as a national epidemic and the harassment of gay students during the high school and college years as a particular cause for alarm.[17]

- A 2012 Nielsen report shows that children aged thirteen to seventeen send an average of 3,417 text messages a month. The Pew Research Center notes that the near ubiquity of handheld devices has had an enormous impact on kids' free time, filling up the "interstitial spaces" in their daily lives. Yale professor Stephen Carter worries that as young people "increasingly fill their free hours with texting and other similarly fast-paced, attention-absorbing activities, the opportunities for sustained reflective thought will continue to fade." One cost of the new world of social media, suggests Carter, may be to accelerate the decline "of what our struggling democracy most needs: independent thought."[18]

## *Ways of Seeing and Managing Difference*

A great deal could be said about any one of the above points or any number of them taken together. I limit myself to three observations, each subject to my own biases and need for greater understanding and conversion, and trust the reader will find (or reject) other possible connections.

First, in all of these snapshots, from music video and national political discourse to the Catholic liturgy, note how prevailing images, language-forms, and ritual practices often serve not to open up the circle of loving encounter between persons in community but rather *to create image and language-worlds that effectively divide, dehumanize, and close the circle of mutual encounter, friendship, and grace.* Young men of color are routinely profiled as "suspicious-looking," often with tragic consequences; black women are "welfare queens," "hoes," and "bitches," and are visualized and treated as such in popular public imagery ranging from political campaign ads to music video; freshmen women in college are targeted as "easy prey" and plied with alcohol to facilitate the easy "hookup" or the traumatic sexual assault; adolescent boys score points and esteem among their peers for their efficiency in gunning down female prostitutes and stealing cars in sexually-charged virtual feedback loops; gay students are bullied and exposed via the Internet to the point of suicide.

In the realm of the church, the Catholic laity cannot be trusted for consultation or insight in matters of faith or worship because "they are not theologically trained"; the sexual abuse crisis is rooted in the "liberal culture of the 1960s" and can further be blamed on the "feminization of worship" and "effeminate priests"; European cultural imagery is "authentically Catholic" while African and Latin American forms of imagery and worship are suspect; God is a reflection of the white European "Holy Father"; and altar girls (it can only follow) are a "liturgical aberration."

While it is true that not all the differences in play here are of the same order—e.g., socially constructed differences such as race and class are not of the same order as biologically inscribed differences such as sex and sexual orientation—nevertheless one can discern a certain tendency or common style of thought epidemic both in society and church in the way language and imagery are used to manage, compartmentalize, and contain difference. As Thomas Merton diagnosed the problem almost fifty years ago, the basic error underlying all manner of dangerous "isms" or phobias of the other—racism, classism, sexism, misogyny, clericalism, homophobia, xenophobia— "is the logical consequence of an essentialist style of thought." Merton laments the degree to which language is used not to facilitate genuine communication or understanding but to *identify and label* the other's "essence," so as to manage and contain our fear of difference:

> [An essentialist style of thought involves] finding out what a man is and then nailing him to a definition so that there can be no change. A White Man is a White Man, and that is it. A Negro, even though he is three parts white is "A Negro" with all that our rigid definition predicates of a Negro. And so the logical machine can devour him because of his essence. Do you think that in an era of existentialism this will get better? On the contrary: definitions, more and more schematic, are fed into computers. The machines are meditating on the most arbitrary and rudimentary of essences, punched into IBM cards, and defining you and me forever without appeal. "A priest," "A Negro," "A Jew," "A Socialist," etc.[19]

Whether conservative or liberal, gay or straight, white or black, Christian or Jew, an essentialist style of thought errs dangerously to the degree it employs language and imagery as an unyielding straitjacket, short-circuiting the imagination and nailing me (and everyone "like me") to a definition, a tautology, an essence, so that the game is up well ahead of time. *There can be no change*, no room for dialogue, no room for encounter, no room for growth, no room for transformation, no room for freedom, no room for curiosity, no room for spontaneity, no room for discovery, no room for risk, no room for error, and above all, no room for mercy or forgiveness. In short, depending on your essence, *you are innocent or guilty*, never both. There can be no room for love.

Second, what scandalizes about many of the above accounts is not just that individuals would be capable of bigotry, willful ignorance and mischaracterization of others, fantastic displays of ego, sexual dysfunction, and violence—all marks of sin, human freedom gone badly awry—but that the very institutions that profess a commitment to human dignity and justice and that hold the power to effect positive transformation in society would fail or refuse to do so when sinful patterns of injustice are brought into the light. Nothing threatens a child's emergent sense of identity and belonging as the realization that his very presence is perceived as a crisis and a threat to his society; that because of his parents' country of origin, his skin color, or the clothes that he wears, he is not only not welcome but according to the prevailing legal system, he is literally disposable. Nothing is more damaging to the church's moral authority in society or more disheartening to the laity than the hypocrisy and willful blindness of some of its shepherds, and the punitive disciplinary measures often employed to silence thoughtful, conscientious dissent. And few practices—though I am open to correction on this point—are more demeaning to the dignity of black persons than the adoption of the racist terms, images, and misogynist practices long used against them in the white "master's house."[20] If language makes a world, the future of hope in families, society, and church depends not a little on the image and language-worlds we choose to inhabit.

Third, while it is difficult to measure or fully understand the impact of television and electronic media in our lives, it is impossible to ignore their enormous sway in the imaginative lives of our children.

What is the status of loving presence—our capacity to "just be" with our spouses, children, or by ourselves in reflective solitude—when there is hardly a moment of the day that we (and our children) are not tethered to an electronic device? What are the prospects for social empathy when the media to which we are addictively present, and through which we so often surrender our capacity for independent thought, fill our imaginations with so much fear, aggression, and unmitigated garbage about those who look and think differently than us?[21]

It is not too strong, I think, nor an evasion of the race question, to suggest that the crisis of culture threatening our very personhood and communal life in America today is not just white racist supremacy but an all-encompassing media supremacy, which is to say, a public and increasingly private atmosphere of imagery and language so rancorously divisive and often violent with respect to difference that it threatens to bury our most basic capacities for empathy, intimacy, and love beneath an avalanche of narcissism, political self-interest, and distraction. All of which add up to a very different kind of presence and power at work in our relational lives and shaping our conception of the real at every level.[22]

Indeed these points come into particularly intense focus when we consider the dominant images and practices shaping our conceptions of sexuality and family life. What are the prospects for sacred eros or erotic love, for example, when so many children, adolescents, and not a few adults are exposed regularly, if not addicted, to sexually charged video games and to pornography, accessed easily via the Internet in ever more fantastic iterations? Even more contentious from a theological perspective is the question of homosexual love. A great many thoughtful people who love the church and who also love their gay and lesbian friends, sons and daughters, and brothers and sisters, are asking for theological clarity on this most vexatious of all issues of human difference.[23]

This is clearly not the place to attempt a discussion of homosexuality in the Scriptures or the Christian tradition, but the question, as an acute problem of difference, merits brief consideration along the lines of reasoning (and imagining) already laid out in this chapter. Can sexual love, this most wondrous of mysteries of our relational life as fashioned in the image of God, be fixed to a *single* image and essence so that the mystery is resolved and contained ahead of time?[24] Is it congruous with our experience that homosexuals, by virtue of biological denotation, are "gravely disordered" and incapable of familial covenantal love or selfless contribution to the common good of society and church? The gathering chorus of Christians who question an essentialist or strictly heterosexual vision of sacred eros evidently do so from the intuition, rooted in the loving witness of gays and lesbians themselves, that homosexual love can be and in practice often is sacramental, an incarnate sign and instrument of covenantal love and divine grace. More and more Christians and Catholics are coming to grasp the issue at its heart (*in* their hearts) as a question not of political correctness, minority rights, or accommodation to liberal culture but rather of theological integrity, wholeness, and doctrinal development. In whose image are homosexual persons made?[25]

Unfortunately even to clear a space for such questions is to wade deeply into the turbulent waters of the culture wars, where efforts at dialogue are often met with scorn and punitive *ad hominem* reprisals. That there is little room in the church to discern such questions safely, openly, and honestly should be a matter of deep concern for every Catholic and Christian, no matter where one's convictions lie on the spectrum of sexuality. Not least because gays and lesbians continue to suffer a terrible existential and theological loneliness, a great many in the heart of the church they love.[26]

How much easier to keep quiet and swallow the beautiful opiate pill of consumerism! Gay or straight, white or black, rich or poor, Christian or Jew, in practice we all seem to agree that what really promises to set us free is money, glorious money, and splendid, self-driven success in the real world of capital. No presence, no mutual vulnerability, no companionship, no attentive silence, no deference to the earth, no making room for the hidden, the sick, the ugly, the forgotten. Just swipe your credit card, hit the gas, and enjoy the ride. "Love: it's what makes a Subaru, a Subaru."

### Love: The Uncontainable Mystery

It may be that our most urgent task today is to take back the word "love" from the corporate spin doctors, best-selling psychologists

and self-help gurus, and self-appointed prophets of religious orthodoxy and return it fully to the boundless mystery of God. The Bible
itself offers not one image or metaphor for love but at least three—
*agape, filios,* and *eros*—and even these with their beautiful and various
shades of meaning cannot fully contain the mystery. The much-
neglected Song of Songs gives us a wondrous affirmation of erotic
love, but still no room for affirming homosexual love as holding a
place in God's heart from the very beginning. Yet if God is Love—not
a fixed and solitary essence but a way of being-in-relationship—and
God remains free and beyond our comprehension, doesn't the burden
lay upon us to make room in our hearts and theological imaginations
for the mystery of love in all its potentially sacramental realizations?
Might that mystery not also include homosexual love?

I ask the question provisionally, granting that the discussion here
is far from complete. Nevertheless, I ask with an eye on the freedom
of God to love in and through different forms of bodily human
agency. If we are going to err in our ignorance, should we not err
freely and willingly on the side of inclusion, both in doctrine and
deed, and not on the side of exclusion so long as the mystery of covenantal love is served? As St. Paul reminds us, "For we know partially
and we prophesy partially"; for now we see only "indistinctly, as in
a mirror," and not yet "face to face" (1 Cor 13:9, 12). One has only to
think of Christianity's historical record with slavery or with the Jews
to discern that the risk of getting it wrong in theological development
is ever outweighed by the demands of love, social solidarity, and
pastoral care: the call to encounter God's presence in those who challenge from difference, and who might yet teach us something beautiful about the mystery of God-made-flesh, something we haven't
before been able to realize.[27]

How might we make ourselves a little more worthy of the great
Welcome Table before our eyes are privileged to see it? We might
begin by taking a critical look at ourselves, and our prevailing images
of God, through the lens of love.

> Love is patient, love is kind. It is not jealous, (love) is not
> pompous, it is not inflated, it is not rude, it does not seek its
> own interests, it is not quick-tempered, it does not brood over
> injury, it does not rejoice over wrongdoing but rejoices with

> the truth. It bears all things, believes all things, hopes all things, endures all things. (1 Cor 13:4-7)

Perhaps these lines are too familiar to Christians for their profound meaning to be really knowable, or contemplated in a sustained way for their implications in every aspect of our lives.

The Christian mystical tradition interprets St. Paul's sublime teachings on love through the lens of the Beatitudes, especially what Jesus calls purity of heart and poverty of spirit. Both purity of heart and poverty of spirit describe an interior disposition that is very difficult to realize outside of grace, namely, the *humility of love as we stand before the other*, a humility that "is not quick-tempered" and "does not seek its own interests." Politically speaking, such a disposition would seem a recipe for disaster! Yet the deep source of all such humility is incarnational: the presumption, in the mystery of faith, that no less than Christ, the incarnate face of God, approaches us in the other. *For Christ plays in ten thousand places, / Lovely in limbs, and lovely in eyes not his / to the Father through the features of men's faces.*[28]

In whose image, specifically, are we made? As a father myself and, more pointedly, as the son of a loving father, the paternal face of God as Father evokes well for me Christianity's sublime teachings about love. For many men, women, and children alike, "Father" has long been and can continue to be a beautiful divine image, a sustaining metaphor of divine presence, constancy, and loving care. (Picture the father, for example, in Rembrandt's incomparable painting "The Return of the Prodigal Son.") But for many people whose experience of "father" is traumatic, domineering, or cold, the image does not evoke or make room enough for love. For many, the line between paternal presence and patriarchal power is much too thin. Clearly it is not enough to insist in perfect tautological fashion that God equals Father. The experience of the Jews, as detailed in chapter 7, ought to have taught Christians that lesson once and for all.

We must remember that God is also Mother, Spirit, and Shekhinah, lest we deny our maternal and feminine experiences of grace, tighten the noose around divine and human wholeness, and foreclose the imaginative flexibility of the Bible itself, not to mention the great intellectual and mystical tradition of the church. Like that of countless Christians from east to west for nearly two millennia, my own prayer life has been enormously enlarged and enriched by the biblical image and memory of God as Sophia, or Holy Wisdom. *For there is [nothing] God loves, be it not one who dwells with Wisdom. . . . Indeed she reaches from end to end mightily and governs all things well* (Wis 7:28, 8:1).

Where the Bible and tradition have been inflexible, making little room for the visage of sacramental love in the marginalized and feared "other"—blacks, Indians, homosexuals, Jews, women, Muslims, "pagans"—we must pray for the courage and grace of discernment in which the Spirit might clear space in our hearts and imaginations for the tradition to develop. Why? Only for the sake of love: to defend and preserve "that little piece of You, God, in ourselves."[29] There is nothing to fear in the intuition that God speaks to us today—preferentially, urgently, intensely—in the Black Madonna; that Christ is crucified and rises again in Trayvon Martin, Matthew Shepard, and Etty Hillesum. We may not have grasped it before, imprisoned by deep cultural fears and longstanding religious prejudices. But surely to resist such a growth in theological imagination today would be to succumb to the poverty of "doubt and small living."[30]

In sum, the error of an essentialist style of thought applies to God no less than to human beings. To affix God to a one-sided image or reflection of a particular human visage or culture—white, male, heterosexual, European—yields a number of "logical" but dangerously unchristian consequences in the life of the church. The Christ of Hopkins's imagination is not (simply) the male Jew from Nazareth whose "essence" we must all physically mirror or whose actions we must all robotically emulate—as if the New Testament presented such a cookie-cutter model of holiness and discipleship (it does not). It is not Christ as essence that we worship but Christ the humanity of God, who hides and "plays" in every person's latent desire, unique God-given gifts, and implicit freedom for love. God gifts us, as God gifted Jesus, with the faculties to grow in wisdom and love.[31] The vulnerability of such a covenantal God, who makes room for the slow flowering of human freedom-in-grace, cannot be overstated.

## *Imagination and Renewal*

In his own reflections on the challenges of theological growth and discernment facing every generation in the church, Blessed John

Henry Newman reminds us why a static or essentialist vision of God will not do for the Catholic sacramental imagination:

> From the nature of the case, all our language about Almighty God, so far as it is affirmative, is analogical and figurative. We can only speak of Him, whom we reason about but have not seen, in terms of our experience. When we reflect on Him and put into words our thoughts about Him, we are forced to transfer to a new meaning ready made words, which primarily belong to objects of time and place. We are aware, while we do so, that they are inadequate, but we have the alternative of doing so, or doing nothing at all. We can only remedy their insufficiency by confessing it. We can do no more than put ourselves on the guard as to our own proceeding, and protest against it, while we do . . . it. We can only set right one error of expression by another. By this *method of antagonism* we steady our minds, not so as to reach their object, but to point them in the right direction; as in an algebraical process we might add and subtract in series, approximating little by little, *by saying and unsaying, to a positive result.*[32]

Theological discernment can never reach its destination so perfectly as a logical syllogism or a smoothly functioning astronomical machine. Because God, the object of theology, is no object at all; and because the human person, too, is an irreducible mystery, theological language needs room to breathe *and* to be caught up breathless; to speak and not to speak; to affirm and to deny; to hold firm and to develop. It is not that theology must begin again in a conceptual vacuum with every new generation. Rather, because our grasp of God is always "analogical and figurative," theology speaks of God, "whom we reason about but have not seen, in terms of our experience."[33]

This means that theology at its catholic best, like Christianity itself, is an organic and living language. We are still learning how to give full (and full-bodied!) voice to the mystery of the incarnation. In our stumbling efforts to realize the mystery we must attend carefully to the Scriptures and appeal methodically to reason, but we also must drink deeply from the wellspring of human experience in all its mosaic diversity, an open realm of discovery much more ambiguous and even "antagonistic" than we should like in speaking of God. To do so is not an act of creativity or daring for its own sake; it is an act of trust in God who breathes life into all things. "Theology," as Newman observes, "makes progress by being always alive to its own fundamental uncertainties."[34]

The alternative—to reduce divine and human mysteries to facts akin to axioms of mathematics or science—is the great temptation and error of religious fundamentalism, the death of theology and the death of authentic Christian hope. Newman writes:

> Our theological philosophers are like the old nurses who wrap the unhappy infant in swaddling bands or boards, put a lot of blankets on him and shut the windows that not a breath of fresh air may come to his skin—as if he were not healthy enough to bear wind and water in due measures. They move in a groove, and will not tolerate anyone who does not move in the same.[35]

Thus again what threatens our grasp of the great human mosaic is the same captivity of imagination that threatens our grasp of the living God. Like the "old nurses who wrap the unhappy infant" for fear she will catch ill, the church risks trading in its theological vitality and growth in wisdom and love to the point of withering slowly in self-contained protectiveness.[36]

Historically the great beauty of Catholicism resides in its intellectual and imaginative capacity to renew itself. A danger point is reached when the language of theology is not permitted to renew itself and becomes, as John Coulson put the matter some forty years ago, even less sensitive than the surrounding culture "to that sense of complexity, even paradox, which, in the public language of our poets, novelists, and dramatists, is, in origin, theological."[37] It is worth pondering this insight very carefully. Wherever the church shuts down—imaginatively, theologically, liturgically—the culture rushes in to fill the void, not least *in the imaginative lives of Christians themselves.*[38] The fertile complexity and paradox to which Coulson speaks refers not only to our encounter with the mystery of God, but so, too, our encounter with the deepest mysteries of human being. How often our poets and filmmakers do a better job attuning our spiritual senses to the wondrous play of Christ, the humanity of God, in all things, than do our increasingly restrictive theologies and liturgies.

Of course, as detailed in the montage above, the secular image-makers also hold the power to get it terribly wrong about the human person, and this fact undoubtedly complicates the relationship between church and culture. Witness the rapacious language-world and pseudo-liturgical aesthetics of the Third Reich; or closer to home, the new universe envisioned by so many Hollywood films, where robots and computers vie to dominate (and liberate) the world, and the boundary between persons and machinery dissolves. What kind of imagination—and dashed hopes in the (merely) human species—would give rise to the enormous popularity of such films? Both for better and for worse, we become creatures of our own image, ritual, and language-worlds. *The machines are meditating on the most arbitrary and rudimentary of essences, punched into IBM cards, and defining you and me forever without appeal.*[39]

As a leavening presence within a domineering technical-economic culture, the church must help people (and then trust them enough) to discern the difference between the sanctification of creation and its profanation. In the realm of sexuality, the church can be a powerful leavening and humanizing force for the good in society wherever it helps people (and finally trusts them enough) to discern the difference between sacred eros and its dehumanizing opposites, the narcissistic and pornographic—not with condemnations and self-inflated rhetoric, but with humility of love, trust in the transcendence of human freedom, and respect for the dignity of conscience.

Let me return, finally, to the central concern of this book. At issue here is not foremost the "individual rights" of peoples of color, women, or gays in the church as an extension or microcosm of liberal democratic society. Rather it is the vocation to theological wholeness and integrity in the church that ought to be out ahead of the game, leavening a secular society by its visible embodiment of love, justice, and unity-in-difference. Is it possible that the fullness of Christ's dwelling place inside us is being halved and quartered from the vine, withering the humane vitality of the whole? What so many racist, patriarchal, and homophobic cultures have yet failed to do, the church can and must do to preserve and live fully into its own inherent but tenuous (because free) theological dignity: "We must help You and defend Your dwelling place inside us to the last."[40] How we imagine, speak of, and perform the presence of God is where that defending and leavening begins. It is where hope bursts forth, or despair sets in, in the heart of the pilgrim community.

This is not to say that engaging such difficult questions in church and society as the empowerment of peoples and cultures of color, the role of women, or the sacramental potentiality of homosexual love will be painless or free of convulsive birth pangs. Far from it! Nor can we predict what the results of such discernment will be, if our pilgrimage in Christ would be free and uncoerced in the Spirit. It is to insist, again, in the words of Etty Hillesum, and with all the saints who have suffered much greater trials before us, that so much that is hard to bear, if we are ready to bear it together with trust and grace, can be "directly transformed into the beautiful."

*And the beautiful was sometimes much harder to bear, so overpowering did it seem. To think that one small human heart can experience so much, oh God, so much suffering and so much love, I am so grateful to You, God, for having chosen my heart, in these times, to experience all the things it has experienced.*[41]

In Christ, God has gifted us with hearts large enough to bear all things in faith, hope, and love. May we show ourselves, one and many in the Spirit, to be worthy of the gift.

# 9

# SONG CIRCLES

There have been times in my life when I just got fed
up with being treated badly and feeling powerless in
the Catholic Church. I struggled with the hypocrisy,
so I would leave . . . not go for a while, because I'm
human, see. The Lord would turn me around and
draw me back, like a magnet. Honey, I have a bruise
on my arm from when Jesus snatched me and brought
me back to the church! He knows where I'm supposed
to be.

> ~ Mrs. Harriett Hazely,
>    St. Mark Catholic Church, Cincinnati, OH

I sit with Shakespeare and he winces not. . . .
I summon Aristotle and Aurelius and what soul I
will, and they come all graciously with no scorn nor
condescension.

> ~ W. E. B. Du Bois, *The Souls of Black Folk*

Sad is the lot of him who arrives inexperienced and
when led to heaven has no power to perceive the
beauty of the Sabbath.

> ~ Abraham Joshua Heschel

*Sr. Thea Bowman, Holy Child Jesus Parish, All Saints Day, 1984. Sr. Thea coaxes a
group of sleepy children to sing. Photo © John Feister.*

I can remember myself vividly as a young boy at Mass, being too small to see over the pew, but it didn't matter. A thousand singing voices lift me into the air, and I'm carried toward the belfry by slow-motion dust particles, dancing in stained-glass light. The music ends and I'm lying again on the kneeler next to my father's perfectly polished shoe. He reaches down to grip my hand during the Lord's Prayer. The back of his hand looks massive folded over mine, its raised arteries pulsing like tributaries of the Nile. I trace them with my finger, and feel his wedding ring press into my palm. His graveled voice resounds in my ears—"Thy kingdom come, thy will be done, on earth as it is in heaven"—as my eyes shutter closed again in illumined darkness.

Decades later, I am at Mass with my wife and kids at a black Catholic parish in South Bend. A young woman named Clare stands up in front of the choir, cradling her newborn baby against her chest. The piano lays down a line, and she begins to sing, "Lord, you are more precious than silver." Her eyes closed, she sways with the baby, singing like both their lives depend on it. The moment is disarmingly intimate, but without a trace of embarrassment. *It's not about her.* Surrounded by a sea of black faces, Clare is the only white woman in the choir. It doesn't matter. We are all one Body, one Presence, one Mother, one Child, a circle opening into the wide-open Heart of God. I can't recall a more prayerful moment in any liturgy my whole life.

## *Life in Community: Embraced by Something More*

"The world is charged with the grandeur of God," wrote the Jesuit poet Gerard Manley Hopkins, as if to shout: wake up, pay attention, you might miss it! The ritual life of public and private prayer—the Jewish Sabbath, the Catholic Mass, solitary meditation, the rosary—may all be seen as different ways of teaching us one thing: namely, the art and discipline of contemplation, of seeing God's hidden presence in the world, through eyes of love. The sacred spaces of the religious world—from the ornate cathedrals of Europe to the humblest chapels and hillside shrines of El Salvador—teach us especially to pay attention to silence. In nearly five decades of participating in the Catholic Mass, what has sustained me most are not the words or creeds spoken there but the sensory interplay of words and images, light and darkness, music streaming through silence.

The rituals and spaces of formal religious worship can be for us and our children a school of wonder and mystery, a saving alternative to a world flattened out by commerce and technology, emptied of mystery or surprise, emptied of beauty, by the everyday drudge and demands of economic survival, by the ubiquitous drug of entertainment and advertising imagery. Regular immersion in sacred ritual is one way to make contact again with that hidden Mystery who breathes within all things, sustaining us into being with every moment. Such contact is never dependent on being in an ornate or beautiful space. I have gazed open mouthed under the dome of St. Peter's Basilica in Rome and prayed in chapels built from little more than mud, straw, or cinder block in Honduras, Mexico, and Haiti. The confrontation with beauty, sometimes a terrible beauty, breaks through wherever two or more are gathered to pray and give thanks—even more, surely, when our feet are touching the receptive earth.

In an American culture that so elevates individualism and stoicism—the self-made man who can overcome any obstacle or burden "by myself, thank you very much"—a church community draws us out of ourselves, beyond the prison of our own ambitions and sufferings, to embrace and even bear the hopes and sufferings of others. The phrase "Do not fear!" appears over three hundred fifty times in Scripture, yet how many of us still struggle with that dread feeling that I have to get right with God before I walk in the door? Church is, or ought to be, where we go to find welcome and support precisely with our brokenness, relational failures, and moral shortcomings.

Indeed our churches could learn a great deal from communities like Alcoholics Anonymous and The Catholic Worker whose rituals of welcome and radical hospitality are built on the foundation of gracious mystery: God surrounds us in mercy not in spite of our moral failures and spiritual struggles but because of them. Moral and spiritual courage comes in the realization that we are loved sinners. Like the disciples on the road to Emmaus, each of us is on the way, struggling to become the loving persons-in-community that God calls us to be. We need room to grow.

It is easy enough to acknowledge my own failings, but does it really help me to be bound together in community with a bunch of other really messed up people? For many regular churchgoers, the honest answer is yes. There is enormous liberation in the realization that I do not have to find my way alone. Unfortunately I was in my late twenties before I began to really internalize this message. And it was not by my own efforts or wisdom that I got it but in the surprising womb of a community that welcomed me, even though I was a complete stranger.

## Behold the Stranger

In the summer of 1989, I completed my studies in music and moved from Boulder to Denver. Able-bodied and desperate to make some money, I somehow lucked into a well-paying job as a construction laborer. Hundreds of miles from family and missing my former life as a student, I felt unmoored and dangerously adrift in a strange city. I needed a place to belong.

I noticed a modest-looking church in the working-class neighborhood where I lived, but seeing the people streaming into the parking lot every Sunday morning, vibrant and friendly though they appeared, I might have easily overlooked it. It was an African American church, about as far from the cathedral church of my white, suburban, Irish Catholic upbringing as one can get. Its humble sign, with paint peeling, proclaimed: Mt. Gilead Baptist Church. I'm not sure what compelled me. The Holy Spirit? Aching loneliness? But it never occurred to me not to go in. One summer evening after dinner, I walked the three blocks from my front door to the church, thinking, "Who knows? Maybe they need a piano player."

As a matter of fact, that evening I walked straight into a rehearsal for the men's choir. There were about thirty African American men of all ages circled about a piano, where an elderly woman—their no-nonsense director, I soon discovered—held court. As I entered the sanctuary she stopped playing, looked up from her music and waited for me to introduce myself. When I got to the part about "hoping to sing and maybe play some piano for you," her countenance broke into a soft smile. "Of course, you are most welcome," she said. "We can always use a piano player." Amazing grace, indeed, how sweet it sounds. For the next six months I sang (and played a little piano) with the men's choir of Mt. Gilead Baptist Church.

Though I did not stay long, the experience at Mt. Gilead planted something deep and beautiful in my religious imagination. After our marriage my wife and I joined an African American Catholic parish in Denver. Our first child was born soon after, and the church community became for us a second home, and to my little boy, a surrogate family.

When one feels oneself a total stranger—even if believing, hoping otherwise—it is a remarkable thing to be welcomed like a brother. It is no small grace to approach a gathering of strangers and, as W. E. B. Du Bois writes, "They come all graciously with no scorn nor condescension." Such graced encounters, such human encounters, occur all the time. But are they not still rare, altogether too rare, between the races? Why should it seem so remarkable, so out of the ordinary, when whites and blacks and all manner of races share table fellowship and prayer?

### *Foretastes of Heaven*

In his classic work *The Sabbath,* Rabbi Abraham Joshua Heschel highlights the inseparable connection between our practices of prayer in this world and our state of preparedness for the next: "[The] Sabbath contains more than a morsel of eternity . . . . Unless one learns how to relish the taste of Sabbath while still in this world, unless one is initiated in the appreciation of eternal life, one will be unable to enjoy the taste of eternity in the world to come. Sad is the lot of him who arrives inexperienced and when led to heaven has no power to perceive the beauty of the Sabbath."[1]

How prepared shall we be when we are seated at the heavenly banquet table? Will we recognize those sitting next to us? (Surely the seating arrangement will be no accident!) Will we know their names, stories, dreams? Will we have prayed with them? The imagination stumbles reluctantly onto one more question: Will I need to ask their forgiveness before the feast is served? Sad will be our lot if we arrive in heaven with no prior experience of the Beloved Community, the multiracial community, and indeed, the multifaith community.

The questions "How do we pray?" and "With whom do we pray?" are closely related to the question "For what do we hope?" Churches that intentionally welcome the stranger may be said to initiate their members into the appreciation of eternal life. Such communities not only anticipate the heavenly banquet, they actualize it in the present. In our Denver parish—about sixty-five percent of African descent, thirty-five percent white, Hispanic, Asian and Native American—visitors were dumbstruck by the sign of peace, which carried on for about ten minutes. In those ten minutes one might have observed that "All heaven breaks loose," and it would be only half a joke. We were part of that community for eight years. Our teenage son still remembers and mourns it like a lost family.

Of course integrated churches are no utopias. Like any community they remain imperfect, on pilgrimage. Perhaps more than racially homogeneous churches, they face unique internal challenges that must be addressed in a healthy manner. At times our Denver parish struggled with conflicts emerging from differences in racial history and culture. The most stubborn problems, however, appeared to stem at least as much from personality clashes as from race. Building trust and shared ownership amid the complexity of feelings around race is not easy. But neither is it impossible. As in any community, strong leadership and frequent opportunities for honest dialogue can keep things vibrant and healthy—and, in our case, the frequent reminder that what we share as Catholics, indeed, with Catholics and Christians worldwide, far outweighs our differences.

The alternative—that no serious effort is made by churches to cross the color line—is hardly worth considering. The fact that by and large most American Christians appear to accept this alternative appears to my mind as a failure of courage, or perhaps, as I have intimated throughout this book, as a failure of theological imagination. In truth, it is probably both.

### *To Rise above the Veil*

Few wrote more poignantly than W. E. B. Du Bois about the torment and irony of race relations. In the world of ideas and books, Du Bois notes, he was free to fraternize with every manner of "smiling men and welcoming women." "I sit with Shakespeare and he winces not."[2] The real world, however, chained him stupidly behind the veil, the veil of race separation and black nothingness. The history of the American Negro, Du Bois observes, is the history of the unreconciled longing to rise above the veil.

But I ask again: Are there not a great many whites, too, who long to rise above the veil? Are there not white Christians and Catholics, and not only among the young, who yearn for a taste of the beloved, multiracial community, and who would rather not wait for the afterlife to find it? Are not some of these flocking into large nondenominational churches where they discover people of many races and economic backgrounds forging relationships and new ways to pray across the color line in this life, right now? I am neither a sociologist nor a demographer, but as a longtime teacher of high school and college students, what I sense over and again in young people is disappointment with the religious status quo, underneath which percolates a vibrant, youthful idealism. Their questions seem to say, "Doesn't it get any better than this?"

To be clear, theirs is not a Pollyannaish desire for "Kumbaya" and interracial lovefests. Young white Christians cannot yet be accused, as their parents have been, of speaking superficially about racial reconciliation solely to assuage their own liberal white guilt. Many of the critically thinking white students whom I teach root their hope for unity across diversity not in political correctness or a sociologically proven optimism—Is there such a thing?—but in a kind of theological cognitive dissonance. In the first place, they accept at least theoretically the value of racial diversity and the inherent dignity and equality of all races. They live, study, and socialize in a rich mix of racial and socioeconomic diversity. This is a notable credit to their parents and grandparents, some of whom marched in the civil rights movement.

But second, against this more positive horizon, they accuse their parents and their parents' churches of hypocrisy. When pressed to examine their limited social horizons and racial biases more critically, they confess to knowing few meaningful experiences of integration or interracial encounter in their neighborhoods or churches. Ironically theirs is much the same critique leveled against liberal white Christians by leaders of the movement fifty years ago. Can such critiques still be effective today, or have they run their course? I don't know.

What I believe is that Christians on every side of the racial divide—blacks, whites, Hispanics, Asians, Native Americans—bear responsibility to the degree that we have resigned ourselves to the contingencies of the so-called real world rather than a hope-driven vision of God's world. By and large Christians have accepted that separate but equal is good enough, and therefore eleven o'clock

Sunday morning remains what Dr. King called the most segregated hour in America.

## Building the Beloved Community

Arguably no person of recent memory has done more to resist and transform the sad legacy of segregation and racism in the Catholic Church than Sr. Thea Bowman, a Franciscan nun who inspired millions with her singing and message of God's love for all races and faiths. Sr. Thea awakened a sense of fellowship in people both within and well beyond the Catholic world first of all by her charismatic presence. But she also did so through her willingness to speak the truth about racial injustice in society and church, and her remarkable ability to express such truths in the context of God's universal love. "We need to tell one another in our homes, in our church and even in our world, I really, really love you."[3] Indeed, how we do need to tell! But as Sr. Thea taught us, we also need to *sing* the beautiful and demanding truth of God's call into the mystery of social love.[4]

At the age fifty-two, confined to a wheelchair by the ravages of late-stage cancer, Sr. Thea spoke before a gathering of the nation's Catholic bishops about the gift and fullness of black spirituality within the Catholic Church. Her "voice clear and resonant, eyes sparkling and hands animated,"[5] she did not hesitate to challenge and even chide the bishops for their complicity in a "church of paternalism, of a patronizing attitude"[6] toward blacks and peoples of color. Most black Catholics would not hesitate, I think, to say that Sr. Thea's words are just as cogent today as they were in 1989.

> What does it mean to be black and Catholic? It means that I come to my church fully functioning. That doesn't frighten you, does it? I come to my church fully functioning. I bring myself, my black self, all that I am, all that I have, all that I hope to become, I bring my whole history, my traditions, my experience, my culture, my African American song and dance and gesture and movement and teaching and preaching and healing and responsibility as gift to the Church.[7]

It is a point of some embarrassment and even shame for me to admit that as a young Catholic I knew nothing about Sr. Thea Bowman during her lifetime. Though her fame extended far and wide even in nonreligious circles, not once do I recall hearing Sr. Thea's name mentioned in the Catholic schoolrooms and parishes of my childhood or young adulthood. Not once. Thus her challenge to another predominantly white audience in 1989 (I was twenty-five) still resounds with prophetic urgency, poignancy, and love, as though she were speaking directly to me: "Are you with us? We can stop and explain this stuff, but I'm asking you, Are you with us?"[8]

Once asked how she was coping with her cancer, she replied, "Part of my approach to my illness has been to say I want to choose life, I want to keep going, I want to live fully until I die."[9] Had she reconciled with cancer? "I don't want to reconcile with cancer, I don't want to reconcile with injustice . . . racism . . . sexism . . . classism. I don't want to reconcile with anything that is destructive." Reflecting further on her life in the face of death, she said: "I wish I had danced more, I wish I had run around more, I wish I had used my body more joyfully and more creatively."[10]

Sr. Thea believed that Catholicism was uniquely equipped to forge empathic relationships across the color line. "The beauty of universality is that the church is able to speak to people in whatever language they understand best—and we're not just talking about verbal language."[11] It is also important to note that Sr. Thea pushed back against that reflex tendency of her fellow Catholics to elevate her or other role models into the status of a "saint," insofar as doing so would relieve us of our own baptismal freedom and Christian responsibility for love. "I know people are looking for sources of hope and courage and strength. I know it's important to have special people to look up to. But, see, I think all of us in the church are supposed to be that kind of person to each other."[12]

How, then, as Sr. Thea so aptly phrased it, to unlock the "power of personal witness," and "get the word out"?[13] How to ignite our baptismal freedom and go and do likewise? "My basic approach," she says, "was to try to promote activities that help different groups get to know one another. As we learn to know one another, we learn to appreciate one another, then we grow to love one another. [You bring people] into situations where they can share your treasure, your art, your food, your prayers, your history, your traditions, the coping mechanisms that enabled you to survive." This kind of mutual sharing opens the way for "points of convergence" to emerge between strangers. Characteristically, she added, "I think a sense of humor and a whole lot of fun can help."

I began this book by recalling one of the most rewarding cross-racial "points of convergence" I can remember: an Advent prayer service organized collaboratively between my students at Regis Jesuit High School, a largely white, wealthy, suburban community, and the youth choir of St. Ignatius Loyola, a mostly black parish in Denver where we were longtime parishioners and where I played the piano. I entered into that experiment, frankly, with trepidation. I came out of it with wonder and renewed hope. I will not soon forget the gathering of both communities on the evening of the service, with parents and grandparents, brothers and sisters, and all manner of folks entering the sanctuary with excitement and uncertainty. I remember the aisles brimming after the service with warm smiles, hugs, laughter, and handshakes. The two choirs, strangers no more, had simply shone when their hands and voices and storytelling came together, and in their shining they had thrown fresh light over the whole congregation. The community had heard again the familiar story of Jesus' birth, but now wholly reimagined in different shades and colors, sung in unfamiliar keys.

To say it once more: Sometimes it is the ineffable God who grasps us from beyond ourselves; sometimes it is the beauty and grandeur of nature; sometimes it is the ineffable human *other*. In every case the question is: Are we are willing to let the circle of familiarity be broken open, and the boundaries give way to the coming of the Lord? Of course such graced encounters are only mustard seeds, bits of leaven in a trenchantly divided society. But in the case of Regis Jesuit and St. Ignatius Loyola, I would never underestimate their latent power for those young people and their families who were involved. Indeed it occurs to me that perhaps the experiment "worked" so graciously because it was imagined and led by the youth of both communities, whose hearts were open to each other from beginning to end, even in their nervousness, hesitation, and fears. They had not yet learned from the adults in their lives that genuine encounters across the color line *simply aren't possible* in the so-called real world.

For what do we hope? And how shall our communal life and prayer reflect that hope? Like Sr. Thea Bowman, I believe that significant numbers of Christians and Catholics of every race would welcome more integrated prayer if they had some idea of where to begin. The young in particular bear an authentic desire in search of a method. What churches and educational institutions are best positioned to provide children and young people right now are opportunities for cross-cultural immersion, service, hospitality, and shared worship led by pastors, lay folks, and teachers committed to working together across the color line. Indeed, many churches are already realizing such a vision, building communities where strangers of every race are made to feel most welcome.[14]

We are called to a way of being in the world, a radically inclusive way, because of who God is. The day is long overdue when any human being, regardless of skin color or creed, might sit down in any Christian church and the community "winces not." When that day comes, when the veil of race separation is destroyed forever, we can sing together, "O Happy Day!" not only in anticipation of the heavenly banquet, but in joyful celebration of its incarnation, here and now.

### In Place of a Conclusion: A Day in the Life (of the Domestic Church)

On any given day in my house you will find two black kids and two white kids driving their two exhausted parents to the brink, and at the same time, filling them with wonder, joy, and even a little youthful vitality. Picture, if you will, the following scene at the local public swimming pool.

A middle-aged, slightly balding, bespectacled, and very white university professor is chasing after a three-year-old black child half his height but clearly with twice his speed and versatility (not to mention muscle mass). Suddenly two white kids, a blonde girl of around nine and a red-headed teenager, sweep in for the rescue, redirecting the little black Dynamo with much laughter and shouting into the water. The temporarily-liberated white guy takes a deep breath and hurries off to locate his other daughter, a beautiful, big-eyed, very black Haitian girl of nine, whom he finds walking with his wife toward the snack shack. Reassured that all are accounted for, our humble professor orders a heaping large raspberry Sno-Cone at the snack shack and sits down in the shade to enjoy it, calculating that in approximately four minutes he'll be on his feet again, chasing the Dynamo. For the next *three* minutes, his face, dripping with red syrup, reflects absolute bliss.

Like many families our daily routine alternates between something like order and thinly veiled chaos. In fact, with the benefit of a little reflection, our days look and feel a lot like what I remember of my own childhood growing up with five brothers and sisters and parents who loved us unconditionally but who rarely could keep up with the whole wild lot of us. It was a graced childhood, to be sure, but far from universally blissful or perfectly loving, as I'm sure my own children will report twenty years from now.

The older I get the more I have come to believe that perfection in love is not the point. It seems to me that the least (and greatest) common denominator in every kind of love is that feeling of an open circle, which I experienced palpably over the long haul as a child: all are welcome here. *You* are welcome, just as you are. There is room enough in our love for you. If not perfectly in daily practice then certainly in general atmosphere, my parents and most of the adults in our neighborhood made it clear that we kids were beautiful to them, that we were valued—enough, indeed, to be frequently corrected—and that we were most welcome, as children, to be children.

I realize that, because of the racialized society we still inhabit, my multiracial family looks different. But surely not so odd or different as we would have appeared just ten or twenty years ago in America. And that fact, too, must be accounted for and celebrated. There are at least two other multiracial families on our street in our unassuming, working class neighborhood, and many more in our parish and in our kids' Catholic school. A young white couple in a small house down the street serve as foster parents for two kids, the oldest black, the youngest white, and are hoping to legally adopt both children. How foster parents are capable of that kind of love and freedom, which would make room for a child in home and heart while knowing that the child, with whom you are falling in love, will likely be returned to his or her birth family—indeed preparing the child for that eventuality—is truly beyond my grasp. So yes, my family is different but not so extraordinary.

Have my wife and I and our two white children, metaphorically speaking, *become black*? In one of the best discussions I have yet seen on "intentional cross-racial solidarity," black Catholic ethicist Bryan Massingale cites several moving testimonials from mixed-race families to illustrate

> how deep interracial friendship and love can shatter the false personal identity built upon the racialized "set of meanings and values" that informs American society. Each one spoke of "becoming black," that is, of a new way of being white and experiencing social reality. Such a person is truly "born again" and lives out of a different identity and social consciousness. Such loving and committed relationships give one the visceral outrage, courage, strength, and motivation to break free from the "rewards of conformity" that keep most whites complacent with white privilege. Transformative love, or compassion, empowers them for authentic solidarity.[15]

In other words, to paraphrase crudely, the general sting and random brutality of racism hits home much more personally and urgently when one has their own "skin in the game."

My wife and I have certainly felt a kind of heightened "social consciousness" and "visceral outrage" in response to manifestations of racism since the adoption of our children. The murder of Trayvon Martin, for example, intensified the already-unhappy awareness that our son Henry, in eight or ten short years, will appear to some like just another "suspicious-looking" black teenager, and may be targeted as such. How I will manage to communicate this news to him remains a question beyond my present capacity to answer. The occasional ignorant remark overheard or posted online by friends or family, even in jest, bears a particularly painful sting. And so, yes, we have "become black" in the sense that we acutely and "personally feel some of the pain that comes from being enmeshed in the racist conditions central to the lives of the oppressed others."[16] It is painful, and also a point of some pride, to imagine how my teenage son might react to any acts of racial animosity directed toward his sister or little brother. But rather than "becoming black" I would simply say that we are, by degrees, becoming more human as a family.

Not to put too fine a point on it, while I appreciate what notions such as "becoming black" and a "new way of being white" aim to communicate, I am not sure such descriptors are quite adequate or helpful at the end of the day in describing the dynamics of cross-racial, transformative love as my family and others we know have experienced it. As Massingale acknowledges, critical race analyses drawn from the social sciences, while "valuable and instructive" for theology, sometimes fall short in their analyses of love, "perhaps because it requires responses that go beyond their horizons."[17] Indeed when I examine the deepest roots, motivations, and the constellation of "accidents" that lay fifteen years deep in our adoption story, insofar as I am conscious of them, they seem to reach well beyond and beneath responses that one could describe as strictly ethical or even compassionate in their source or motivation, though these dimensions are certainly present.

Briefly, the best I can say is that over the course of many years, numerous global immersion experiences among the poor, and after several painful reproductive losses, my wife and I felt a deep desire to make room in our lives for more children, especially for children in need. Because of the blessings we have been given in life we were able pragmatically and prayerfully to consider adoption. It felt like a tremendous grace to do so. Whether the unseen child of our future family would be brown, black, or white, healthy, whole, or handicapped, was secondary, so long as it was a child who otherwise would have no stable family. (Our initial intention was to adopt a single infant.) Once Haiti entered our consciousness, it was no longer a question of "if" but only a matter of "when" we would discover the child who needed us. After seeing their pictures and learning their stories, we were overjoyed to be matched with our two children, neither of whom had any foreseeable future outside of an orphanage. The process began in earnest and accelerated dramatically after a devastating earthquake struck Haiti on January 12, 2010. Twelve days later, our kids were boarded onto an airplane with dozens of other children and brought to the United States, where we greeted them with tears of joy in an airport hangar in Denver.

Since then we have not only become metaphorically blackenized but also considerably Haitianized. One could also say that our two Haitian children are becoming metaphorically Anglicized: in their culinary tastes, distinctly Italian; in temperament, distinctly Irish; and in cultural tastes—if my wife has her way—budding Denver Broncos fans. In their dance moves, I am happy to report they are still very much Haitian. More to the point, our extended family and all manner of folks in our local community have welcomed them with open arms, from the African American checkout lady at the grocery, who greets Henry by name with smiles and shouts clear across the store, to Sophia's kindergarten teacher who made room, literally and metaphorically, for this once-shy, Creole-speaking child to join her class in the middle of the school year. Our neighbors held a block party to welcome the children to their first spring in Cincinnati, and not a few strangers have approached us in public, asking to meet the children and hear something of their story.

In sum, as Massingale suggests, there is something sacramental and even prophetic in the act of intentional cross-racial solidarity within a racist culture. And that is a beautiful thing to behold. Even more, it is an extraordinary grace to be part of. Yet the motivation for such acts might be much simpler, or more mysteriously *human*, than what the sociologists have yet found adequate language for, because they merge into that ineffable and not-so-strictly-rational realm of the invitation to surrender ourselves, even in uncertainty and suffering, to the all-encompassing way of love. We feel ourselves called to a way of being family in the world because of who God is.

The Second Vatican Council was prophetic, I think, in an understated but crucial way, when it spoke of the family as the "domestic church," the seedbed of the universal church, where faith is passed on by word and example not only within the home but also by the family's witness beyond the home. "There should be found in every Christian family," wrote Pope Paul VI, "the various aspects of the entire church."[18] That is a statement worth pondering. Indeed the church is a global, multicultural, multiracial church. What could Paul VI have meant by such a bold claim?

It is not difficult for me to see how our parish community, with its multiracial families and friendships across the color line, is a kind of microcosm of the global church and for us a concrete instrument of God's love. Nor is it hard for me to see how my children, in the evolution of their relationships with each other, are teaching me every day the meaning of transformative love, the kind that is spontaneous, costly, and free. My daughter Grace, who freely welcomed a stranger into her room, her wardrobe, and her life, and who has since discovered a beloved sister; my son Isaiah, who, as I write these lines, is out in the driveway teaching his little "brother from a different mother" how to ride his first Big Wheel; and Sophia and Henry, who came to us from Haiti by some chain of miracles I will never understand, and who will probably lead us all tonight, including their father with two left feet, in a song and dance circle of their own devising. Tonight, in a word, we are going to have some church.

I conclude with my heartfelt thanks to the reader for joining me in this conversation. May God sustain us in the work of solidarity and racial justice, in our discovery of new friendships across the color line, and in our pilgrimages together in the wider womb of grace. May we live fully until we die, until that happy moment when God draws us together again around the Welcome Table.

For resources for further reflection, study, and conversation please consider visiting: http://www.HopeSingsSoBeautiful.org.

# AFTERWORD

# "OUR SKIN IN THE GAME"

Dogmas are the poor mind's share in the divine. A creed is almost all a poor man has. Skin for skin, he will give his life for all that he has. Yea, he may be ready to take other people's lives, if they refuse to share his tenets.

~ Abraham Joshua Heschel,
"Depth Theology"[1]

This much I will say: My latent ambition to be a true Jew under my Catholic skin will surely be realized if I continue to go through experiences like this, being spiritually slapped in the face by these blind and complacent people of whom I am nevertheless a "collaborator."

~ Thomas Merton to Abraham Heschel,
September 9, 1964[2]

Each of us faces the world in our skin. Christopher Pramuk gives us hope, and documentary evidence, that spiritual beauty unites us in ways discovered by the arts (especially music), by nature, and by religion. But the path is as fraught with sorrow as with grace.

*Lauri, author's wife, with children, rural Guatemala, 2012. Photo provided by author.*

With this book, *Hope Sings, So Beautiful*, Pramuk again welcomes us, all of us, into the large community, larger than race and religion, but not larger than life itself. Here he applies the theology of an earlier work, *Sophia: The Hidden Christ of Thomas Merton*, to both affirm and liberate the foundational dogma of salvation through Jesus Christ and Catholic faith. He writes of incarnation as a quality we all share, whatever our religious or ethnic origins. Grace and hope surpass the boundaries of doctrine as he draws upon the wisdom literature of the Hebrew Bible, the faith of Eastern Orthodox Christianity, John Henry Cardinal Newman and Rabbi Abraham Joshua Heschel, and his own insights as a devout Catholic. With *Hope Sings, So Beautiful*, Christopher Pramuk reminds us to get "our skin in the game," as he surveys the deplorable racial divide in American Christianity and in American culture at large. He writes: "Most white people remain blind to racism, as the logic goes, because whites in America have the luxury and privilege of not seeing. They have no skin in the game."

Along with his bold social critique, Pramuk highlights many treasures of our multiethnic world such as the desert paintings of Georgia O'Keeffe, the music of Stevie Wonder (which inspired him as a boy), the death camp diaries of Etty Hillesum (whose erotic energy gives us hope), as well as Jonathan Kozol's relentless examination of the lethal inequities of American public education. One of the many highlights, for me, is Pramuk's stirring account of the Jewish author of Billie Holiday's excruciating song of lynching, "Strange Fruit."

This book is unusual as it combines moments of personal disclosure with scrupulous academic analysis and documentation. Among several grace-filled insights is a worship event he describes which took place in a black Catholic parish in South Bend, as a white mother sings while cradling her newborn child: "Surrounded by a sea of black faces, Claire is the only white woman in the choir. It doesn't matter. We are all one Body, one Presence, one Mother, one Child, a circle opening into the wide-open Heart of God. I can't recall a more prayerful moment in any liturgy my whole life." The author's language is so Catholic, and yet so universal. We get to know Chris, his wife, and their four children, two of whom were orphaned from earthquake-devastated Haiti. *Hope Sings* is a celebration of what is best in American culture, as well as what needs to be confronted bravely and healed.

Chris invited me to respond to his book since we have much in common. I have spent most of my adult years studying and writing about the life and works of Abraham Joshua Heschel (1907–72), mystical theologian and prophetic activist, who was also close to the Rev. Martin Luther King, Jr. As a Jew I am also fascinated with Thomas Merton, the Trappist monk who combined a dynamic faith and criticism of worldly morality with a life of prayer and contemplation. As if to prepare me for these two major influences, as a young man I was privileged to spend time with Howard Thurman (1899–1980), the African American mystic and counselor to many in the civil rights movement. All along over forty years of teaching French literature and religious studies, I have tried to affirm the values of my father, Kivie Kaplan (1904–75), who did not go to college, but who was a successful businessman, national president of the NAACP, and a leader of the Reform Jewish social action commission.

Perhaps the very fact that Christopher and I are of different generations, with entirely different religious backgrounds, underscores how these and other differences are absorbed by faith, or the search for faith, and certainly by love of humankind, love of God, and reverence for the divine human image. At the very least, "graced encounters across the color line."

Our common ground is a "pre-theological" situation, in Heschel's terms, the individual's facing God before the formulation of any creed. Such a leap is necessary for me, as a Jewish reader and thinker, loyal to the God of Israel and to the Jewish people. Pramuk's repudiation of all forms of racism, color prejudice, and homophobia echoes the generous vision of Vatican II. And in this we are more than partners; we are family.

Edward K. Kaplan
Brandeis University

# NOTES

## Foreword

1. Thomas Merton, *Seeds of Contemplation* (Norfolk, CT: A New Directions Book, 1961), 72.

2. Marie-José Mondzain, *Image, Icon, Economy: The Byzantine Origins of the Contemporary Imaginary*, trans. Rico Franses (Stanford: Stanford University Press, 2005), 57.

## Introduction

1. *Gaudium et spes*, no. 1, *Vatican Council II: The Basic Sixteen Documents*, ed. Austin Flannery (Northport, NY: Costello, 1996), 163; all references to Vatican II documents are from this edition. The principle is brought home beautifully in *Gaudium et spes*, no. 22, which centers on the mystery of God's incarnation and revelation in the person of Jesus and, by extension, in every human being: "For, by his incarnation, he, the Son of God, has in a certain way united himself with each individual. He worked with human hands, he thought with a human mind. He acted with a human will, and with a human heart he loved. Born of the Virgin Mary, he has truly been made one of us, like to us in all things except sin" (185).

2. My approach in this book accords well with St. Anselm's classic formulation of *theology* as "faith seeking understanding," though I would supplement Anselm's definition with Jesuit Anthony De Mello's description of theology, in a more narrative key, as "the art of telling stories about the Divine. Also the art of listening to them." See Anthony De Mello, *The Song of the Bird* (New York: Doubleday, 1982), xvi. Both underscore the active, dynamic, searching dimension of theological inquiry, a task which never ends because its final "object" is no object at all but the transcendent mystery of God, who lay beyond our full grasp. In this sense I would describe theology as a lifelong conversation with wonder and mystery, a searching that is both personal and communal at once, inseparable from the corporate memory and life of the church.

By *spirituality* I mean broadly the everyday "way of life" flowing forth from one's deepest beliefs, desires, and internalized values; it is a way of living into our calling and identity as human beings. Everyone "has" a spirituality insofar as every person builds his or her self-understanding and patterns his or her behavior around core beliefs and values. *Christian spirituality* describes the daily, communal expression of one's faith in Jesus Christ, marked by openness to the love of God, self, neighbor, and the world through Jesus and in the power of the Spirit. It is the way of life flowing from the graced encounter with Jesus, who reveals the heart of God to be Love. There is no single correct Christian spirituality but there are many ways, unique to the gifts of each person, of following Jesus.

A related term at play in this book is *mysticism* (from the Greek *mystikos*: hidden; secret), which I take to mean the experience of the immediate presence of God or holy Mystery, a sense of real Presence that is both hidden and revealed in the world, opening our eyes to possibilities that lay beneath the empirical surface of things. De Mello defines mysticism as "the art of tasting and feeling in your heart the inner meaning of such stories [of the Divine] to the point that they transform you." The point to emphasize from a Catholic perspective is that all of these terms, while distinct, are inseparable. Theology, spirituality, and mysticism all find their roots in the encounter with God and holy Mystery as it breaks into human consciousness in historical time and space, an encounter that is both personal and communal and which ultimately lies beyond all our attempts to define, contain, or manage it.

3. By "imagination" I do not mean the realm of make believe or fantasy. Following John Henry Newman, William Lynch, and many others, I understand imagination as the dynamic mode of cognition which selects and organizes experience into a meaningful whole; the imagination is not separate from reason, but rather enables us to *reason differently* by enlarging and reordering our perception of reality, providing a new unity to our understanding and knowledge. What I mean by the "artistic spirit" is difficult to pin down, but I have never seen it better expressed than in Robert Henri's classic, *The Art Spirit* (New York: Basic Books, 2007; originally 1923, J. B. Lippincott Co). A flourishing body of scholarship is advancing the engagement of theology, imagination, and the arts. Recent works include David C. Robinson, ed., *God's Grandeur: The Arts and Imagination in Theology*, College Theology Society Annual 52 (Maryknoll, NY: Orbis, 2006); Richard Viladesau, *Theology and the Arts: Encountering God through Music, Art and Rhetoric* (New York: Paulist, 2000); Jeremy Begbie, ed., *Beholding the Glory: Incarnation Through the Arts* (Grand Rapids: Baker Academic, 2001); Kimberly Vrudny and Wilson Yates, eds., *Arts, Theology and the Church: New Intersections* (Cleveland, OH: Pilgrim Press, 2005); and Don E. Saliers' small but shimmering gem, *Music and Theology* (Nashville: Abingdon, 2007). My own work tends toward the integration of political (or liberationist) and mystical (or aesthetic) approaches to theology.

4. In writing this book I faced a question confronted, at some point, I think, by every scholar writing on race: namely, whether and to what degree I should introduce my own story to readers. Academic culture often looks with suspicion

on personal narrative: too subjective! As a white scholar I am acutely aware of certain other risks of personal disclosure. Readers may wonder, for example, if I mean to use my family's adoption story and, by extension, my kids to establish my racial *bona fides* ("I have skin in the game"). But when I ask the question simply as a human being, as a whole person with a story to tell, the answer seems clear. My story is relevant, just as the memories and experiences of every reader of this book are significant. The crucial question is whether we are willing to reflect on our stories *critically*, with a persistent eye on the need for growth, conversion, and transformation in love.

5. German political theologian Johannes Baptist Metz, much like his teacher, the great Jesuit theologian Karl Rahner, laments the too-sharp divide in much Catholic thought between theology and spirituality, or mystical biography, which he describes as "the articulation of one's life's story in God's presence." Johannes Baptist Metz, *Faith in History and Society: Toward a Practical Fundamental Theology*, trans. J. Matthew Ashley (New York: Crossroad, 2007), 198–207. My method here, and my invitation to readers to reflect critically on their own stories, accord with Metz's desire to view fundamental theology and mystical biography as part of a single cloth. On this point Merton especially stands out for his witness to an integral theological vision and spirituality that is self-critically aware *and* radically catholic, which is to say, radically open to the mystical biographies of others. For a close study of Merton's life and theological vision, see Christopher Pramuk, *Sophia: The Hidden Christ of Thomas Merton* (Collegeville, MN: Liturgical Press/ Michael Glazier, 2009).

## *Chapter 1*

1. I am indebted to Rowan Williams for this phrase and for the image of "breaking silence" from his discussion of the tension in Christian life, and specifically in the life of Thomas Merton, between contemplative silence and prophetic speech. See "The Only Real City: Monasticism and the Social Vision," in *A Silent Action: Engagements with Thomas Merton* (Louisville, KY: Fons Vitae, 2011), 55–68, at 65.

2. For major papers from the conference see *Uncommon Faithfulness: The Black Catholic Experience*, ed. M. Shawn Copeland, with LaReine-Marie Mosely and Albert J. Raboteau (Maryknoll, NY: Orbis, 2009). See also Jon Nilson's groundbreaking address to his colleagues at the Catholic Theological Society of America, "Confessions of a White Catholic Racist Theologian," *Origins* 33 (2003): 130–38, and Jon Nilson, *Hearing Past the Pain: Why White Catholic Theologians Need Black Theology* (New York: Paulist, 2007). Nilson's work and witness have led the way for white Catholic scholars in the field of academic race discourse.

3. The term "white privilege" is a way of conceptualizing racial inequalities that focuses as much on the advantages that white people accrue from society as on the disadvantages that people of color experience. The general claim is

that solutions to problems of racial inequality can only be achieved by explicitly discussing the implicit (often unconscious) advantages that whites as a group hold in American society. Sociologist Peggy McIntosh describes white privilege as "an invisible package of unearned assets that I can count on cashing in each day, but about which I was 'meant' to remain oblivious. White privilege is like an invisible weightless knapsack of special provisions." From her seminal essay, "White Privilege and Male Privilege: A Personal Account of Coming to See Correspondences through Work in Women's Studies (1988)," in *Race, Class, and Gender: An Anthology,* ed. Margaret Andersen and Patricia Hill Collins (Albany: Wadsworth, 1998): 94–105, at 94–95. McIntosh's famous checklist of fifty practical examples of skin privilege ("Unpacking the Invisible Knapsack") can be found at http://www.amptoons.com/blog/files/mcintosh.html.

In his pastoral letter on racism, "Dwell in My Love" (April 4, 2001), Cardinal Francis George of Chicago names institutional racism and white privilege as evils calling for personal and structural conversion. Helpful primers on white privilege include Richard Delgado and Jean Stefancic, *Critical Race Theory: An Introduction* (New York: New York University, 2001); Stephanie M. Wildman, *Privilege Revealed* (New York: New York University, 1996); Birgit Brander Rasmussen et al., eds., *The Making and Unmaking of Whiteness* (Durham, NC: Duke University, 2001); Tim Wise, *White Like Me: Reflections on Race from a Privileged Son* (Berkeley, CA: Soft Skull, 2007); and Laurie M. Cassidy and Alexander Mikulich, eds., *Interrupting White Privilege: Catholic Theologians Break the Silence* (Maryknoll, NY: Orbis, 2007).

4. The preferential option for the poor implies a twofold commitment: first, to interpret scripture, tradition, and the contemporary signs of the times from the perspective of the poor; second, to love the least of society with an active love, in solidarity with the struggles of the poor for justice. Developed explicitly by Latin American liberation theologies and implicitly by black theology in the United States during the 1960s, and embraced by the Latin American and Canadian bishops and eventually in many statements of Pope John Paul II, the preferential option has become an integral pillar of Catholic social teaching. Of course the question of how to live the principle in specific social contexts remains alive and not a little controversial. For an excellent historical and theological overview, see Gregory Baum, *Amazing Church: A Catholic Theologian Remembers a Half-Century of Change* (Maryknoll, NY: Orbis, 2005), 53–82.

5. Gregory Baum offers a helpful distinction between "guilt by personal implication," which means to knowingly participate in sinful structures or refuse to resist them, and "guilt by common heritage," which applies to persons or communities who, even if not guilty by personal implication, may still "willingly share in the burden of guilt" because they share "a common heritage and are spiritually identified" with those who are (or were) personally responsible. As an example of the latter, Baum points to young Germans today who were not alive during World War II and yet strongly believe that they must assume the heavy burden of past evils. Why? "Without grieving over the past, they argue, people cannot come

to a truthful understanding of the present nor adopt a responsible orientation toward the future." An analogous dynamic comes to play in reflecting on white privilege and the legacy of racial injustice in US society. To assume a share of culpability, as Baum suggests, is not always about guilt in the proper sense, though it may be that; often "it is more aptly described as grieving or sorrowing," the readiness to mourn and "a keener sense of personal responsibility." See Gregory Baum, *Essays in Critical Theology* (Kansas City: Sheed & Ward, 1994), 199–200.

6. The term *lo cotidiano* refers to the quotidian or everyday quality of racism, its palpable atmosphere or impending threat for nonwhites in US society. For peoples of color every day presents "a situation . . . a choice, of how to stand in relation to oppression, whether to live as subsumed by [it] or to live as active resistance toward liberation." Ada Maria Isasi-Diaz, *Mujerista Theology* (Maryknoll, NY: Orbis, 1996).

7. The following overview is adapted from three Wikipedia entries: "Hispaniola"; "The United States and the Haitian Revolution"; and "Touissant Louverture." As in all overviews, a great deal of complexity is left out. My wife and I are especially indebted to the following: Tracy Kidder, *Mountains Beyond Mountains: The Quest of Dr. Paul Farmer, A Man Who Would Cure the World* (New York: Random House, 2003); Paul Farmer, *The Uses of Haiti* (Monroe, NE: Common Courage Press, 2004); Jean-Robert Cadet, *Restavec: From Haitian Slave Child to Middle-Class American* (Austin: University of Texas, 1998); Mark Curnutte, *A Promise in Haiti: A Reporter's Notes on Families and Daily Lives* (Nashville: Vanderbilt University, 2011); Kathie Klarreich, *Madame Dread: A Tale of Love, Vodou, and Civil Strife in Haiti* (New York: Nation Books, 2005); *Egalite for All: Toussaint Louverture and the Haitian Revolution*, PBS Home Video (Koval Films, 2009).

8. Founded in 1973, the remarkable story, vision, and discography of Sweet Honey in the Rock can be found at http://www.sweethoneyintherock.org.

9. Thomas Merton, *Bread in the Wilderness* (New York: New Directions, 1953), 107.

10. Not to overdraw the distinction, the liberal arts aim to serve an analogous function in universities, seeking to engage the whole person and not just the intellect of the student. That the survival of the liberal arts model appears to be much in question today does not bode well, I think, for the cultivation of social empathy in our youngest generation.

11. Merton, *Bread in the Wilderness*, 75. When we pray and sing the psalms, says Merton, the Holy Spirit "is at the same time the poet, the poetry and the reader of the poetry; the music and the musician, the singer and the hearer . . . . We are transformed in the midst of a discovery."

12. Ibid., 38; emphasis original. Elsewhere Merton describes this paradoxical experience as the "eschatological secret" at the heart of the Christian Gospel: "not solving the contradiction, but remaining in the midst of it, in peace, knowing that it is fully solved, but that the solution is secret." See Thomas Merton, *Conjectures of a Guilty Bystander* (Garden City, NY: Doubleday, 1966), 211–12.

13. The phrase is borrowed from black Catholic theologian M. Shawn Copeland whose work we will consider in chapter 2. "Racism and the Vocation of the Christian Theologian," *Spiritus* 2 (2002): 21.

14. Truth- and hope-telling in the prophetic tradition, writes Walter Brueggemann, "must be told, in image, in figure, in poem, in vision. It must be told sideways, told as one who dwells with the others in the abyss." *Disruptive Grace: Reflections on God, Scripture, and the Church*, ed. Carolyn J. Sharp (Minneapolis: Fortress, 2011), 153. So it is with the psalms of joy and lament, Mary's *Magnificat*, the wisdom sayings of Jesus, and the "dream" of Martin Luther King, Jr.: all speak from heart to heart, as between exiles travelling shoulder to shoulder on a wondrous but perilous journey.

## *Chapter 2*

Portions of this chapter were first developed in Christopher Pramuk, "Living in the Master's House: Race and Rhetoric in the Theology of M. Shawn Copeland," *Horizons* 32, no. 2 (Fall 2005): 295–331. This material is used with permission and has been substantially revised.

1. Howard Thurman, *With Head and Heart: The Autobiography of Howard Thurman* (New York: Harcourt Brace, 1979), 226.

2. Howard Thurman, *Howard Thurman: Essential Writings*, Selected with an Introduction by Luther E. Smith (Maryknoll, NY: Orbis, 2006), 39; emphasis original.

3. Ibid., 40; cf. 136–37.

4. Ibid., 39.

5. Ibid., 38.

6. Psychologist Abraham Maslow described the "peak experience" as a state of blissfulness, more or less characteristic of natural processes of self-actualization, and innately available to everyone. Researcher Edith Cobb developed her groundbreaking theory of the "ecology of imagination in childhood" after discovering striking similarities in the biographies of some three hundred artistic or "creative geniuses," each of whom had experienced their natural surroundings in an intense, life-determining way as a child.

7. Thurman, *Essential Writings*, 40; Abraham Joshua Heschel, *Man is Not Alone: A Philosophy of Religion* (New York: Farrar, Straus and Young, 1951), 75.

8. Thurman, *Essential Writings*, 40–41.

9. Ibid., 41. Thurman's linking of mystical experience and ethical practice resonates not a little with the writings of Peruvian liberation theologian Gustavo Gutierrez, for whom *gratuitousness* is the wellspring of religious experience and pervasive biblical theme from which compassion and solidarity with the poor flow. See *Gustavo Gutierrez: Spiritual Writings*, ed. Daniel Groody (Maryknoll, NY: Orbis, 2011), 66–71. Likewise for German political theologian Johann Baptist Metz, religion addresses a primary need in us, not peripheral or based on the

market principle of exchange, but rooted in and flowing from gratuity. Metz describes both mourning and joy, for example, as categories of "resistance to the growing inability to celebrate gratuitous meaning." See Johann Baptist Metz, *Faith in History and Society: Toward a Practical Fundamental Theology*, trans. and ed. J. Matthew Ashley (New York: Crossroad, 2007), 49–51, 67.

10. Thurman, *Essential Writings*, 66.

11. Ibid., 68–69.

12. Ibid., 69.

13. Ibid., 61.

14. Ibid., 64.

15. Ibid., 61.

16. Ibid., 54. The point calls to mind Martin Luther's striking image of the sinner: *incurvatus in se*—turned in on the self.

17. Thurman, *Essential Writings*, 159.

18. "Man in his strength and in his weakness," writes Niebuhr, "is too ambiguous to understand himself, unless his rational analyses are rooted in a faith that he is comprehended from beyond the ambiguities of his own understanding." Reinhold Niebuhr, *Faith and History* (New York: Scribner's, 1949), 70. What Genesis portrays as rebellion and Augustine calls pride, Niebuhr calls vanity of imagination and the illusion of omnipotence. Revelation "will not be convincing except to the soul which has found the profoundest enigma of existence not in the evil surrounding it *but in itself*" (101); it takes root in those who know "what they are," like the "moral derelicts" of the Gospel—e.g., the criminals crucified with Jesus, and not the Pharisees (142–44).

19. Howard Thurman, *The Search For Common Ground* (New York: Harper and Row, 1973), 104.

20. The realization of creation's interconnectedness is not, of course, limited to religious or mystical insight and exploration. To cite one of a billion possible examples from the realm of natural science, consider the yearly migration of sea turtles across thousands of miles of ocean by means (we think!) of the lunar cycle.

21. Thurman, *Essential Writings*, 41.

22. "Slavery is the anvil on which the African American Catholic community was forged," writes black Catholic historian Cyprian Davis. "Contrary to what many Catholics think, the Catholic church in the South was implicated in slavery as an institution among the laity, the religious orders, and all ranks of the clergy." *The History of Black Catholics in the United States* (New York: Crossroad, 1990), 119. There are currently about three million black Catholics in the United States (two to three percent)—more than the combined membership of many Protestant denominations—some 250 black priests and 16 black bishops. While the experience of black Catholics is highly diverse and far from monolithic, many feel themselves hidden, their history marginalized, and their presence an anomaly to the institutional church and in the eyes of most white Catholics. See *Plenty Good Room: The Spirit and Truth of African American Catholic Worship* (USCCB, 1991), no. 43–46.

23. M. Shawn Copeland, cited in Margot Patterson, "A Theology of the 'Human Other': Interview with M. Shawn Copeland," *National Catholic Reporter* (July 18, 2003), 17.

24. Thomas Merton, *New Seeds of Contemplation* (New York: New Directions, 1972), 72.

25. Copeland defines racism as the "systematized oppression of one race by another. [The] various forms of oppression within every sphere of social relations . . . that make up a whole of interacting and developing processes which operate so normally and naturally and are so much a part of the existing institutions of society that the individuals involved are barely conscious of their operation." M. Shawn Copeland, "Racism and the Vocation of the Christian Theologian," *Spiritus* 2 (2002): 16, citing James Boggs. That racism operates "so normally and naturally" is not because racism *is* normal and natural; rather, it feeds on the breakdown of responsible understanding and knowing in individuals and communities, especially the common error of equating knowing *with looking*, what Copeland calls a "picture-thinking mentality" or "naive racist empiricism." Like the Catholic understanding of original sin, racism points to a social malaise that, while rooted in personal freedom, extends well beyond the attitudes or actions of a few individuals. To highlight the social character of racism Copeland employs the term *racial formation* from sociology: children are not born racists, they must be taught to be so. This means that they can be taught *not* to be so through new experiences, critical education, cross-cultural awakenings. See Copeland, "Racism and the Vocation," 17; citing Michael Omi and Howard Winant, *Racial Formation in the United States, From the 1960s to the 1990s* (New York: Routledge, 1994).

26. M. Shawn Copeland, "The New Anthropological Subject at the Heart of the Mystical Body of Christ," *CTSA Proceedings* 53 (1998): 24–47, at 37; revised in M. Shawn Copeland, *Enfleshing Freedom: Body, Race, and Being* (Minneapolis: Augsburg Fortress, 2010), 95–101. Copeland employs the fictitious name "Fatima Yusif" to protect the woman's real identity; she also notes "the danger that my analysis, however well intentioned, might foster negative stereotypes and reproduce the injury" the woman has suffered.

27. Copeland, "New Anthropological Subject," 38.

28. Ibid., 39.

29. M. Shawn Copeland, "The Interaction of Racism, Sexism, and Classism in Women's Exploitation," *Women, Work, and Poverty*, ed. Elisabeth Schussler Fiorenza and Anne Carr (Edinburgh: T&T Clark, 1987), 19-27, at 22.

30. Copeland, "New Anthropological Subject," 39; emphasis added.

31. Copeland, "Racism and the Vocation," 18; emphasis original.

32. Ibid., 20. As noted in the introduction, prejudice and racial formation bear out not only between different races but also *within* the same racial community or ethnic group. Much African American literature attests to the prevalence of "colorism," the comparing and ranking of shades of blackness within the black community.

33. Copeland, "New Anthropological Subject," 40.

34. Ibid., 38.

35. Ibid.

36. Editorial, "Wasting Time on Hate," *America* 170, no. 11 (April 2, 1994), 3. "For too many of the Orthodox settlers of Kiryat Arba," the editors conclude, "the study of Torah has been contaminated by this 'soil and blood' racism. . . . Of all people in the world they ought to have known better."

37. See Martin Luther King, Jr., *A Testament of Hope*, ed. James M. Washington (San Francisco: HarperSanFrancisco, 1986), 342.

38. Copeland, "New Anthropological Subject," 31–32.

39. Ibid., 39. As Copeland notes, the word *ressentiment* "is borrowed from the French and was introduced into philosophy by Nietzsche."

40. At the height of the Cold War, British pop musician Sting penned the song "Russians": "We share the same biology / regardless of ideology / Believe me when I say to you / I hope the Russians love their children too."

41. Copeland, "Racism and the Vocation," 21.

42. Thomas Merton, *Seasons of Celebration* (New York: Farrar, Straus and Giroux, 1965), 118.

43. Copeland, "New Anthropological Subject," 41.

44. Ibid., citing Canadian Jesuit theologian Bernard Lonergan. Copeland draws richly from the cognitional theory of Lonergan to develop her analysis of racism, sexism, classism, homophobia, and other forms of group or socially constructed biases, as well as her theological vision of solidarity in the mystical body of Christ. For her the traditional Catholic imagery of the "Mystical Body of Christ" is never just "mystical" but always both mystical and political, never triumphal but always rooted in "the anguish of the victims." See Copeland, *Enfleshing Freedom*, 101–5. For a thorough discussion of these dynamics in her thought, see Christopher Pramuk, "Living in the Master's House: Race and Rhetoric in the Theology of M. Shawn Copeland," *Horizons* 32, no. 2 (Fall 2005): 295–331.

45. Cited in Edward K. Kaplan, *Holiness in Words: Abraham Joshua Heschel's Poetics of Piety* (Albany: State University of New York, 1996), 16. A Jewish scholar of French literature at Brandeis University, Kaplan has also dedicated much of his career to the study of Heschel, Merton, and Thurman. Raised in a family deeply committed to the civil rights movement, Kaplan knew both Thurman and Heschel from his childhood, and throughout his career has taught all manner of students across religious traditions on the interplay of mysticism, poetics, and prophecy in their work. See, e.g., Edward K. Kaplan, "A Jewish Dialogue with Howard Thurman: Mysticism, Compassion, and Community," *Cross Currents* 60 (Dec. 2010): 515–25; and Kaplan's afterword at the end of this book.

46. Abraham Joshua Heschel, *Man is Not Alone: A Philosophy of Religion* (New York: Farrar, Straus and Young, 1951), 35.

47. The word "liminal" comes from the Latin *limen*, meaning "doorway" or "threshold." One of the more striking aspects of Johann Baptist Metz's political

theology is its attempt to reclaim for Christian spirituality what Metz identifies as a distinctively Jewish, Hebrew, or "Israelite" sense of urgency and imminent expectation with respect to God's irruption into history; that sensibility in which a moment in time "becomes the gate through which the Messiah enters into history" (Metz, *Faith in History and Society*, 161, citing Walter Benjamin).

## *Chapter 3*

Portions of this chapter were first developed in " 'Strange Fruit': Black Suffering / White Revelation," *Theological Studies* 67 (June 2006): 345–77; and "Living in the Master's House: Race and Rhetoric in the Theology of M. Shawn Copeland," *Horizons* 32, no. 2 (Fall 2005): 295–331. This material is used with permission and has been substantially revised.

1. Jonathan Kozol, *Amazing Grace: The Lives of Children and the Conscience of a Nation* (New York: Crown, 1995), 3.

2. Ibid., 99.

3. Ibid., inside jacket.

4. The example that comes to mind is the murder of fourteen-year-old Emmett Till in 1955 and, on his mother's insistence, the publication of photographs of his mutilated body in *Jet* magazine—a revelatory moment that prompted not only widespread mourning and protest but also inspired a whole generation of youth (of every color) to dedicate their lives to the civil rights movement and the cause of justice.

5. Daniel P. Grigassy, "Reconciliation," *The HarperCollins Encyclopedia of Catholicism*, ed. Richard P. McBrien (New York: HarperCollins, 1995), 1083.

6. Gerard Manley Hopkins, "As kingfishers catch fire," *Gerard Manley Hopkins: The Major Works* (Oxford: Oxford University, 1986), 129.

7. Thomas Merton, *The Intimate Merton: His Life from His Journals*, eds. Patrick Hart and Jonathan Montaldo (New York: HarperCollins, 1999), 40; entry from November 24, 1941.

8. Jon Sobrino, *Spirituality of Liberation*, trans. Robert Barr (Maryknoll, NY: Orbis, 1988), 22.

9. Jamie T. Phelps, "Communion Ecclesiology and Black Liberation Theology," *Theological Studies* 61 (2000): 672–99, at 695. Compelling resources for readers less familiar with blacks' "personal and collective history of joy and sorrow," include *This Far By Faith: African American Spiritual Journeys* (PBS Video/Blackside Inc.); *My Soul Has Grown Deep: Classics of Early African-American Literature*, ed. John Edgar Wideman (New York: Ballantine, 2001); and Diana Hayes, *Forged in the Fiery Furnace: African American Spirituality* (Maryknoll, NY: Orbis, 2012).

10. Sobrino, *Spirituality of Liberation*, 31.

11. Gen 1:27; Matt 5:43-48; Matt 25:31-46.

12. Malcolm X, *The Autobiography of Malcolm X*, told to Alex Haley (New York: Ballantine, 1964), 346; emphasis original.

13. Ibid., 348.

14. Ibid., 345.

15. Ibid., 347; emphasis original.

16. Ibid.; emphasis original. From this point forward Malcolm's social vision and rhetoric became more conciliatory toward whites, as James H. Cone demonstrates in his masterful study, *Martin and Malcolm and America: A Dream or a Nightmare* (Maryknoll, NY: Orbis, 1992).

17. Malcolm X, *Autobiography*, 347; emphasis original.

18. Virgilio P. Elizondo, *Guadalupe: Mother of the New Creation* (Maryknoll, NY: Orbis, 1997), x.

19. This radically undivided and *unforgetting* scope of concern between the living and the dead is what Johann Baptist Metz calls the "mystical-political" dimension of Christianity: "mystical, because it does not give up its interest in the salvation of past, unreconciled suffering; political, because it is precisely this interest in universal justice that continually commits it to justice among the living." *A Passion for God: The Mystical-Political Dimension of Christianity*, trans. J. Matthew Ashley (New York: Paulist, 1998), 162. The electrifying and often confrontational use of language by Martin Luther King, Jr., Malcolm X, and black preachers today such as Rev. Jeremiah Wright illustrates the disruptive, volatile, and politically transforming character of this particular cloud of witnesses. For King the acute memory of suffering was exactly why blacks—indeed, why America—could not wait for justice any longer. "We have waited for more than 340 years for our constitutional and God-given rights." King's community, the "we" of his imagination, is clearly a mystical-political community of both the living and the dead. "Three hundred years of humiliation, abuse and deprivation cannot be expected to find voice in a whisper." Martin Luther King, Jr., *A Testament of Hope: The Essential Writings and Speeches of Martin Luther King, Jr.*, ed. James Melvin Washington (New York: HarperSanFrancisco, 1986), 292; 519.

20. Jonathan Alter, "Poverty, Race, and Katrina: Lessons of a National Shame," *Newsweek* (September 19, 2005), 42–48.

21. See chapter 1, no. 3.

22. Of course a similar indictment is often leveled against middle class or "upwardly mobile" blacks, evidence of the fact that the chasm between the haves and the have-nots in the United States is not simply a racial problem but a phenomenon of both race and class.

23. One may wonder why it takes a national crisis to witness such outpourings of goodwill and solidarity across racial, economic, and religious boundaries. It seems the last comparable movement, if more sustained and dramatically more dangerous, was the civil rights movement, which saw, for example, thousands of young people boarding buses from college campuses in the north to put their bodies on the line in the Freedom Riders movement. See the superb documentary *Freedom Riders*, PBS Video, dir. Stanley Nelson (American Experience, 2011).

24. Michael Eric Dyson, *Come Hell or High Water: Hurricane Katrina and the Color of Disaster* (New York: Basic Civitas, 2006), 180, cited from Selwyn Crawford, "Storms as Wrath of God?," in the *Dallas Morning News*, October 5, 2005.

25. Ibid., 180–81, from Eric Deggans, "Add to Katrina's Toll Race-Tinged Rhetoric," *St. Petersburg Times*, September 14, 2005.

26. Ibid., 181, citing from Deggans, "Add to Katrina's Toll."

27. Ibid. Commenting on public discourse in America today, novelist Marilynne Robinson recently wondered: "On average, in the main, we are Christian people, if the polls are to be believed. How is Christianity consistent with the generalized contempt that seems to lie behind so much so-called public discourse?" See "Imagination and Community," *Commonweal* 89:5 (March 9, 2012).

28. Sobrino, *Spirituality of Liberation*, 19; Niebuhr calls such willingness "the contrite recognition of the real."

29. *Gaudium et spes*, no. 1, in *Vatican Council II: The Basic Sixteen Documents*, ed. Austin Flannery (1996).

30. See David K. Shipler, *A Country of Strangers: Blacks and Whites in America* (New York: Knopf, 1997), especially 223–226; and Jean Bethke Elshtain and Christopher Beem, "Race and Civil Society: A Democratic Conversation," in Dwight N. Hopkins, *Black Faith and Public Talk: Critical Essays on James H. Cone's Black Theology and Black Power* (Maryknoll, NY: Orbis, 1999), 211–16.

31. Martin Luther King, Jr., *Strength to Love* (Philadelphia: Fortress Press, 1963), 72. In her introduction to this volume, Coretta Scott King describes her husband's belief "in a divine, loving presence that binds all life" as the central element of his philosophy of nonviolence and the spiritual force beneath his efforts "to eliminate social evil."

32. Cone, *Martin and Malcolm*, 80. It also anointed the black community with a prophetic self-identity, as Cone notes: "go forth knowing that you as a people have been called by God to redeem the soul of America."

33. The Catholic bishops in the United States have issued a number of documents on racism, most notably the USCCB's *Brothers and Sisters to Us* (1979). Especially compelling is *Plenty Good Room: The Spirit and Truth of African American Catholic Worship* (1991), published by the Secretariat for the Liturgy in collaboration with the Secretariat for Black Catholics. For a balanced appreciation and critique of bishops' statements in the last fifty years see Bryan Massingale, *Racial Justice and the Catholic Church* (Maryknoll, NY: Orbis, 2010), 43–82. Sometimes overlooked in sweeping categorical or broadside critiques of racism in the Roman Catholic Church is the degree to which Catholic institutions such as urban schools and hospitals, most founded and staffed by religious sisters and dedicated laity, have incarnated compassionate presence and social advocacy in more hidden ways but with far-reaching social impact in American society. This dimension of the story is powerfully chronicled in the exhibit "Women and Spirit: Catholic Sisters in America," which debuted in Cincinnati in 2009 and continues to travel the country. See http://www.womenandspirit.org/.

34. Witness the case of Bill Cosby, who was both praised in the black community for "speaking the truth" in his controversial speech to the NAACP and excoriated by others such as Michael Eric Dyson for "further victimizing the most vulnerable among us" and "lending credence to the ancient assaults they've endured from the dominant culture." From an interview with Dyson on National Public Radio (www.npr.org/templates/story/story.php?storyId=4628960) in reference to his book *Is Bill Cosby Right? Or Has the Black Middle Class Lost Its Mind?* (New York: Basic Civitas, 2006).

35. Adam Clark, "Honoring the Ancestors: Toward an Afrocentric Liberation Theology" (*The Journal of Black Studies*, pub. pending), 3; used with permission. From 2005–12, 86 percent of homicides in my city of Cincinnati were cases of black-on-black violence, up from 75 percent in the years 2000–2004; these numbers are reflected nationally.

36. In her breathtaking study of Philadelphia's Mural Arts Project, *If These Walls Could Talk: Community Muralism and the Beauty of Justice* (Collegeville, MN: Liturgical Press, 2012), white Catholic theologian Maureen H. O'Connell offers a sober yet hopeful view of life at street level, illuminating the pressures exerted both from above and from below on persons, especially the young, in blighted urban landscapes. Hers is the kind of personally engaged, cross-disciplinary scholarship much needed today in academia, especially among white scholars.

37. Copeland, *Enfleshing Freedom*, 93; cf. Metz, *Faith in History and Society*, 60–84; 208–14.

38. Gustavo Gutierrez, *A Theology of Liberation*, rev. ed., trans. and ed. Sr. Caridad Inda and John Eagleson (Maryknoll, NY: Orbis, 1988), 116–120.

39. A good starting point in addressing this question in local contexts is http://www.beyondwhiteness.com/.

40. Phelps, "Communion Ecclesiology," 72–79; Massingale, *Racial Justice and the Catholic Church*, 137–40; Copeland, *Enfleshing Freedom*, 55–84.

41. Clark, "Honoring the Ancestors," 3.

42. It bears noting that analogous internal tensions have long simmered in Hispanic and Native American communities, where preserving the beliefs and practices of the ancestors or elders is seen by many as a crucial defense against the diluting and destructive influence of American society with its "white," putatively Christian cultural values of radical individualism, materialism, and so on; more on this tension from the Indian perspective in chapter 5.

43. See O'Connell, *If These Walls Could Talk*, 91–98; also Mark Curnutte, "Street Code: Revenge," *The Cincinnati Enquirer* (October 28, 2012).

44. For changing US demographics and pastoral implications in the Catholic Church see Alejandro Portes and Ruben G. Rumbaut, *Immigrant America: A Portrait, 3rd Edition* (Berkeley: University of California, 2006); Timothy Matovina, *Latino Catholicism: Transformation in America's Largest Church* (Princeton, NJ: Princeton University Press, 2012); Dean Hoge and Marti Jewell, *The Next Generation of Pastoral Leaders: What the Church Needs to Know* (Chicago: Loyola, 2010);

Carol Ganim, ed., *Shaping Catholic Parishes: Pastoral Leaders in the Twenty-First Century* (Chicago: Loyola, 2008).

45. Recent studies suggest that only about five percent of the nation's churches are racially integrated, and many of these appear to be in the process of becoming all black or all white. See Curtiss Paul DeYoung et al., *United by Faith: The Multiracial Congregation as an Answer to the Problem of Race* (New York: Oxford University, 2003). Columnist Leonard Pitts celebrates the United Church of Christ as one of the few denominations to make transcending the color line integral to its mission and self-identity. "The UCC was the first church I'd ever seen that seemed to take seriously the idea that inclusion is a Christian value" (*Miami Herald*, December 5, 2004).

46. Thomas Merton, *Conjectures of a Guilty Bystander* (New York: Doubleday, 1965), 156.

47. Ibid., 156–57.

48. George Steiner, "To Speak of Walter Benjamin," *Benjamin Studies: Perception and Experience in Modernity* (Amsterdam: Rodopi, 2002), 13–23, at 22.

49. Thomas Merton, *New Seeds of Contemplation* (New York: New Directions, 1962), 72.

50. Walter Burghardt, "Contemplation: A Long Loving Look at the Real," in *An Ignatian Spirituality Reader*, ed. George W. Traub (Chicago: Loyola Press, 2008), 89–98; originally published in *Church* (1989).

51. Sallie McFague, *The Body of God: An Ecological Theology* (Minneapolis: Fortress, 1993), 210.

52. Ibid., 211, citing Iris Murdoch.

53. Alice Walker, *In Search of Our Mothers' Gardens* (San Diego: Harcourt Brace Jovanovich, 1983), 241.

54. The doctrine of the resurrection of the body is most profound when merged with the concrete memories of persons like Bernardo and Emmett Till, those whose bodies have been brutalized on this side of history. The vision of these glorified bodies on the other side will be wondrous and terrible indeed.

55. See Christopher Pramuk, "A Dream of Life: Revisiting Bruce Springsteen's 'The Rising,'" *America online* (September 12, 2011).

56. Thomas Merton, *Bread in the Wilderness* (New York: New Directions, 1953), 53.

## Chapter 4

Portions of this chapter were first developed in Christopher Pramuk, "'Strange Fruit': Black Suffering / White Revelation," *Theological Studies* 67 (June 2006): 345–77; Pramuk, "'Strange Fruit': Contemplating the Black Cross in America," ARTS 20, no. 1 (Spring 2009): 12–20; and Pramuk, "Beauty Limned in Violence: Experimenting with Protest Music in the Ignatian Classroom," *Transforming the World and Being Transformed: Justice in Jesuit Higher Education* (New York: Fordham University, 2013).

This material is used with permission and has been substantially revised. I am especially grateful to Professor Chris Bollinger and his colleagues at Texas Lutheran University who invited me to present early formulations of this material to undergraduates during their annual Krost Symposium in September 2006. Their kindness, receptivity, and critical feedback were a great gift to me.

1. Reinhold Niebuhr, *Faith and History* (New York: Scribner's, 1949), 170.

2. Catherine Keller, *Apocalypse Now and Then* (Boston: Beacon, 1996), 23, citing Julia Kristeva.

3. Lewis Allan (a.k.a. Abel Meeropol), "Strange Fruit" (1939); Billie Holiday, *The Best of Billie Holiday: 20th Century Masters* (Hip-O Records, 2002).

4. The documentary film *Strange Fruit*, dir. Joel Katz (San Francisco: California Newsreel, 2002), brings powerfully to life the song's historical significance as well as its varied and often contentious reception in different live performance contexts. The film is well-suited for use in classroom or church discussion groups, where it might mediate conversations about race relations in society and church today.

5. David Margolick, *Strange Fruit: Billie Holiday, Café Society, and an Early Cry for Civil Rights* (Philadelphia: Running Press, 2000), 16.

6. Ibid., 50; see also Stuart Nicholson, *Billie Holiday* (Boston: Northeastern University, 1995), 112–16.

7. Margolick, *Strange Fruit*, 21, 17. As Margolick notes, Holiday first sang "Strange Fruit" sixteen years before Rosa Parks refused to yield her seat on a Montgomery, Alabama bus.

8. Cited in ibid., 17.

9. Ibid., 75.

10. Ibid., 21.

11. Cited in Robert O'Meally, *Lady Day: The Many Faces of Billie Holiday* (New York: Arcade, 1991), 136.

12. Margolick, 36–37; cf. "The Strange Story of the Man Behind 'Strange Fruit,'" http://www.npr.org/2012/09/05/158933012/.

13. Interview in *Strange Fruit*, dir. Joel Katz.

14. Margolick, 29.

15. Cited in O'Meally, 136.

16. David Tracy's account of the "classic" is fitting here: "When a work of art so captures a paradigmatic experience of [an] event of truth, it becomes in that moment normative. Its memory enters as a catalyst into all our other memories, and, now subtly, now compellingly, transforms our perceptions of the real." David Tracy, *The Analogical Imagination: Christianity and the Culture of Pluralism* (New York: Crossroad, 1998), 115. Perhaps even more apropos is Walter Benjamin's notion of the "dialectical image," which refers to marginalized or discarded images ("ruins") from the past that, when suddenly interjected into the present, produce a shock to our reigning assumptions about reality, offering insight into what might have been and opening up new possibilities of political agency for what might still be. See Max Pensky, "Method and Time: Benjamin's Dialectical

Images," in *The Cambridge Companion to Walter Benjamin*, ed. David S. Ferris (New York: Cambridge University Press, 2004), 177–98.

17. Web-based archives of *Time*, December 31, 1999. The praise is not a little ironic given that six decades earlier *Time* had described the ballad as "a prime piece of musical propaganda for the NAACP," and Holiday herself as "a roly poly young colored woman with a hump in her voice," who "does not care enough about her figure to watch her diet, but [who] loves to sing" (Margolick, 74).

18. German theologian Johann Baptist Metz uses this phrase to describe the disruptive character of Jesus' death and resurrection and, by extension, the remembrance of all the forgotten victims of history. Even Christian creeds and dogmas for Metz are "formulas of *memoria*," which—in a society "ever more devoid of history and memory"—"break the spell of the dominant consciousness" in a "redemptively dangerous way." *Faith in History and Society: Toward a Practical Fundamental Theology*, trans. and ed. J. Matthew Ashley (New York: Crossroad, 2007), 182–85.

19. On "negative capability" and "negative space" see Nathan Mitchell, "The Cross That Spoke," *The Cross in Christian Tradition*, ed. Elizabeth A. Dreyer (Mahwah, NJ: Paulist, 2000), 72–92, at 87.

20. See Edward Schillebeeckx, *Church: The Human Story of God* (New York: Crossroad, 1990), 5–6. The revelatory dimension of a negative contrast experience resides in its participatory (not merely passive or objective) dynamic: like liturgical, artistic, or narrative remembrance it is deep, evocative, moving. For the transcendental framework generally presupposed in this chapter, see Thomas F. O'Meara, "Toward a Subjective Theology of Revelation," *Theological Studies* 36 (1975): 401–27; note especially the language of God as Presence and Eschatological Summoner, 408–12.

21. Margolick, 60–61.

22. Jon Sobrino, *Christ the Liberator* (Maryknoll, NY: Orbis, 2001), 43.

23. Ibid., 44.

24. Michelle Alexander's critically acclaimed book, *The New Jim Crow: Mass Incarceration in the Age of Colorblindness* (New York: New Press, 2010), details the devastating effects of mass incarceration on communities of color in the United States. The staggering growth of the prison population and the sprawling prison industry in the United States in the last thirty years corresponds directly with the so-called War on Drugs, which has disproportionately targeted communities of color. More on Alexander's work in chapter 6.

25. "There are no islands [where we do not already] bear the stamp of the guilt of others, directly or indirectly, from close or from afar." Karl Rahner, *Foundations of Christian Faith* (New York: Crossroads, 1978), 109.

26. Thomas Merton, *Raids on the Unspeakable* (New York: New Directions, 1966), 17.

27. William David Hart makes this point while noting that prior to the Civil War the victims of lynching were predominantly white. See his review of Anthony

B. Pinn, *Terror and Triumph: The Nature of Black Religion* (Philadelphia: Fortress, 2003), in *Journal of the American Academy of Religion* 72 (2004): 795–97.

28. Metz describes mourning as a solidarity that "looks backward" to include a love and desire for justice on behalf of the dead and vanquished (*Faith in History and Society*, 67).

29. Paul Evdokimov, *The Art of the Icon: A Theology of Beauty* (Redondo Beach, CA: Oakwood, 1990), 166.

30. To Holiday's act of memory and resistance we could add many more, most unseen and unsung, a few iconic: a lone Chinese protester standing before an advancing row of tanks in Tiananmen Square; Tommie Smith raising his fist on the gold medal stand during the 1968 Mexico City Olympics; the Argentinian "Mothers of the Disappeared," dancing in silence for their missing sons, husbands, and fathers. British pop artist Sting honors these women in his haunting tribute, "They Dance Alone," likewise the Irish rock band U2 in their hypnotic "Mothers of the Disappeared." The mothers appeared onstage with Sting in Buenos Aires in 1988, and years later with U2; in both cases their missing relatives' photographs were projected on large screens before the audience, and their names invoked one by one in a kind of litany as the artist and audience together sang the song. Video footage of these events, extraordinary moments of global solidarity through music, is readily accessible for viewing in the classroom via YouTube.

31. Cited in Margolick, 43. As Walter Brueggemann says of the prophets, "God's future rests on the lips of the truth-tellers." *Disruptive Grace: Reflections on God, Scripture, and the Church*, ed. Carolyn J. Sharp (Minneapolis, MN: Fortress, 2011), 129–54.

32. Few writers have voiced the tension between memory and hope (and the ambiguities of Christianity for blacks) with greater pathos than James Baldwin, in his *The Fire Next Time* (New York: Dial Press, 1963).

33. The ontology of race and victimization is a contentious subject in race discourse, both within and between racial groups. Emilie M. Townes worries about a "rhetoric of victimization" in black discourse that "fails to acknowledge the individual and collective choices we make in how we live our lives—even in the midst of death-dealing socio-economic and cultural realities." Emilie M. Townes, "Searching for Paradise in a World of Theme Parks," *Black Faith and Public Talk: Critical Essays on James H. Cone's Black Theology and Black Power*, ed. Dwight N. Hopkins (Maryknoll, NY: Orbis, 1999), 105–25, at 116; see also Victor Anderson's critique of womanist and black theological hermeneutics, in *Beyond Ontological Blackness* (New York: Continuum, 1995).

34. Richard Pryor, Eddie Murphy, Bill Cosby, Chris Rock, to name a few. On the paradoxical convergence of joy and sorrow in Christian experience and in the black church, see James Martin, "Rejoice Always," *America*, October 3, 2011; for introducing black art and literature to youth, I recommend the beautifully realized *Children of Promise: African American Literature and Art for Young People*, ed. Charles Sullivan (New York: Harry N. Abrams, 1991).

35. One of the most striking characteristics of the church described by Vatican II's *Lumen gentium*, the Dogmatic Constitution on the Church, is Christ-like poverty, suffering, and humility. Quoting St. Augustine, the great African father of the church, chapter 8 offers what might be taken for a hauntingly prophetic description of the black church that looks to Augustine as a forebear. "The church, 'like a stranger in a foreign land, presses forward amid the persecutions of the world and the consolations of God,' announcing the cross and death of the Lord until he comes. But by the power of the risen Lord it is given strength to overcome, in patience and in love, its sorrows and its difficulties, both those that are from within and those that are from without, so that it may reveal in the world, faithfully, although with shadows, the mystery of its Lord until, in the end, it shall be manifested in full light.'" One can identify this passage with the black church (inclusive of black Catholics) on the basis of historical fact—*like a stranger in a foreign land*—and do so without romanticizing the black community or ignoring its limitations and failings. By contrast, it would seem to require a great deal of sentimentality to find in this description even the remotest family resemblance—*he emptied himself, taking the nature of a slave*—to the more affluent white churches of middle class America and Europe.

36. By black theology I mean the black theology of liberation with roots in the civil rights and Black Power movements, the thought of Martin Luther King, Jr. and James Cone. Cone's classic study of African American music, *The Spirituals and the Blues: An Interpretation* (Maryknoll, NY: Orbis, 1992), corresponds closely with the spirit of this chapter; see also Cone, *The Cross and the Lynching Tree* (Maryknoll, NY: Orbis, 2011).

37. Elisha A. Hoffman (d. 1929) and John H. Stockton (d. 1877), in *Lead Me, Guide Me: The African American Catholic Hymnal*, ed. James P. Lyke, Thea Bowman, and J-Glenn Murray.

38. Following Jesus himself, St. Paul is the first in the nascent Jewish-Christian community to articulate a positive theology (or theopoetics) of the cross, as it were, a metaphysics of mercy in which life springs forth paradoxically from suffering and the way of sacrificial love. But we must never forget that Paul's sublime hymns to the love of God poured out in Jesus were also hymns to the human community that bears Jesus' name (see 1 Phil 2:1-11).

39. It is one of the distinctive geniuses of *The Spiritual Exercises* of St. Ignatius to render the desire to do something for the crucified Christ as a drama, an ongoing discernment that plays itself out in solidarity with the world, especially with those who suffer, like Jesus, the ignominies of a senseless death. Jesuit Jon Sobrino is right to insist that today the climactic question of the first week of the exercises becomes this: "What must I do to help take the crucified peoples down from the cross?" See Jon Sobrino, *The Principle of Mercy: Taking the Crucified People From the Cross* (Maryknoll, NY: Orbis, 1994).

40. June 19, 1965; cited in Phil Ochs, *Farewells and Fantasies* (Elektra R273518), liner notes, 31.

41. Cited in Ochs, *Farewells and Fantasies*, liner notes, 42.

42. "On the white steed of aesthetic rebellion," Ochs declared in 1966, "I will attack the decadence of my future with all the arrogance of youth" (ibid., 53).

43. Ochs, *Farewells and Fantasies*, inner sleeve. Compare to Thomas Merton's oft-quoted letter in May of 1966 to Jim Forest, a young Catholic Worker peace activist, which begins: "Do not depend on the hope of results," and ends with an appeal to Forest's faith that God can and will make a way out of no way: "The real hope, then, is not in something we think we can do, but in God who is making something good out of it in some way we cannot see. If we can do His will, we will be helping in this process. But we will not necessarily know all about it beforehand." Thomas Merton, *The Hidden Ground of Love: Letters*, ed. William H. Shannon (New York: Farrar, Straus and Giroux, 1985), 294–97.

44. The Christian way of wisdom "is no dream, no temptation and no evasion," writes Merton, "for it is on the contrary a return to reality in its very root. . . . It does not withdraw from the fire. It is in the very heart of the fire, yet remains cool, because it has the gentleness and humility that come from self-abandonment, and hence does not seek to assert the illusion of the exterior self." *Faith and Violence: Christian Teaching and Christian Practice* (Notre Dame, IN: University of Notre Dame, 1968), 218. Merton penned these words not long after publishing his book on Gandhi; he frequently celebrated both Gandhi's spirit and Jesus' way of nonviolence in the life of Martin Luther King, Jr.

45. The music of Bruce Springsteen and the films of Martin Scorsese are two good cases in point. See Andrew Greeley, "The Catholic Imagination of Bruce Springsteen," *America* 158, no. 5, February 6, 1988, 110–15; Christopher Pramuk, "A Dream of Life: Revisiting Bruce Springsteen's 'The Rising,' " *America*, September 12, 2011; Robert E. Lauder, "His Catholic Conscience: Sin and Grace in the Work of Martin Scorsese," *America*, February 27, 2012, and Scorsese's response, "Letters to the Editor," *America*, April 9, 2012.

46. Once again *The Spiritual Exercises* of St. Ignatius tutor the retreatant in the way of entering into the gospel stories holistically, imaginatively, such that we may *feel* Jesus' journey from the vantage point of Jesus himself and those who knew him intimately, and thus grow in the desire to accompany him in the way of love, even to the cross.

47. Pedro Arrupe, *Pedro Arrupe: Essential Writings*, ed. Kevin F. Burke (Maryknoll: Orbis, 2004), 8.

48. "The poet," writes Merton, "has to be free from everyone else, and first of all from himself, because it is through this 'self' that he is captured by others. Freedom is found under the dark tree that springs up in the center of night and of silence, the paradise tree, the axis mundi, which is also the Cross." *Day of a Stranger* (Salt Lake City: Gibbs M. Smith, 1981), 19.

## Chapter 5

1. William Hart McNichols, interview with the author, May 2012; used with permission. Fr. Bill compares this kind of "knowing by unknowing" to praying before icons, which speak to us—insofar as we are willing to let them so speak—by eluding rational explanation. Fr. Bill's icons can be viewed at http://www.fatherbill.org/.

2. Erna Fergusson, *Dancing Gods: Indian Ceremonials of New Mexico and Arizona* (Albuquerque: University of New Mexico, 1931), 131. The kiva or ceremonial lodge may be entirely underground, as is typical in Taos and Hopi villages, or entirely above ground, as in many other Pueblos dotting the course of the Rio Grande from Arizona to New Mexico. Novelist Frank Waters, whose books detail the juxtaposition and frequent conflict of cultures in the American Southwest, describes the kiva in one passage as follows: "And now after a thousand years these great feminine, womb-like kivas sunk deep in Mother Earth still existed as Indian America's church, in contrast to the traditional church of Euro-America with its masculine, phallic spire aggressively thrusting into the sky." *The Woman at Otowi Crossing* (Athens, OH: Swallow, 1987), 95. Erna Fergusson echoes Waters's observations about the kiva in mythical-physical terms, observing that, to the Indians, "both the Garden of Eden and heaven lie underground." *Dancing Gods*, xxii.

3. Ibid., 34–35.

4. Ibid., 35.

5. Thus Jesus prefaces many of his enigmatic sayings with the words, "let those with eyes to see and ears to hear," an appeal not just to the head but to the whole person of the listener. In effect the wisdom teacher is inviting us to sit in the belly of a paradox: listen to the silence, hear the forgotten histories, let things unseen and silent speak to you.

6. Unlike Mabel Dodge, who came to know Indian culture intimately through her marriage to Tony Luhan, a leader of Taos Pueblo, what I know about the Indians I know mostly through the pages of books. Yet even in books there is music to be heard, enough to sow the seeds of empathy with peoples and histories far removed from my own. In what follows I rely on cultural anthropologist R. C. Gordon-McCutchan's meticulous and spellbinding study, *The Taos Indians and the Battle for Blue Lake* (Santa Fe: Red Crane Books, 1991). At the time of its publication the author was a long-time resident of Taos and an advisor to the Taos Indians, assisting them in their relationship with the larger community.

7. Gordon-McCutchan, *Taos Indians*, 93.

8. Mabel Dodge Luhan, *Winter in Taos*; cited in Gordon-McCutchan, *Taos Indians*, xx.

9. Gordon-McCutchan, *Taos Indians*, 157.

10. Ibid., 158–59.

11. Ibid., 9.

12. Ibid., 13.

13. Ibid., 119.

14. Ibid., 16–17.

15. Ibid., 90.

16. Ibid., 153.

17. Ibid., 136.

18. Ibid., 184. The immediate object of the Cacique's criticism here is Senator Clinton Anderson of New Mexico, though his words speak more broadly to white ignorance and contempt toward the Indians. The sentiment reminds me of Stevie Wonder's biting critique of the white politician in the song "Big Brother," which opens chapter 6.

19. Ibid., 189.

20. Ibid.

21. Gordon-McCutchan's assessment is less theological but no less inspired: "'If you have a mission, and if you capture the imagination of the people . . . and you have a cause that really is just, sometimes good really does prevail'" (*Taos Indians*, 219; citing Bobbie Greene).

22. The image is borrowed from Rowan Williams describing Thomas Merton, whose "poverty" resides in the way his writings ultimately direct the readers' attention away from himself and toward the hidden God he seeks. Rowan Williams, *Silent Action: Engagements with Thomas Merton* (Louisville: Fons Vitae, 2012), 19. Even more the image reminds me of the central character in French author Jean Giono's magical parable *The Man Who Planted Trees*. Elzear Bouffier is a solitary shepherd who, though he has "lost the habit of speech," transforms a barren, war-ravaged landscape into a lush forest and verdant valley by his patient responsiveness to and care for the earth. Giono's story has been translated by Canadian animator Frederic Back into a stunning Academy Award winning short film (CBC-Radio Canada, 2004).

23. "Koyaanisqatsi," Wikipedia, last modified October 14, 2012, http://en.wikipedia.org/wiki/Koyaanisqatsi. "Godfrey Reggio," Wikipedia, last modified May 2, 2012, http://en.wikipedia.org/wiki/Godfrey_Reggio.

24. Ibid. In a seminal essay Catholic theologian David Tracy laments the darker side of modernity in which "we have seen our lifeworlds, in all their rich difference, increasingly colonized by the forces of a techno-economic social system that does not hesitate to use its power to level all memory, all resistance, all difference, and all hope. Religion becomes privatized. Art becomes marginalized. All the great classics of our and every culture become more consumer goods for a bored and anxious elite. Even the public realm—the last true hope of reason in its modern and classical Western forms—becomes merely technicized." David Tracy, "On Naming the Present," *Concilium* 1990, no. 1(Maryknoll, NY: Orbis, 1990): 3–24.

25. The classic study is Walter Brueggemann, *The Prophetic Imagination*, 2nd ed. (Minneapolis: Fortress, 2001); see also Brueggemann, *Disruptive Grace: Reflections on God, Scripture, and the Church*, ed. Carolyn J. Sharp (Minneapolis: Fortress, 2011), especially 17–37, 129–54; also Abraham Joshua Heschel's *The Prophets*.

26. To Reggio's trilogy I would add the music of Canadian singer Bruce Cockburn and the writings of Kentucky farmer Wendell Berry as contemporary artistic works that open disarming insight into the signs of the times and provoke fruitful reflection in the classroom. Al Gore's *An Inconvenient Truth* (Paramount, 2006) "breaks silence" on global warming by weaving together personal narrative with discourse from the scientific community. The controversy surrounding the film echoes not a little of the polarized rhetoric seen in the Blue Lake story.

27. South African writer Rosemary Kearney contemplates a similar wisdom rising from the ancient inhabitants of her land: "The San people living in the Karoo region of South Africa were the ancestors of humanity. At night the stars still sing but few can hear. The silence out here is palpable. The stony Karoo—a San word for 'dry ground'—holds another kind of silence which surrounds the genocide of the /Kam. The San occupied this land for 30,000 thousand years using the stars for both a calendar and direction. /Kam cosmology seems strangely allied with modern science in claiming that we share a physical origin with everything in the universe and that we are all descended from a single mother who lived in Africa about 150,000 years ago. . . . [Contemplating this thought] I am filled with the same almost painful emotion I experienced when I saw our blue planet from outer space: 'Here in the birthplace of all humanity is where we might come home to each other, come home to ourselves, come home to the cosmos.' " Cited from http://www.themagdalenetestament.com /blog.html, May 11, 2012.

28. Again I am indebted to Rosemary Kearney (n. 27) for helping me frame these wider questions.

29. Lois Palken Rudnick, introduction to Mabel Dodge Luhan, *Edge of Taos Desert: An Escape to Reality* (Albuquerque: University of New Mexico, 1987), xiv.

30. For an extended treatment of this insight, both scholarly and powerfully personal, see Belden Lane, *The Solace of Fierce Landscapes: Exploring Desert and Mountain Spirituality* (New York: Oxford, 1998). Also for historical perspective, see Douglas Burton-Christie, *The Word in the Desert: Scripture and the Quest for Holiness in Early Christian Monasticism* (New York: Oxford, 1993).

31. Thomas Merton, *Conjectures of a Guilty Bystander* (Garden City, NJ: Doubleday, 1966), 294.

32. Georgia O'Keeffe, quoted in Henry Seldis, "Georgia O'Keeffe at 78: Tough-Minded Romantic," *Los Angeles Times West Magazine* (January 22, 1967): 22.

33. Cited in Fergusson, 13. Reflecting on the African slave trade Catholic theologian Mary Doak rightly notes that "the genocide committed against Native Americans is also a foundational American sin." Mary C. Doak, "Cornel West's Challenge to the Catholic Evasion of Black Theology," *Theological Studies* 63, no. 1 (Mar. 2002): 87–107, n. 34.

34. Joe S. Sando, *Pueblo Profiles: Cultural Identity Through Centuries of Change* (Santa Fe, NM: Clear Light, 1998), 7.

35. Fergusson, *Dancing Gods*, 44.

36. Ibid., 15. In one of many lucid moments of cross-cultural exegesis, Fergusson compares Native ceremonials with the Roman Catholic Mass: "In a sense the mass is still a stately dance, the theatrical production is descended from a prayer. The ancestor of both was the ritual presenting a symbolic act in dramatic form before the altar. David danced before the Lord" (xviii). A fruitful study could likewise be made of the resonances between the Pueblo dances and the African American "ring shout," in which participants "shift their feet and move their bodies in a circle, to symbolize the connection between the past, present, and future"—and especially the ways that both of these religious-artistic forms provided their participants with a secretive means of *resistance to* and *transformation of* the Christianity of their white oppressors. Both forms also teach a profound affirmation of the body, a powerful sense that "my body matters"—hands, feet, voice—"it wasn't just doctrine, creeds, words, it was what you felt." Alonzo Johnson, in a segment titled "The Ringshout" from *This Far By Faith: African American Spiritual Journeys* (PBS Video/Blackside Inc.).

37. Sando, 8.

38. Just as W. E. B. Du Bois (*The Souls of Black Folk*) unforgettably describes the "double-consciousness" of the American Negro, so does Erna Fergusson observe the "dual nature" of the Pueblo Indian: "The white man's Indian is trained in a government school and turned out as a fairly good carpenter, farmer, and Christian. . . . The other face of him, however, is turned away from the white man and everything he typifies." *Dancing Gods*, 27. Strategies of "silence and concealment" marked the performance of ancient religious practices in the face of severe punishments meted out by Christian missionaries "for practicing the old religions"; alternately, those religious ceremonies conducted openly "were combined with the observance of Catholic feast-days in the extraordinary mixture of faiths which still prevails" (22).

39. Ibid., 276.

40. Ibid., 199.

## Chapter 6

Portions of this chapter were first developed in Christopher Pramuk, "'The Street is for Celebration': Racial Consciousness and the Eclipse of Childhood in America's Cities," *The Merton Annual* 25 (Louisville, KY: Fons Vitae, 2012): 91–103. This material is used with permission and has been substantially revised.

1. Stevie Wonder, *Songs in the Key of Life* (Motown Records, 1976).

2. The phrase is borrowed from Eduardo Bonilla-Silva's superb study, *Racism without Racists: Color-Blind Racism and Racial Inequality in Contemporary America* (Rowman and Littlefield, 2010).

3. Thomas Merton, *The Behavior of Titans* (New York: New Directions, 1961), 83–84.

4. Several factors contribute, in my view, to Merton's enduring trustworthiness on matters of race. First, he never described black experience (or "Negro experience," in the parlance of the day) in a monolithic, naively romantic, or sociologically detached way. That Merton saw and rejected the dangers of race essentialism (black or white) is clear (see chapter 8). Second, removed from the public fray as he was, Merton's commentary was comparatively clear-eyed and free of bias. He could be just as critical of the nihilist rhetoric of the Black Power movement as he was of the ignorance and complicity of white Christian liberals. In fact, he was suspicious of any rhetoric that elevated ideals, principles, or social constructs (including race) over *persons*. Third, Merton recognized with epistemic humility that he was in many respects an alien and stranger to the struggles of the city, an outsider looking in, a guilty bystander. Reflecting on Malcolm X in 1967, for example, he noted, "I realize I don't fully know what I am talking about" (*Learning to Love: The Journals of Thomas Merton*, vol. 6: *1966–1967: Exploring Solitude and Freedom*, ed. Christine M. Bochen [San Francisco: HarperCollins, 1997], 233). Nevertheless he risked the attempt to understand life as it is for blacks in this country, even where his social location prevented full comprehension. "I ought to learn to just shut up and go about my business of thinking and breathing under trees," he wrote in 1967. "But protest is a biological necessity" (*Learning to Love*, 240).

5. For the considerable impact of Harlem on Merton's consciousness and emerging sense of vocation during these years—especially the influence of Catherine de Hueck Doherty—see Thomas Merton, *The Seven Storey Mountain* (New York: Harcourt Brace Jovanovich, 1999), 337–52, 357–60; *Run to the Mountain: The Journals of Thomas Merton Volume 1: 1939–1941* (New York: HarperCollins, 1996), 384–85, 448–51, 455–56, 464–65; also "Holy Communion: the City" and "Aubade-Harlem," in *The Collected Poems of Thomas Merton* (New York: New Directions, 1977), 39–40, 82–83.

6. Thomas Merton, *Seeds of Destruction* (New York: Farrar, Straus and Giroux, 1964), 60.

7. See Thomas Merton, *Conjectures of a Guilty Bystander* (Garden City, NY: Doubleday, 1966), 156–58; also Thomas Merton, *A Search for Solitude: Pursuing the Monk's Life. Journals, vol. 3: 1952–1960*, ed. Lawrence S. Cunningham (San Francisco: HarperCollins, 1996), 181–82.

8. Merton, *Conjectures of a Guilty Bystander*, 158. Today in Louisville at the corner of Fourth and Walnut—now "Fourth and Muhammad Ali Boulevard"—there is a commemorative sign marking Thomas Merton's famous "Revelation." A few blocks away a mural-sized image of Merton with His Holiness the Dalai Lama graces the side of a building.

9. Thomas Merton, *Dancing in the Water of Life, Volume Five: 1963–1965: Seeking Peace in the Hermitage*, ed. Robert E. Daggy (San Francisco: HarperCollins, 1997), 114–15.

10. Thomas Merton, *Dancing in the Water of Life*, 130.

11. Thomas Merton, *Love and Living*, ed. Naomi Burton Stone and Patrick Hart (New York: Harcourt Brace Jovanovich, 1985), 46–53. The essay was originally intended to serve as the preface for a picture book on Monsignor Robert Fox's work in Spanish Harlem entitled *Summer in the City*. Though the book was never published, Merton certainly had this setting in mind when writing the essay.

12. Thomas Merton, *Seeds of Destruction* (New York: Farrar, Straus and Giroux, 1964), 3–71.

13. Thomas Merton, *Love and Living*, 46–48; emphasis original.

14. Jonathan Kozol, *Amazing Grace: The Lives of Children and the Conscience of a Nation* (Harper, 1996); Kozol, *The Shame of the Nation: The Restoration of Apartheid Schooling in America* (Broadway, 2006); Michelle Alexander, *The New Jim Crow: Mass Incarceration in the Age of Colorblindness* (New Press, 2010).

15. For "And the Children of Birmingham," written before the bombing, see Thomas Merton, *Emblems of a Season of Fury* (New York: New Directions, 1963), 33–35; for "Picture of a Black Child with a White Doll," see Thomas Merton, *Collected Poems* (New York: New Directions, 1977 ), 626–27. See also John Howard Griffin's *Black Like Me* (New York: New American Library, 2003), a riveting account of Griffin's experiment in "becoming black" in the deep South during the 1950s. A close friend of Merton, Griffin's story is one of the most compelling, yet strangely overlooked, narratives of cross-racial solidarity during the civil rights era. The book and a recent documentary, *Uncommon Vision: The Life and Times of John Howard Griffin*, dir. Morgan Atkinson (Duckworks, 2010), are superb for classroom use, perhaps above all for exposing the question of social empathy— both our capacity for it and our resistance to it as persons and communities in US society.

16. See Howard Thurman, *Howard Thurman: Essential Writings*, Selected with an Introduction by Luther E. Smith (Maryknoll, NY: Orbis, 2006).

17. Merton, *Love and Living*, 50. The film *Crash*, dir. Paul Haggis (Lions Gate, 2005), brilliantly exposes intersecting racial tensions and the cumulative impulse to violence across the color line in contemporary Los Angeles.

18. Ibid., 48–49; emphasis original.

19. Ibid., 53.

20. Ibid.; emphasis original.

21. Ibid., 52.

22. In "Gandhi and the One-Eyed Giant," Merton cites Lauren Van Der Post's thesis "that the white man's spiritual rejection and contempt for the African is the result of the rejection of what is deepest and most vital in himself." Thomas Merton, *Gandhi on Non-Violence* (New York: New Directions, 1965). Framing the race problem even more broadly Merton suggests that the crisis of civilization in our "post-modern" era is partly rooted in our failure as a global human community to reconcile the wisdoms of the East and the West. "The marriage was wrecked on the rocks of the white man's dualism and of the inertia, the incomprehension, of ancient and primitive societies." Author James Douglass takes

his cues from Merton's prophetic unmasking of state violence in the book *Raids on the Unspeakable* to examine both Gandhi's and John F. Kennedy's resistance to Western militarism. See James W. Douglass, *Gandhi and the Unspeakable: His Final Experiment with Truth* (Maryknoll, NY: Orbis, 2012); Douglass, *JFK and the Unspeakable: Why He Died and Why It Matters* (Maryknoll, NY: Orbis, 2008).

23. Merton, *A Search for Solitude*, 182–83; from the original Fourth and Walnut passage.

24. Thomas Merton, "Hagia Sophia," in *Emblems of a Season of Fury*, 63; also "The Time of the End is the Time of No Room," in *Raids On the Unspeakable* (New York: New Directions, 1966). For a close study of Wisdom-Sophia in Merton's life and thought, see Christopher Pramuk, *Sophia: The Hidden Christ of Thomas Merton* (Collegeville, MN: Liturgical Press/Michael Glazier, 2009). While "The Street is for Celebration" has no explicit references to children, the book for which the essay was intended was focused largely on the youth of Harlem (see n. 11 above).

25. Thomas Merton, *The Sign of Jonas* (New York, Octagon, 1983; orig. 1953), 341.

26. Merton, *Conjectures of a Guilty Bystander*, 158. The theme of innocence and the image of the child figure significantly in Merton's theological anthropology (see Pramuk, *Sophia*, 200–2). Closely related and also prominent in the Fourth and Walnut passage is the phrase *le point vierge*, roughly the "virgin point" or secret heart of creation where God invites all things into being. With such terms Merton does not mean to suggest a regression to the freshness of childhood, in a naïve or narcissistic sense, still less a denial of sin. They speak rather to the divine image or spark in us, deeper and more primordial than sin, at once both gift (already given) and invitation (not fully realized). It is "a new birth, the divine birth in us" that grounds our freedom and creativity in history as co-creators before God.

27. Thomas Merton, *Learning to Love*, 147; citing theologian Karl Rahner.

28. Merton, *Learning to Love*, 262.

29. Innumerable gospel passages leap to mind: Jesus' encounter with the rich young man, the parable of the Good Samaritan, the judgment scene of Matthew 25, and so on. The term love as I use it here is analogous to solidarity and the preferential option for the poor, persistent themes of Catholic social teaching. Solidarity is not simply an ethical command so much as a *response* to the gift and wonder of life itself and God's love for us. We love because we have come to know God's love and mercy for us intimately through Jesus (1 John 4:19).

30. See *Uncommon Faithfulness: The Black Catholic Experience*, ed. M. Shawn Copeland, with LaReine-Marie Mosely and Albert J. Raboteau (Maryknoll, NY: Orbis, 2009), for Phelps's seminal essay on Catholic identity and mission with respect to social and racial transformation.

31. Thomas Merton, *Seeds of Destruction*, 17. Note the phrasing of the question: what matters first is the *person*, this "other Christ," who "happens to be black." We might also say that what matters ultimately for whites is not one's socially constructed whiteness but the discovery of one's true, Christ-like self, who also

happens to be white. And yet for whites the need for heightened racial consciousness is especially acute since, as Merton long ago observed, whites are most inclined to be unconscious of the hidden privileges of their "normative" whiteness. Thus what Merton wrote in 1964 seems to me no less true today: "Most of us are congenitally unable to think black, and yet that is precisely what we must do before we can hope to understand the crisis in which we find ourselves" (*Seeds of Destruction*, 60).

32. A recent study suggests that the traditional image of suburbia as a hub of white affluence is no longer simply a given, as America's suburbs have become more racially diverse. The authors caution, however, that resegregation always looms by means of white flight from multiracial suburbs or the breaking away of wealthier white enclaves into separately incorporated municipalities. See Myron Orfield and Thomas Luce, "America's Racially Diverse Suburbs: Opportunities and Challenges," Institute on Metropolitan Opportunity at the University of Minnesota Law School (July 20, 2012); available at http//:www.umn.law.edu.

33. Gustavo Gutierrez, *A Theology of Liberation*, rev. ed., trans. and ed. Sr. Caridad Inda and John Eagleson (Maryknoll, NY: Orbis, 1988), 82.

34. I speak here from my experience as a high school and college teacher in predominantly white schools. To the degree this analysis rings true for many (certainly not all) whites, surely it applies to many nonwhites also, since everyone in the "master's house" (Audre Lorde) is subject to the same dehumanizing ideologies, albeit in radically different ways.

35. Thus Friedrich Schleiermacher writes, "Any man who is capable of being satisfied with himself as he is will always manage to find a way out of the argument." *The Christian Faith* (Edinburgh: T&T Clark, 1989), 69.

36. On the paschal dimension of solidarity, see James B. Nickeloff, "Church of the Poor: The Ecclesiology of Gustavo Gutierrez," *Theological Studies* 54 (1993): 512–35. On solidarity as a "personalization of grace," see Thomas F. O'Meara, "Toward a Subjective Theology of Revelation," *Theological Studies* 36 (1975): 419.

37. On the power of immersion experiences for privileged young people, see John Savard, SJ, "The Heart Feels What the Eyes See: The Impact of Service-Immersion Programs," *Conversations On Jesuit Higher Education* 42 (Fall 2012): 49–50, and related essays in this volume; also Stephen M. Belt, *Men and Women for Others: A Phenomenological Investigation of University Member's Stories of International Cultural Immersion and Jesuit Mission* (PhD dissertation, University of St. Louis, 2012).

## Chapter 7

1. See William Lynch, SJ, *Images of Hope: Imagination as a Healer of the Hopeless* (Notre Dame, IN: University of Notre Dame, 1990).

2. Adolfo Nicolas, SJ, "Depth, Universality, and Learned Ministry: Challenges to Jesuit Higher Education Today," Mexico City (April 23, 2010): 4, http://www.sjweb.info/curiafrgen/curia_frgen.cfm.

3. Ibid.

4. Sue Monk Kidd, *The Secret Life of Bees* (New York: Viking Penguin, 2002).

5. Etty Hillesum, *An Interrupted Life and Letters from Westerbork* (New York: Henry Holt, 1996), 135–36.

6. Robert Ellsberg, *All Saints: Daily Reflections on Saints, Prophets, and Witnesses from Our Time* (New York: Crossroad, 1997), 522. Ellsberg notes that Etty's diary, published four decades after her death, "was quickly recognized as one of the great moral documents of our time" (521).

7. Etty Hillesum, *An Interrupted Life*, 176.

8. Ibid., 171.

9. Ibid., 89; cf. 48–50.

10. Ibid., 178.

11. Ellsberg, *All Saints*, 522.

12. Ibid.

13. For Etty to share in humanity's suffering meant accepting the contradictions of light and darkness, good and evil, within ourselves, no less than in our enemy or persecutor. "Yes, we carry everything within us, God and Heaven and Hell and Earth and Life and Death and all of history" (154). Etty also writes of the freedom from fear that comes through embracing life's gratuity from moment to moment, a freedom the Germans could not take away (144–45). In many such passages Etty sounds remarkably like a *satyagrahi*: one who has wholly internalized the truth-force of loving nonviolence as taught and lived by Mahatma Gandhi and by Jesus' life and teachings in the Sermon on the Mount.

14. Eva Hoffman, foreword to *An Interrupted Life*, vii.

15. Ibid.

16. Etty Hillesum, *An Interrupted Life*, 360.

17. To be clear, she also addresses God throughout the diaries in more traditionally masculine terms.

18. From the teachings of Isaac Luria (1534–72), or the *Lurianic Kabbalah*. Among Christian theologians the notion of *zimzum* has been explored in connection with Sophia-Shekinah and the theme of divine *kenosis* by Jurgen Moltmann (*God in Creation: The Gifford Lectures 1984–1985*) and, albeit more implicitly, the great Russian Orthodox theologian Sergius Bulgakov in his dogmatics of the humanity of God, or divine-human Sophia.

19. Melissa Raphael, *The Female Face of God in Auschwitz: A Jewish Feminist Theology of the Holocaust* (New York: Routledge, 2003).

20. The literature on biblical Wisdom-Sophia in the Jewish and Christian traditions is vast, rich, and not without controversy. For a superb overview see Leo D. Lefebure, "The Wisdom of God: Sophia and Christian Theology," *Christian Century* 111, no. 29 (October 19, 1994): 951–57; in Western Christian feminist retrievals the definitive study is Elizabeth Johnson's magisterial *She Who Is: The Mystery of God in Feminist Theological Discourse* (New York: Crossroad, 1992).

21. Raphael criticizes prevailing androcentric Jewish theologies in the wake of the Holocaust for effectively condemning God for "God's failure to be patriarchal enough" (*Female Face of God*, 35). Her thesis, rendered with humility and deference to the inexplicable horrors of Auschwitz, hinges on the need to challenge patriarchal assumptions about how God's power and presence are (and are not) manifest in the world: "There has been too much asking '*where* was God in Auschwitz?' and not enough '*who* was God in Auschwitz' " (54).

22. Raphael, *Female Face of God*, 68.

23. Ibid., 157.

24. Ibid., 58.

25. Ibid.

26. Ibid., 71.

27. Ibid., 74; with a nod to Rudolph Otto's famous description (*The Idea of the Holy*) of religious experience as the *mysterium tremendum et fascinans*.

28. Ibid., 139.

29. Ibid., 80.

30. Ibid., 142.

31. Ibid., 79.

32. Sergius Bulgakov, as cited in Bernice Rosenthal, "The Nature and Function of Sophia in Sergei Bulgakov's Prerevolutionary Thought," *Russian Religious Thought*, ed. Judith Kornblatt and Richard Gustafson (Madison, WI: University of Wisconsin, 1996): 154–75, at 167. In the Russian Bible, Rosenthal notes, Genesis 3:19 reads: "for earth thou art and to earth shalt thou return." Bulgakov's celebration of the mutual relationship between the "holy flesh" of humanity (Adam) and "matter-mother" (the Earth) is often hymnic—"In you we are born, you feed us, we touch you with our feet, to you we return"—yet never sentimental or merely bucolic. Indeed his constructive theological justification of the natural world presages contemporary environmental theologies by some fifty years. "The fate of nature, suffering and awaiting its liberation, is henceforth connected with the fate of man . . . the new heaven and new earth now enter as a necessary element into the composition of Christian eschatology."

33. Etty Hillesum, *An Interrupted Life*, 152.

34. Raphael, *Female Face of God*, 58; citing Victor Frankl's *Man's Search for Meaning*, 69. The image of divine presence in a tree stripped bare may, for some Christian readers, evoke patristic and medieval meditations on the cross as linked with the tree of life from Genesis. Raphael is careful to draw a distinction between the Jewish memory and experience of Shekhinah as "the real presence

of a suffering God" and a "quasi-Christian incarnation of God crucified in Auschwitz." She cites Jurgen Moltmann's theology (*The Crucified God*) as a Christian depiction "that is close but not identical" to her own, noting that in Jewish understanding "the suffering is that of one who, being among us, suffers with us, but does not suffer vicariously *for* us" (54–55). To be sure, great care must be taken not to easily conflate Jewish and Christian interpretations of a suffering God, particularly in the case of the Shoah. Much depends, from the Christian side, on precisely *how* we understand Jesus' crucifixion to be redemptive (see chapter 4).

35. Etty Hillesum, *An Interrupted Life*, 198.

36. See Nicolas Kristof and Sheryl Wu Dunn, *Half the Sky: Turning Oppression into Opportunity for Women Worldwide* (New York: Vintage, 2010); Sue Monk Kidd, *The Secret Life of Bees* (New York: Penguin, 2003); Sojourner Truth, "Ain't I A Woman," http://www.fordham.edu/halsall/mod/sojtruth-woman.asp; Georges Bernanos, *The Diary of a Country Priest*, trans. Pamela Morris (New York: MacMillan, 1937); James Chapin, cited in *Time*, September 28, 1953, http://www.time.com/time/magazine/article/0,9171,818933,00.html; Somaly Mam, *The Road of Lost Innocence: The True Story of a Cambodian Heroine* (New York: Spiegal and Grau, 2008); Rosanne Murphy, *Martyr of the Amazon: The Life of Sister Dorothy Stang* (Maryknoll, NY: Orbis, 2007), and *They Killed Sister Dorothy*, dir. Daniel Junge and Henry Ansbacher (First Run Features, 2009).

37. Thomas Merton, *Hagia Sophia*, in *Emblems of a Season of Fury* (New York: New Directions, 1963).

38. Sue Monk Kidd, *The Secret Life of Bees*, 140–41.

39. Ibid., 289.

40. During an informal retreat with Catholic religious sisters in 1967, Thomas Merton offered a vision of community rooted in trust and presence. "We want to be present to each other and then trust what happens. Presence is what counts. It's important to realize that the Church itself is a presence, and so is contemplative life. Community is presence, not an institution." Thomas Merton, *The Springs of Contemplation: A Retreat at the Abbey of Gethsemani* (New York: Farrar, Straus and Giroux, 1992), 3.

41. Rita Gross, cited in Raphael, *Female Face of God*, 150. In a similar spirit, Kristof and Wu Dunn open their study of global women's oppression (n. 36) with a Chinese proverb: *Women hold up half the sky*. When Kristof and Wu Dunn ask "Is Islam misogynistic?" (149–66), they pose one of the pivotal theological questions of our time, with far-reaching social and political implications. Of course whether Catholicism is misogynistic also continues to be worth asking.

42. To Luise Oestreicher, November 17, 1944; cited in *Ultimate Price: Testimonies of Christians Who Resisted the Third Reich*, selected by Annemarie S. Kidder (Maryknoll, NY: Orbis, 2012), 65–66.

43. See *Ultimate Price*, which gathers select writings of Dietrich Bonhoeffer, Franz Jagerstatter, Alfred Delp, Sophie Scholl, Jochen Klepper, Bernhard Lich-

tenberg, and Rupert Mayer. Also highly recommended is *Sophie Scholl: The Final Days*, dir. Marc Rothemund (Zeitgeist, 2006). By engaging these witnesses it is impossible not to feel profoundly humbled and to ask oneself, what would I have done? What am I doing now?

44. John Kane, "Men (and Women) Finding God's Feminine Presence," *Leaven* e-vol. 3:3 (Jan 2011). The affirmation of covenantal promise and noncoercive divine presence even "in the valley of the shadow of death" (e.g., Ps 22–23) seems to me the profoundest seed of biblical good news that both Jews and Christians must embrace and bring into dialogue with others in an increasingly fragmented and violent world. Whether Muslims might have recourse to such analogical or sacramental imagination through elements of the Qur'an or Sufic mysticism, for example, I cannot say with certainty. But on this point hinge, I think, a great many theological (and political) difficulties, which converge on the realization of humankind's ontological unity and freedom in God, the deep ground for dialogue, justice, and peace. For Islamic perspectives on divine-human relationality and the divine feminine see Seyyed Hossein Nasr, "The Male and Female in the Islamic Perspective," *Studies in Comparative Religion* 14: 1–2 (Winter–Spring, 1980); and Laurence Galian, "The Centrality of the Divine Feminine in Sufism," *Proceedings of the 2nd Annual Hawaii International Conference on Arts and Humanities (2004)*, available at http://www.hichumanities.org/.

## *Chapter 8*

1. Adolfo Nicolas, SJ, "Depth, Universality, and Learned Ministry: Challenges to Jesuit Higher Education Today," Mexico City, April 23, 2010, http://www.sjweb.info/curiafrgen/curia_frgen.cfm, p. 4.

2. Ibid.

3. Karl Plank, "The Eclipse of Difference: Merton's Encounter with Judaism," in *Merton and Judaism: Recognition, Repentance, and Renewal*, ed. Beatrice Bruteau (Louisville: Fons Vitae, 2003), 67–82, at 81–82.

4. Jesse Washington, Associated Press, "Black Male Code Still—Sadly—Needs to be Handed Down," in *The Cincinnati Enquirer*, March 24, 2012.

5. *Dreamworlds 3: Desire, Sex and Power in Music Video*, dir. Sut Jhally (Northhampton, MA: Media Education Foundation, 2007), DVD.

6. Greg Toppo, *USA Today*, "Kids Spend Nearly 8 Hours a Day on Electronic Media," in *The Cincinnati Enquirer*, January 18, 2010; John F. Kavanaugh, *Following Christ in a Consumer Society: The Spirituality of Cultural Resistance* (Maryknoll, NY: Orbis, 2006).

7. John Jay College Research Team, "The Causes and Context of Sexual Abuse of Minors by Catholic Priests in the United States, 1950–2010" (May 2011), http://old.usccb.org/mr/causes-and-context.shtml.

8. The Editors, "Anything But Clear: A Report on Campus Sexual Assaults," *Notre Dame Magazine* (Winter 2011–12); Jean Porter, in Melinda Henneberger,

"Reported Sexual Assault at Notre Dame Campus Leaves More Questions Than Answers," *National Catholic Reporter Online*, March 6, 2012, http://ncronline .org/news/accountability/reported-sexual-assault-notre-dame-campus-leaves -more-questions-answers.

9. See Sut Jhally, dir., *Dreamworlds 3*.

10. See http://www.freedomcenter.org/slavery-today/.

11. See http://dreamact.info/.

12. Bryan Massingale, *Racial Justice and the Catholic Church* (Maryknoll, NY: Orbis, 2012), 81; cf. 46.

13. Interview with the author, April 2012. The priest, for obvious reasons, wishes to remain anonymous.

14. Editors, "Save the Altar Girls," *America* (October 10, 2011), http://www .americamagazine.org/content/article.cfm?article_id=13056; Tom Gallager, "No Girl Servers at Latin Masses," *National Catholic Reporter Online* (June 9, 2011), http://ncronline.org/blogs/ncr-today/vatican-no-girl-servers-latin-masses; Alice Popovici, "Catholics Protest Altar Server Policy," *National Catholic Reporter Online* (December 3, 2011), http://ncronline.org/news/women-religious /catholics-protest-altar-server-policy.

15. John Coleman, "Church Loyalty Oaths Revisited," *America* online (June 29, 2012), "In All Things," http://www.americamagazine.org/blog/entry. cfm?blog_id=2&entry_id=5221; Michelle Boorstein, "Arlington Diocese Parishioners Question Need for Fidelity Oath," *The Washington Post* online (July 11, 2012), http://www.washingtonpost.com/local/sunday-school-teachers-balk -at-oath-agreeing-to-all-church-teachings/2012/07/11/gJQAcAvGeW_story .html.

16. Bruce Jancin, "Video Games: What You'd Really Rather Not Know," *Pediatric News* 46, no. 3 (March 2012).

17. Wikipedia, "Suicide Among LGBT Youth," last modified October 5, 2012, http://en.wikipedia.org/wiki/Suicide_among_LGBT_youth, and references therein.

18. Greg Toppo, "Kids Spend" (n. 6 above); Stephen L. Carter, "A Little Less Texting, A Little More Thinking," in *The Cincinnati Enquirer* (March 24, 2012).

19. Thomas Merton, *Dancing in the Water of Life: Seeking Peace in the Hermitage*, ed. Robert E. Daggy (San Francisco: HarperSanFrancisco, 1997), 200–201. That Merton also saw and resisted the dangers of gender essentialism for both women and men, especially within the life of the church, is patently clear in his strikingly prescient comments on "The Feminine Mystique," inspired partly by Merton's reading of Betty Friedan's groundbreaking 1963 book of the same title, given to a gathering of religious sisters in 1967. *The Springs of Contemplation: A Retreat at the Abbey of Gethsemani* (Notre Dame, IN: Ave Maria, 1992), 125-35.

20. See the influential essay by Audre Lorde, "The Master's Tools Will Never Dismantle the Master's House," *Sister Outsider: Essays and Speeches by Audre Lorde* (Trumansburg, NY: The Crossing Press, 1984), 114–23.

21. This is not to deny the potential for good of the Internet and other forms of electronic media as tools of communication and building community, especially where person-to-person means are impossible, even forbidden. It is also important to note that the factors contributing to excessive television and media exposure among children are socially variable and complex, such as in neighborhoods unsafe for children to be outdoors or in households where parents work multiple jobs and have neither the leisure nor the disposable income to keep their kids engaged in more creative or healthy activities.

22. According to Jesuit Superior General Adolfo Nicolas, one of the greatest challenges facing university educators today is what he calls the "globalization of superficiality," partly a consequence of our ability to instantly access unlimited quantities of information via the Internet without personal engagement, depth of thought, or intellectual labor. "People lose the ability to engage with reality, a process of dehumanization that may be gradual and silent, but very real." Nicolas, "Depth, Universality, and Learned Ministry," n. 1 above.

23. Among my college students there are few issues that generate more intensive discussion than homosexuality and the question of how to account for gay and lesbian persons, theologically, in God and in the life of the church. Sexual diversity raises the theological dilemma of difference in ways arguably more primordial than race, insofar as it manifests differences that are biologically inscribed and not just, or primarily, socially constructed.

24. The relevant church teachings, available at www.usccb.org, include *The Catechism of the Catholic Church*, nos. 2331–2400; *Homosexualitatis problema*, "On the Pastoral Care of Homosexual Persons" (1986); "Always Our Children: A Pastoral Message to Parents of Homosexual Children and Suggestions for Pastoral Ministers" (1997); especially influential among younger Catholics are John Paul II's conferences on the "theology of the body." For a balanced summary of "gender essentialism" and "complementarity of the sexes" in church teachings, see Beth Haile, "Catechism Commentary: The Sixth Commandment," at http://catholic moraltheology.com/catechism-commentary-the-sixth-commandment/.

25. "What are gays and lesbians to do with their bodies, their selves?" asks M. Shawn Copeland, one of a few Catholic systematic theologians to publicly call for the development of Catholic theological anthropology with respect to homosexual embodiment, in her case through the lens of Christology. See M. Shawn Copeland, *Enfleshing Freedom: Body, Race, and Being* (Minneapolis: Fortress, 2010), 55–84, and references therein. Also Todd A. Salzman and Michael G. Lawler, *The Sexual Person: Toward a Renewed Catholic Anthropology* (Washington, DC: Georgetown University, 2008).

26. Bishop Thomas Gumbleton has openly supported Catholic ministries to gays and lesbians while emphasizing primacy of conscience. See Thomas Gumbleton, "A Call to Listen: The Church's Theological and Pastoral Response to Gays and Lesbians," in *Sexual Diversity and Catholicism: Toward the Development of Moral Theology*, ed. Patricia Beattie Jung with Joseph Andrew Coray

(Collegeville, MN: Liturgical Press, 2001), and other essays in this volume. Catholic priest and theologian James Alison and Jesuit author James Martin have also written eloquently on this topic; see, e.g., James Alison, *On Being Liked* (New York: Crossroad, 2004), and James Martin, "Respect, Compassion, and Sensitivity" (Jan. 12, 2012) and "She Loved Prophetically" (Jan. 9, 2013), both available at www.americamagazine.org.

27. To put it another way, counterbalancing our "negative theology" (our respect for the limits of human comprehension and language before the mystery of God) we need to uphold a "negative anthropology," a deep respect for the mystery and mosaic diversity of human persons, each of whom holds a unique place in God's heart eternally, from before the very beginning. It is worth noting that this principle is inscribed into the religious beliefs and practices of many Native American tribes who make room for gender fluidity beyond strict male-female binaries. See Will Roscoe, *Changing Ones: Third and Fourth Genders in Native North America* (New York: St. Martin's Press, 1998). On the development of moral teaching in the church and implications for ecclesial practices, see John Noonan, *A Church That Can and Cannot Change: The Development of Catholic Moral Teaching* (Notre Dame, IN: University of Notre Dame, 2005); also Dennis M. Doyle, Timothy J. Furry, and Pascal D. Bazzell, eds., *Ecclesiology and Exclusion: Boundaries of Being and Belonging in Postmodern Times* (Maryknoll, NY: Orbis, 2012).

28. Gerard Manley Hopkins, "As Kingfishers Catch Fire," in *Gerard Manley Hopkins: The Major Works* (Oxford: Oxford University, 1986), 129.

29. Etty Hillesum, *An Interrupted Life and Letters from Westerbork* (New York: Henry Holt, 1996), 178; see chapter 7.

30. From *The Secret Life of Bees*, see chapter 7. The icon of Matthew Shepard that precedes this chapter moves the argument from head to heart. Shepard, a twenty-one-year-old college student in Laramie, Wyoming, was tortured and left to die hanging from a fence post by two attackers because he was gay. During his funeral in his hometown of Casper, Wyoming, protestors from the Westboro Baptist Church in Topeka, Kansas, were on hand to deliver their "God Hates Fags" message to Shepard's family and friends. Their picket signs read: "No Tears for Queers," and "Fag Matt in Hell." The harassment of young gays around the country—and in not a few cases their subsequent suicide—is described by many observers today as epidemic.

31. In Eastern Orthodox doctrine reaching back to Irenaeus, Clement of Alexandria, Athanasius, Maximus the Confessor, and others, the paradoxical formula at the heart of Christology (truly human/truly divine) expresses a mystery that applies not only to Jesus Christ but also analogically, if not physically-ontologically, to all persons everywhere by virtue of the incarnation, and the potency for divinization or *theosis* that the incarnation inscribes into human being. Without denying the crippling reality of sin, in Orthodoxy there is a countervailing sense in which the gift of divinization has, so to speak, already

been planted in human soil through the incarnation. "He became human so that we might become God" (Athanasius).Though the gift both constitutes and always awaits our free human response, the point is—the *good news* is—human beings are really capable of Christ-like love.

32. *Theological Papers on Faith and Uncertainty* 1.102, emphasis original; cited in Terrence Merrigan, "Newman and Theological Liberalism," *Theological Studies* 66 (2005): 605–21, at 619.

33. This dynamic, cumulative, holistic, and "antagonistic" manner of appropriating the mystery of God, this process of growing into the truth, Newman calls "the illative sense." Where scientific rationality proceeds by linear, deductive, or syllogistic thinking, imaginative rationality (the illative sense) is closer to literary or poetic cognition, involving a more delicate and organic process of discernment which Newman compares to the sensibilities of the climber on the rock face—we advance "not by rule, but by an inward faculty." For a more detailed discussion of Newman on the imagination and its role in doctrinal development see Christopher Pramuk, " 'They Know Him By His Voice': Newman on the Imagination, Christology, and the Theology of Religions," *Heythrop Journal* 48 (Jan 2007): 61–85.

34. Cited in John Coulson, "Belief and Imagination," *The Downside Review* (1972): 1–14, at 13.

35. Newman, *Letters and Diaries*, as cited in Merrigan, "Newman and Theological Liberalism," 614–5.

36. Newman describes wisdom as "the clear, calm, accurate vision, and comprehension of the whole course, the whole work of God'; it "implies a connected view of the old with the new; an insight into the bearing and influence of each part upon every other; without which there is no whole, and could be no centre." *Fifteen Sermons Preached Before the University of Oxford* (Notre Dame, IN: University of Notre Dame, 1997), 287–93.

37. Coulson, "Belief and Imagination," 14.

38. Witness the enormous commercial success of films like *Avatar*, my teenage son's fascination with the *Transformers* films, and his concomitant dread of attending Mass.

39. Merton, *Dancing in the Water of Life*, 201. Or, as Metz has it: "So-called modern man stands in danger of becoming increasingly faceless and (to speak biblically) nameless. . . he is being bred back more and more into a cleverly adaptable animal, into a smoothly functioning machine." Johann Baptist Metz, *Faith in History and Society: Toward a Practical Fundamental Theology*, trans. and ed. J. Matthew Ashley (New York: Crossroad, 2007), 80.

40. Etty Hillesum, *An Interrupted Life*, 178; see chapter 7.

41. Ibid., 198.

## Chapter 9

Portions of this chapter were first developed in Christopher Pramuk, "O Happy Day! Imagining a Church Beyond the Color Line," *America* 189, August 18, 2003: 8–10. This material is used with permission and has been substantially revised.

1. Abraham Joshua Heschel, *The Sabbath* (New York: Farrar, Straus and Giroux, 1951), 74.

2. W. E. B. Du Bois, *The Souls of Black Folk* (Boston: Bedford Books, 1989), 109.

3. Cited in Charlene Smith and John Feister, *Thea's Song: The Life of Thea Bowman* (Maryknoll, NY: Orbis, 2009), 239.

4. Thomas Merton describes "the mystery of social love" as a call "not only to love but to be loved. The [person] who does not care at all whether or not [s/he] is loved is ultimately unconcerned about the true welfare of the other and of society. Hence we cannot love unless we also consent to be loved in return. . . . The life of 'the other' is not only a supplement, an adjunct to our own. Our companion is our helper, and it is in helping one another that we give glory to God." *The New Man* (New York: New Directions, 1961), 91.

5. Catholic News Service reporter Jerry Filteau, cited in Smith and Feister, *Thea's Song*, 260.

6. Thea's words, cited in ibid., 262.

7. Ibid., 261. Compare to Mrs. Harriet Hazely, a parishioner at St. Mark's Catholic Church in Cincinnati, whose words open this chapter. Cited in *Tracing Your Catholic Roots: Celebrating National Black Catholic History Month, November 1990–2008* (Archdiocese of Cincinnati, 2008), 92.

8. Smith and Feister, *Thea's Song*, 270.

9. Ibid., 244.

10. Ibid., 246.

11. Ibid., 245–46.

12. Ibid., 271.

13. Ibid., 245.

14. See Curtiss Paul DeYoung et al., *United by Faith: The Multiracial Congregation as an Answer to the Problem of Race* (New York: Oxford University, 2003).

15. Bryan Massingale, *Racial Justice and the Catholic Church* (Maryknoll, NY: Orbis, 2010), 116–120, at 120.

16. Ibid., 118; citing Joe Feagin (*Systemic Racism: A Theory of Oppression*) on stages of white development on the way toward interracial solidarity and transformative love.

17. Ibid.

18. *Evangelii nuntiandi* no. 71; expanding on Vatican II's *Lumen gentium*, no. 11.

## *Afterword*

1. Abraham Joshua Heschel, "Depth Theology," *The Insecurity of Freedom* (New York: Farrar, Straus & Giroux, 1996), 121.

2. Bruteau, ed., *Merton and Judaism* (Louisville KY: Fons Vitae, 2003), 109. Merton is reacting to the first drafts of a statement circulated by curial officials during the Second Vatican Council on the question of the church's relationship with the Jewish people, which repeated traditional Catholic teachings calling for the conversion of the Jews. Heschel was instrumental in moving the council fathers to reject such teachings.

# INDEX